The World of
Shakespeare's Sonnets

The World of Shakespeare's Sonnets

An Introduction

ROBERT MATZ

McFarland & Company, Inc., Publishers
Jefferson, North Carolina, and London

LIBRARY OF CONGRESS CATALOGUING-IN-PUBLICATION DATA

Matz, Robert.
    The world of Shakespeare's sonnets : an introduction / Robert
Matz.
        p.   cm.
    Includes bibliographical references and index.
    ISBN-13: 978-0-7864-3219-6
    softcover : 50# alkaline paper ∞

    1. Shakespeare, William, 1564–1616. Sonnets.   2. Sonnets,
English — History and criticism.   I. Title.
PR2848.M33   2008
821'.3 — dc22   2007037638

British Library cataloguing data are available

On the cover: Nicholas Hilliard, *Henry Wriothesley, 3rd Earl of
Southampton* [1573–1624], 1594, miniature watercolour on vellum
(The Fitzwilliam Museum); background ©2008 Shutterstock

Manufactured in the United States of America

McFarland & Company, Inc., Publishers
  Box 611, Jefferson, North Carolina 28640
  www.mcfarlandpub.com

IN MEMORY OF
Karen Sara Erdman,
1964–2004

Acknowledgments

My thanks to many friends and colleagues who have generously read parts of this book and helped make it better: Scott Berg, Zofia Burr, Art Duval, Eric Eisner, Devon Hodges, Rosemary Jann, Deborah Kaplan, Gareth Lea, Cynthia Rogers, Sarah Schneewind, Alok Yadav, and Terry Zawacki. Special thanks to Denise Albanese, for taking on the whole thing. I have also benefited from the help of three terrific undergraduate research assistants: Linda Fauteux, Amaris Price and Alison Strubb. The staff of the Folger Shakespeare Library has likewise been of great help. George Mason University provided a semester's study leave to write this book, and the English Department at George Mason has been a congenial place to work. Many thanks to my parents, Lorraine and Joseph Matz, for their love and support, and to my sisters, Judith Matz and Ellen Frankel, for the same, as well as their good writing advice. My children, David and Rachel Matz, give me much joy. Teresa Michals guides me in my work and in most things else. No acknowledgment could answer all her gifts to me. This book is dedicated to the memory of Karen Sara Erdman, one of the sharpest and bravest thinkers I have ever known, and a fabulous teacher of English. Karen gave me early encouragement to write this book, and I always expected her to read a final draft of it. It would be a better book if she had, but I hope it nevertheless reflects something of her spirit, conversation and friendship.

Table of Contents

Section III: "A Woman Coloured Ill"

Section IV: "So Long Lives This"

Preface

How did sonnets get written in Shakespeare's day? Here's one story. In the fall of 1599 Queen Elizabeth dined with Francis Bacon, the ambitious writer, courtier and royal counselor. Her visit to Bacon's country retreat at Twickenham Park was unusual, and for Bacon probably nerve-racking. The times were tense. The queen was furious at the Earl of Essex, one of the most powerful men in England and, formerly, one of her favorite courtiers. He was under house arrest for what the queen saw as his failures and disobedience in the conduct of a military campaign in Ireland. Essex was also the patron of Bacon and his brother. The very estate where Bacon would entertain the queen was a gift from the earl. So, a nightmare dinner party: Bacon caught between Essex and Elizabeth, both of whom he depended on for his political advancement. What did Bacon do in this difficult situation? He wrote a sonnet. Its purpose, he later recalled, was to reconcile these warring giants. The sonnet, Bacon wrote, was a mere "toy" (or as we would say, "trifle"), but sometimes "men's inclinations are opened more in a toy, than in a serious matter."[1]

Two years later fortune's wheel had gone full turn. Bacon would write for Elizabeth about Essex again. But this time it was an essay, written at the queen's request, published by her printer, and intended to justify Elizabeth's execution of the earl, who was beheaded for treason after a desperate attempt to seize the throne. Bacon was well placed to write this justification of the queen's actions, having also participated in the prosecution of his former patron. And he benefited from the service. Elizabeth granted Bacon £1,200, a huge sum at the time, raised from the fine of one of Essex's convicted co-conspirators.[2]

1

Bacon's sonnet and the fall of Essex seem worlds away from Shakespeare's poetry of love. Yet they have much in common. Bacon's sonnet has political purpose. Shakespeare's sonnets, too, have social as well as literary and emotional significance. Bacon's sonnet is written to Queen Elizabeth, but it concerns the Earl of Essex, whose supporters cultivated erotically charged friendships with the earl and with one another.[3] Likewise, most of Shakespeare's sonnets are written to an aristocratic young man, whom the sonnets address as a friend, lover and patron. Bacon appeared to many to have betrayed Essex. So, too, the bond between Shakespeare and the aristocratic young man of the sonnets is haunted by betrayal on both sides.

Bacon's sonnet has not survived, but his explanation of its specific subject and motive has. We have Shakespeare's sonnets, but we lack a similarly clear explanation of their subjects and motives — either from the sonnets themselves, or from Shakespeare or anyone else. For this reason I do not treat the sonnets as Shakespearean autobiography. But I also do not write as if the sonnets tell no story. Rather than revealing particular biographical events or persons, my goal in discovering that story is to identify the customs and beliefs that shaped the sonnets, Shakespeare's life, and his world.

Many discussions of the sonnets emphasize their timeless expression of love. This book, by contrast, argues for the value of understanding the sonnets *in their time*. It explores Shakespeare's brilliant, edgy sonnets through their roots in the equally brilliant, edgy culture of the English Renaissance. Each section shuttles between the poems and this cultural world. For example, I show what the interest in the sonnet at the Renaissance court has to do with the new fashion for the handkerchief there, while my discussion framing the sonnets' homoeroticism ranges from love letters passed between King James and the Duke of Buckingham to what contemporary college students count (or don't count) as sex. Along the way readers will also discover:

- The relationship between the sonnets and the tipsy excess of Renaissance rhetorical style
- The connection of the sonnets to the revisionary history of sexuality that informed *Lawrence v. Texas*, the 2003 Supreme Court case that declared U.S. anti-sodomy laws unconstitutional
- Seventeenth-century women's surprisingly modern responses to Renaissance antifeminist stereotypes
- And why one eighteenth-century critic, reflecting the general opinion of the time, praised the sonnets' *exclusion* from a collection of Shakespeare's works ("For where is the utility of propagating compositions which no one can endure to read?").

Readers interested in the sonnets as primarily formal works of art might turn to Helen Vendler's *The Art of Shakespeare's Sonnets*. As Vendler's work shows, the sonnets contain many riches that formal literary analysis helps us to appreciate. While I also explore the literary qualities of the sonnets, I believe it important and illuminating to connect the sonnets to their world. This book has more in common with two recent introductions to the sonnets (both titled *Shakespeare's Sonnets*, the one by Paul Edmondson and Stanley Wells, the other by Dympna Callaghan) but it emphasizes more the relationship between the sonnets and Renaissance culture than do these books. And though also introductory, it offers a more particular argument about the sonnets.

Over the past twenty-five years research on Shakespeare's sonnets, Renaissance poetry and Renaissance culture has allowed us to appreciate the sonnets in new and exciting ways that offer an alternative to the either/or of literary or biographical study. Most of this work remains unfamiliar or uninviting to general readers, however. I hope that readers who are familiar with this scholarship will find new detail, interpretation and argument in this book. But I also hope to make this scholarship more accessible to non-specialists, and in doing so to provide these readers with fresh ways of enjoying Shakespeare's sonnets, and a new understanding of their historical and cultural significance.

All quotations of Shakespeare are from *The Norton Shakespeare*, ed. Stephen Greenblatt et al. (New York: Norton, 1997). I have followed the practice of the *Norton*, and most contemporary editions of Shakespeare, by modernizing the spellings and punctuation of other English Renaissance texts that I quote, if an editor has not already done so. An exception is the poetry of Edmund Spenser, since Spenser intentionally wrote in an "antique" style.

Introduction

Shakespeare's sonnets have been called the "greatest love-poetry in the world," and individual poems such as "Shall I compare thee to a summer's day," "Let me not to the marriage of true minds" and "My mistress' eyes are nothing like the sun" are among the most familiar and beloved in the English language. [1] When it comes to basic facts about the sonnets, however, it is remarkable how much about them we do not know: to whom Shakespeare wrote his sonnets, when he wrote them, whether he ever meant them to be published, and whether the order in which they currently appear is the one Shakespeare intended. There are enough facts about the sonnets to sustain hundreds of years of speculation about them but not enough facts to put an end to that speculation or think that we ever will.

This chapter provides an introduction to the sonnets. It is not my hope in it to end hundreds of years of debate. Instead I outline some of the most credible responses that have been given to these basic questions. In the rest of this book I look at Shakespeare's sonnets in ways less narrowly bibliographical and biographical. Not that these kinds of questions aren't interesting. But they are limited by our inability to answer them definitively — and by their failure to get at the whole story of the sonnets. Even to the extent that we can answer when, who and how about the sonnets, we still need to know why and what did it mean. For those kinds of questions we have to look at the sonnets in light of the times in which they were written, as I do in the rest of this book. But first to the who, when and how.

Shakespeare's sonnets consist of 154 individual sonnets, a poetic form typically consisting of fourteen lines of rhymed, metrical verse. The story these sonnets tell is as tantalizing as the facts of their composition. They don't tell so little a story as to make it uninteresting or impossible to ponder. But they don't tell so much of a story that one can follow it completely.[2] Given their brevity, sonnets usually communicate some single feeling rather than a narrative. When grouped together in what's called a sonnet sequence a narrative can emerge. But often the reader is left with large gaps in the story, and such is the case with Shakespeare's sonnets.

The sonnets are written to two beloveds, an unnamed man and an unnamed woman. The man is usually referred to as "the young man" or the "friend." I refer to him as the "young man," since Shakespeare describes him in both these terms. He also calls the young man his "friend," his "love" and his "boy." These names would be possible as well, and each comprises part of Shakespeare's sense of the young man, just as we may call someone we know different names depending on our mood or the moment. "Boy" and "friend" are likely to confuse modern readers. "Boy" need not refer to a preadolescent, as it most commonly does today. Rather, the word was used in the Renaissance in the same way "girl" is sometimes used today: we would not assume that the men watching "The Girl from Ipanema" were pederasts. While the word "friend" does not exclude a sexual relationship, it also encompasses a popular Renaissance ideal of male fidelity and equality that I believe Shakespeare found very important. The woman is most often referred to today as the "dark lady," but I call her the "black mistress," since Shakespeare describes her as black several times but dark only once, and since he never calls her a lady — just the opposite — but he does refer to her as his mistress a number of times.[3]

The sonnets begin with a group of sixteen urging a young man to marry and have a child. This group, numbers 1 through 17 (15 is the exception), are often referred to as the "procreation sonnets." The sonnets from 18 to 126 turn to Shakespeare's own relationship to the young man. Most famously, Shakespeare in these sonnets declares the faithfulness of his love for the young man, and celebrates the power of his poetry to preserve the young man's memory. The sonnets in this large group also often express a more anxious relationship to the young man. Shakespeare laments his own inadequacies — he is old and his profession of actor or writer demeaning — and declares his absolute dependence on his beloved, who has youth, beauty, social rank, and the admiration of others on his side. Many of these sonnets present Shakespeare faithfully yearning for the absent young man. In some sonnets Shakespeare further complains — though usually gently or even abjectly — that his attentions to the young man are not returned, or that the young man is betraying his love. In other sonnets, however, Shakespeare confesses to his own betrayal of the young man.

Some groups of sonnets to the young man provide a glimpse of a more definite set of events. Notable among these are sonnets are 33–35, in which Shakespeare describes how the young man has first made him feel secure in his love and then betrayed him, perhaps by sexual infidelity; sonnets 40–42, in which Shakespeare describes a love triangle among the young man, himself and his mistress; sonnets 78 to 86 (except for 81), in which — in what are often called the "rival poet" sonnets — Shakespeare complains that the young man has begun to favor another, more flattering poet; sonnets 97–103, in which Shakespeare describes being absent from the young man and ceasing for a time to compose sonnets to him; and sonnets 109 and 110 and 117–120, in which Shakespeare further apologizes not just for neglect but for some betrayal, perhaps sexual, on his part (120 suggests that Shakespeare and the young man are now equal in their betrayals of one another). This part of the sequence ends at sonnet 126 (which, lacking two lines, is not "officially" a sonnet) with Shakespeare contemplating the young man's inevitable death. In section two of this book I consider at length the significance — sexual and otherwise — of Shakespeare's decision to write most of his sonnets to a man rather than a woman.

Shakespeare does write about a woman in the remaining 28 sonnets, from 127 to 154. In contrast to the young man, whom Shakespeare frequently describes as fair in behavior and appearance, this woman is repeatedly described as black in these same respects. Sonnets in this part of the sequence are less complementary and more sexually explicit than the sonnets to the young man. Though a few praise the black mistress, more describe Shakespeare's frustrated sexual desire for her or berate her for her sexual promiscuity. Some describe a love triangle involving her, Shakespeare and the young man, which suggests that sonnets 40–42 also concern the black mistress.

The sequence concludes with two bawdy sonnets about sexual desire, humorously couched in a primly dignified language of mythic cupids and mystical baths. Sonnets 153 and 154 are similar translations of the same sixth-century Greek poem.[4] The tone of these sonnets, which describe unquenchable sexual desire for a mistress, matches that of the black mistress sonnets. Nonetheless, the source of these sonnets in a poem already 1,000 years old when Shakespeare was writing provides a last frustration to our desire to find a complete and simply biographical story in Shakespeare's sonnets.

That doesn't mean readers haven't tried.

Much of the biographical speculation has focused on the identities of the young man, black mistress and rival poet, who are never identified by their proper names.[5] For the young man, there have long been two leading contenders. Both are English Renaissance noblemen, since the young man of the sonnets appears to be of higher birth than Shakespeare. Moreover, poets in the English Renaissance often wrote or dedicated their poems to aristocratic men or women, because of the potential for prestige and literary patronage that writing for an aristocrat brought.[6]

The first of these two noblemen is Henry Wriothesley (no one knows just how the surname was pronounced), who was the Earl of Southampton.[7] Advocates for Southampton point to the fact that Shakespeare explicitly dedicated to the earl his poems *Venus and Adonis* and *The Rape of Lucrece*. In fact, the language of sonnet 26 closely echoes that of Shakespeare's dedication of *Venus and Adonis*. Details about Southampton's personal life also fit the sonnets. Around the time Shakespeare may have been starting his sonnet sequence, the earl, like the young man of the sonnets, was refusing to get married, and another poet had already composed a poem for the earl that implicitly counseled him to do so. Shakespeare might have followed suit.[8]

The second chief candidate for the young man is William Herbert, Earl of Pembroke. Shakespeare never dedicated any poetry to Pembroke as he did to Southampton. Nor is there direct evidence that he knew Herbert. However, the first compilation of Shakespeare's plays, published after Shakespeare's death in 1623, was dedicated to William Herbert and his brother Philip. The two men who wrote the dedication, actors and friends of Shakespeare, might have known of a relationship between Shakespeare and Herbert. They referred to the Herbert brothers as having favored Shakespeare's plays and their author. However, their claim may have merely been an ingratiating gesture on the occasion of dedicating their publication to Pembroke.[9] Like Southampton, Pembroke also resisted marriage, to no less than four proposed brides.[10]

The mysterious dedication of the sonnets by their publisher Thomas Thorpe to a "Mr. W.H." has also played a role in the debate over the young man's identity. Advocates of William Herbert point to the initials of the earl's name as evidence that he is the sonnets' dedicatee and thus presumably the young man to whom they are written. The identification of W.H. has never been clear cut, however. Those who believe the initials stand for Herbert must explain the "Mr.," since an earl would be much more conventionally and appropriately entitled a "Lord." By imagining the sonnets' printer mistakenly reversed W.H.'s initials Henry Wriothesley works, too, but the problem of the "Mr." remains. One recent scholar has suggested that "Mr. W.H." is a printer's error for "Mr. W. Sh."—that is William Shakespeare—with the "S" accidentally dropped when the type for the book was set. Shakespeare, of lower social status, would more appropriately be entitled "Mr." A sillier suggestion for W. H. (though likewise implying Shakespeare as dedicatee) has been William Himself![11]

The identity of the black mistress has been still more difficult to discern. There are no initials narrowing the field, nor can the pool be limited to aristocratic women, since, though she is now conventionally called "the dark lady," nothing in the sonnets suggests her high social status. A lady-in-waiting of Queen Elizabeth's named Mary Fitton who had an affair and illegitimate child with the earl of Pembroke was once a popular candidate, at least among Pembroke advocates, but she has never been particularly plausible.[12] Neither has Aemelia Lanyer, a published poet (a rarity for women during Shakespeare's day). Lanyer was mistress of Henry Carey, Lord Hunsdon. Though not one of the two major candidates for the young man (Southampton or Herbert), Hunsdon was patron of Shakespeare's acting company the Lord Chamberlain's men from 1594 until his death in 1596. And Lanyer had been described as "very brown in youth." Alas, closer inspection of these handwritten words revealed them to be "very brave in youth."[13]

More interesting recent speculation has centered around whether the black mistress was racially black rather than a light-skinned brunette, as has been traditionally supposed. A racially black candidate for the mistress has been proposed: a London brothel-keeper nicknamed Black Lucy. Problems remain with this identification as well, however. It appears there were *two* London brothel-keepers during Shakespeare's lifetime with that nickname. One of these, who we know from court records was active in the late 1570s, could have been racially black — she was part of a prostitution ring that had "blackamoor" clients and operated in a part of London in which blacks were living. But she was by no means certainly black, and was probably too old to be the black mistress by the time Shakespeare wrote the sonnets. The other Black Lucy was active in the 1590s, but she was, despite her nickname, white. Most importantly, whether black or white, old or young, nothing directly links either of these women with Shakespeare.[14]

Though the identification of the black mistress with a particular black woman remains speculative, the idea that "black" in the sonnets refers to race is more plausible. *Othello* is clear evidence that "black" had this meaning for Shakespeare, and the play suggests Shakespeare's interest in interracial relationships as well. It is true that brunettes and black-eyed women populated sixteenth-century sonnets, antidotes to the by-then stereotypical praise of the sonnet lady for her fair hair and complexion (a "pure white dove" is how the famous fourteenth-century poet Petrarch describes his Laura). But it is equally true that by the mid-seventeenth century there was a whole set of love poems written by white Englishmen about women who were racially black. The sonnets might have helped initiate the later tradition as much as followed the earlier one.[15]

More plausible still is that Shakespeare knew he was associating the black mistress with racial blackness, whatever her actual race. Certainly the author of *Othello* — whose habit in the sonnets is to let words mean as much

as they can — would have been aware that his repeated emphasis on the word
"black" could call a black woman to mind, among the other meanings of
that word. Shakespeare dramatizes just this response in *A Midsummer Night's
Dream*, in which Lysander insults Hermia as an "Ethiope," for being darker
than her fair rival Helena.[16] Similarly, one of the Black Lucies was also called
in one instance "Lucy Negro" (negro always referred to racial blackness in
Renaissance English), either because she was black or because a loose woman
with a "blackened" reputation was readily associated with a foreign race and
ethnicity.[17]

About the rival poet's identity little can be said. Many famous and not
so famous Elizabethan poets have been proposed. Among these, in alphabet-
ical order, are: Barnes, Chapman, Daniel, Davies, Davison, Drayton, Griffin,
Jonson, Marlowe, Markham, Nashe, Peele, Ralegh, Shakespeare (it's com-
plicated), Spenser and Watson. However, the evidence for any of these poets
goes from circumstantial to silly. It usually involves noting that the poet
wrote for either Southampton or Pembroke, that he has qualities Shakespeare assigns to the rival poet (such as greatness), and/or that some particular words or phrases in the sonnets about the rival recalls him. By freely
associating between the evocative language of the sonnets and the whole
body of European literature even such chronologically and geographically
improbable candidates as Chaucer and Dante (not to mention the Italian
Renaissance poet Torquato Tasso) have found themselves snagged in the rival
poet net![18]

On the other hand, there would seem to be one personage in the sonnets who could be confidently identified, the writer who says "I," that is,
Shakespeare. Generations of modern students of poetry, however, have
learned not to mix up the poem's "persona," the first-person speaker of a
poem, with the poem's author. The persona of the poem might be the fiction
of the author. And if the speaker of the sonnets is Shakespeare's fiction, then
all the other personages in the sonnets are likely fictions as well. Perhaps the
poet, the young man, the black mistress, and the rival poet are simply drawn
from the conventions of sonneteering — with persuasive vividness by a great
dramatist. Thus the hunt for the young man and the others is futile and the
assumption that the sonnets are autobiographical is unwarranted. Over the
years many readers of the sonnets have held this position.[19]

This view, however, can be argued with. It is true that poets of the sixteenth and seventeenth centuries, like many modern poets, created fictional
speakers. A good number of English Renaissance sonnet ladies have names —
Phyllis, Chloris, Zepheria, Parthenophe, Fidessa — probably drawn from literature (of Greece or Rome) rather than from life. Composing sonnets was
a literary exercise and a sign of learning and gentility, not necessarily an

expression of true feeling.[20] One sonneteer observed that "a man may write of Love, and not be in love; as well as of husbandry [i.e. farming], and not go to the plough."[21] Comparing the poetry of love to poems about farming, the writer was referring to the georgic, a classical poetic tradition that dealt with agriculture.

Other Renaissance sonnet sequences, however, are more truly autobiographical. Sir Philip Sidney's sonnets, the most influential in the Elizabethan period, were written about a real woman, Penelope Devereux. One of these sonnets was not initially published because it played on her married name, Penelope Rich. In his sonnet sequence *Amoretti* the Elizabethan poet Edmund Spenser refers to other poetry that he has been writing and has one sonnet in which he praises three Elizabeths: his queen, his mother and his beloved. And indeed he did marry Elizabeth Boyle.[22] Even literary names could coyly disguise real women. There may have been no actual "Parthenophe," but "Stella" (from the Latin for star) was Sidney's name for Penelope Rich.

Shakespeare's sonnets appear closer to this autobiographical side of Renaissance sonneteering. They repeatedly draw attention to their writer's life. Sonnet 111, for example, complains that fortune "did not better for my life provide / Than public means which public manners breeds." The lines have been interpreted to refer to Shakespeare's profession as an actor and certainly seem to refer to some specific, autobiographical fact about their writer, whatever it is. Sonnets 135 and 136, repeatedly play on Shakespeare's first name, Will. Sonnet 136, in fact, ends "my name is Will."

In this book I take Will at his word, and refer to the "I" of the sonnets as Shakespeare, not "the speaker" or "the poet." It is true we should not confuse Hamlet with his author, but sonnets are more autobiographical than plays and Shakespeare's sonnets especially so. Even if these sonnets were pure fiction, Shakespeare seems to have wanted to persuade us that they were autobiography, that they were about a writer of poetry named "Will." I grant it possible — though don't think it likely — that Shakespeare was counting on readers to respond knowingly to the most apparently truth-felt passions of the sonnets as the aesthetic product of a dramatic master — but if so he does little to signal the sonnets' aesthetic distance, such as using classical names. And he was taking a risk. The sonneteer who wrote "a man may write of Love, and not be in love," felt the need to warn against assuming the opposite. And his sonnet sequence — entitled *Licia* with a subtitle calling attention to his "imitation of the best Latin poets, and others" — sounds much less self-revelatory than Shakespeare's.

Another question about the autobiographical status of the sonnets' story hovers around the sonnets' "you"s: the young man and black mistress. The

sonnets never, after all, actually refer to their names. Readers have made up
the names young man or dark lady (or black mistress) as a convenience, but
perhaps names lend a unity to sonnet "characters" that do not really exist.
Even if the sonnets' anonymous "you"s are not fictional, they could be multiple. That is, Shakespeare could on different occasions have written sonnets
to more than one man or woman. Only the composition of these sonnets
into a sequence creates the illusion of stable characters. Stephen Greenblatt
in his Shakespeare biography, for example, wonders whether the earlier
"young man" sonnets were written to the earl of Southampton, the later to
the earl of Pembroke.[23]

   We cannot know whether in the creation of a sonnet sequence multiple
male or female recipients were reduced to one man or woman. We can say
that the sonnets themselves do not encourage the idea of multiple young men
or black mistresses. Because other features of the sonnets — their repetitions
of word, image or theme — encourage us to read the sequence as a unified
whole, we are led to treat their recipients in the same way. Moreover, faithful and even obsessive love for a single person is a fundamental aspect of
sonnet love convention.[24] The sonnets' doubled male and female beloveds
powerfully complicate this convention. But a sequence of passionate avowals
of love to not just two but multiple "you"s would sound increasingly hollow, rather than compelling. It is sometimes said that we reduce the sonnets'
rich variety when we turn their potentially multiple "you"s into a single
"young man" or "black mistress." But variety is not complexity.[25] The con-
centration of various attitudes toward two "you"s, rather than the dispersal
of that variety over many, creates the feeling that the sonnets record a dense,
and dynamic, experience.[26]

   In sum: readers who are inclined — and able! — to read Shakespeare's
sonnets and imagine their "I" as a persona, not Shakespeare, are welcome to
imagine the "Shakespeare" in this book as a persona, too. Likewise, readers
who are able to read the "you"s of the sonnets — the young man and black
mistress — as fabrications of the sonnet sequence, may do the same with my
invocations of these names. Since my ultimate interest in this book is not
Shakespearean autobiography but literary and cultural criticism, it matters
less to me whether the story the sonnets tell is literally true. Even fiction needs
to speak some kind of imaginative truth, if it is to be compelling. Hamlet
may not have been real, but indecision and adultery are. A sensitive, expres-
sive poet born into patronage culture will write differently than one born
into a world dominated by the marketplace. And perhaps Shakespeare did
not really love a young man — but he seems to have believed that his readers would believe that he could.

   It should be added as a corollary that all autobiography is shaped by the writer and his cultural experience. It is never the unmediated truth — but this does not mean that it is simply untrue. To qualify autobiography in this way is not to disqualify it. Shakespeare may have really been involved in a love triangle. But he was also selecting a story that would have powerful cultural resonances in the Renaissance as well.[27] The sonnets are highly wrought poetry. Yet the ability and desire to write this kind of poetry itself says something important about the conditions under which the author wrote.[28]

A number of bibliographical unknowns about the sonnets make their biographical puzzles still more difficult to solve. We do not know, first of all, whether the sonnets were published with Shakespeare's permission. Many have believed that they were pirated, a fate occasionally met by literary works at a time when they were often passed around and copied among friends in manuscript. If the original manuscript or a copy of it fell into a publisher's hands, authors' rights in their creative work were not protected (Renaissance copyright law instead protected publishers from the infringements of other publishers).[29] For example, two of Shakespeare's sonnets (138 and 144) were published in 1599 in an unauthorized volume called *The Passionate Pilgrim* — with work lifted from other contemporary poets added in for good measure, and all attributed to Shakespeare.

Those who believe Thorpe pirated the sonnets cite the unlikelihood that Shakespeare would have allowed such private and possibly scandalous poems to be printed, that Thorpe's edition of the sonnets had many printing errors, which their author would have corrected had he overseen its publication, and that the edition carries the printer's dedication — that enigmatic one to Mr. W.H.— not Shakespeare's. Authors typically dedicated their poetry to a potential patron, as Shakespeare himself did when he published his poems *Venus and Adonis* and *The Rape of Lucrece*. The debate about authorization has also revolved around the reputation of Thorpe. Was he the kind of publisher who pirated authors' works?[30]

Fewer literary historians have argued that Shakespeare authorized publication of the sonnets. A recent proponent of this view, however, has been the Shakespeare scholar Katherine Duncan-Jones, who suggests that Shakespeare published his work when threat of plague closed the theater, leaving Shakespeare without the income he usually received from it.[31] Shakespeare published *Venus and Adonis* and *The Rape of Lucrece* during plague years when the theaters were closed. Duncan-Jones points out that the year of the sonnets' publication, 1609, was likewise a plague year with the theaters again closed. She also argues that Thorpe was not a pirate but a highly reputable publisher whom Shakespeare would be likely to use, since he had published the work of many literary notables of the day, including Shakespeare's friend and rival playwright Ben Jonson. Thorpe may have written the dedication, Duncan-Jones suggests, because Shakespeare had already left London to escape the plague. Finally, she and others have argued that the number of printing errors in the sonnets was not unusual for the time.[32]

Whether or not Shakespeare authorized the sonnets' publication, there is no doubt that the case against it has been fueled by a reluctance to believe that Shakespeare *would* have allowed these sonnets to be published, since they chronicle relationships — adulterous and possibly homosexual — that have disturbed many readers.[33] Much of this literary historical work was done in the nineteenth and earlier twentieth centuries. Literary historians today, no longer embarrassed by the content of sonnets, may be more willing to look for evidence that Shakespeare authorized the sonnets' publication.

If we knew whether Shakespeare authorized publication of the sonnets then we could decide more conclusively whether the sonnets are in the correct order. That order now almost always derives from Thorpe's first edition of the sonnets, which is usually referred to as the 1609 quarto (quarto refers to the format of the book). If Shakespeare gave the sonnets to Thorpe to publish, then it's likely they're in the order that Shakespeare wanted. If Thorpe pirated the sonnets, it becomes more likely that the order of the 1609 quarto was Thorpe's and not Shakespeare's. Even if they were pirated, however, the sonnets' order might still be Shakespeare's. Thorpe might have printed them from a manuscript that Shakespeare himself prepared, which then passed out of his hands and somehow into Thorpe's.[34]

Uncertainty about the order of the sonnets once led many editors and critics to propose their own reordering of them. In the words of Shakespeare's *King Lear*, "that way madness lies."[35] So many of the sonnets are thematically linked one way or another, and the threads of the narrative are so slight, that many new combinations can and have been proposed without being sufficiently persuasive to convince most readers that the new order is the correct one. Editors today thus usually leave be the order of the 1609 quarto, which seems as persuasive from a narrative point of view as the new ones, and, because it is the earliest, has the most likely claim to represent Shakespeare's intentions. An editor who reorders the sonnets, on the other hand, must trust to his or her ability to intuit Shakespeare's mind.[36]

The question of sonnet order is an especially loaded one since most of the sonnets are gender neutral: they do not specify a man or woman as their subject or recipient. One cannot know for certain in most of the sonnets whether Shakespeare is expressing love to a man or a woman. Nonetheless, based on the order of the 1609 quarto the sonnets are frequently divided between those written to or about the young man (numbers 1–126) and those written to or about the black mistress (numbers 127–154). This break is marked by sonnet 126, which is missing two lines and thus functions as a kind of coda, and sonnet 127, which introduces the black mistress. If the sonnets are out of order, however, some of the gender neutral sonnets currently in the young man group might really be written to the black mistress. This possibility has sometimes appealed to those uncomfortable with the erotic tone of the first 126 sonnets who suppose that the more ardent among these sonnets were written to the black mistress and then got mixed up into the first group.[37] The reverse, however, could just as well be true: some of the more highly sexual sonnets in the black mistress group that are gender neutral could have been written to the young man.[38]

Skepticism of the sonnet order has lately gained some notable adherents. For example, in their recent introduction to the sonnets, Paul Edmondson and Stanley Wells caution against assuming that there aren't poems to a woman in the young man section, or vice versa.[39] I believe however that the 1609 order of the sonnets is at least roughly correct. Sonnets 1–126 share stylistic similarities, as do sonnets 127–154. The first 126 sonnets, thought to be to the young man, are generally more loving and reverential, while the last 28 sonnets, thought to be to the black mistress, are generally more cynical, angry and sexual. Moreover, in each group the sonnets that explicitly specify the gender of their recipient reproduce this division.[40] Criticism of the gendered division of the sonnets would be more persuasive if even one sonnet definitively addressed to a male or female disrupted this pattern. But none does. It remains possible that Shakespeare diverted from this stylistic pattern only when he *also* wrote sonnets that did not identify the gender of their recipient, but there's no apparent reason to make such an assumption.

Further, this tonal division is consistent with those sonnets that explicitly compare Shakespeare's "two loves" in a single sonnet. For example, sonnet 144 ("Two loves I have, of comfort and despair") juxtaposes Shakespeare's unequal loves for a "man right fair" and "a woman coloured ill." The love triangle sonnets 40–42 likewise emphasize Shakespeare's greater love for the young man than for the woman who comes between them. Sonnets such as these provide a kind of map for the sequence as a whole and again suggest the 1609 quarto is correct in its grouping of the more positive "fair" sonnets to the young man and the more negative sonnets to the black mistress, a woman "coloured ill" in her complexion and behavior.

Since in this book I do not try to tell a narrowly biographical story, it is less important to me whether some sonnets within each group are out of place. I do stress the gender divide of the sonnets, which I find discernible in the sonnets themselves and consistent with habits of thought in Shakespeare's day to treat men and women as different and unequal. As I argue in part three of this book, the sonnets to the black mistress in particular echo —

and sometimes challenge — Renaissance stereotypes about women's "black" behavior and male fears of losing sexual control over women and themselves.[41] In fact, unlike their forbears, contemporary skeptics of the 1609 sonnet order appear troubled by the prospect of a Shakespeare who hates women, rather than one who loves men. After all, homosexual desire in the sonnets only makes these poems more universal.[42]

When did Shakespeare write the sonnets? He likely composed at least some of them by 1598 (Shakespeare would have been thirty-four), when a writer named Francis Meres, in the course of likening Shakespeare to the Roman poet Ovid, commended Shakespeare's "sugred Sonnets among his Private friends."[43] Meres's remark suggests that by this time some of the sonnets were circulating in manuscript.[44] We also know that a year later sonnets 138 and 144 were published in *The Passionate Pilgrim*. All the rest were first published in 1609 (when Shakespeare was forty-five), which provides an end date to the sonnets' composition. These dates do not tell us however how long before 1598 Shakespeare was writing sonnets — suppositions go to as early as 1582 — or how many of the sonnets published in 1609 might have been written (or revised) after 138 and 144 appeared in print in 1599.[45]

One way scholars have tried to date the sonnets more precisely is by comparing the sonnets to other writing by Shakespeare whose dates of composition are better known — a method called "stylometry," and usually conducted today with the aid of statistics and computers. For example, if a sonnet shares the vocabulary and style of *Venus and Adonis*, a poem Shakespeare published and likely composed in the early 1590s, then, the argument goes, that sonnet was probably written during that period as well. Recent stylometric studies suggest that the order of the sonnets as published is not the order in which they were written, but these studies do not agree on the dates of composition. One dates the sonnets from 1590 to 1604, one from 1598 right up to their publication in 1609, and another from 1591 to their 1609 publication.[46]

Scholars have come to these different results because of the difficulties that complicate stylometric analysis. Stylometry likes things neat, but writing is a messy process. For example, since Shakespeare likely revised at least some of the sonnets, a word shared between a sonnet and a play Shakespeare wrote in the seventeenth century might be the result of revision, rather than evidence of the sonnet's seventeenth-century composition. The different genres in which Shakespeare wrote might also have influenced his words and styles. A sonnet written at the same time as a play would not necessarily share the play's language or style. And Shakespeare when he composed a sonnet could have simply recalled a word (or more) from a long-completed play, or vice versa. A linguistic correspondence does not guarantee a temporal one, especially given Shakespeare's powerful memory for words. Finally, individual sonnets within groups could have different dates.[47] Nonetheless, while the date ranges assigned to the sonnets vary considerably, these analyses generally agree that 127–154 are the earliest sonnets, with 1–103 somewhere in the middle, and 104–126 the last written.

The conclusion that 127–154 are earlier than the rest of the sonnets lends support to the idea that these sonnets are part of a distinct group. At the same time, the dates of this group overlap with the young man sonnets, just as particular sonnets within both groups contain overlapping relations among Shakespeare, the young man and a woman (explicitly the "black mistress" in 144, likely her in 40–42).[48] Most striking is the reversal of order and chronology for the black mistress sonnets, written first but placed last. Why did Shakespeare — if it was he — do this? I address this question in the section of the book on those sonnets.

An alternative means for determining the date of the sonnets has been to search for their correspondences not to other texts but to identifiable historical or literary historical contexts. For example, since the earl of Southampton was seven years older than the earl of Pembroke, readers who believe the young man was Southampton need to assume an earlier date for the sonnets if the young man is to be of a marriageable age, while readers who prefer Pembroke assume a later date. But since the identity of the young man remains uncertain, so must this way of dating the sonnets.[49]

Rare references to mentions of particular events within the sonnets have also been seized upon. But these references are hardly clear. Most tantalizing has been sonnet 107, which enigmatically declares "the mortal moon hath her eclipse endured" and "peace proclaims olives of endless age." It sounds like Shakespeare means something specific, but what? Many possibilities have been suggested, including the 1588 defeat of the Spanish Armada under Queen Elizabeth, Elizabeth's 1596 "grand climacteric" (when she turned sixty-three, a year with great astrological significance), the 1601 revolt against Elizabeth by the Earl of Essex, and the 1603 succession of the crown from Elizabeth to James.[50] The range of possibilities covers the entire period when the sonnets might have been written.

Finally, some critics argue for an earlier date for the sonnets based on the assumption that Shakespeare wrote them, as did many another Elizabethan poet, during the height of the sonnet fad in the early to mid 1590s. But Shakespeare's sonnets are atypical in a number of respects, and might be in their date of composition as well. Moreover, Shakespeare might have started the sonnets during the sonnet craze, and then kept writing or revising them into the seventeenth century, as did the sonneteers Samuel Daniel and Michael Drayton.[51]

Shakespeare's sonnets offer little in the way of names, dates, places or events yet they are rich in feelings, ideas and experiences. And it is as poems of a timeless experience of love that the sonnets are now most often read and celebrated. But how timeless are Shakespeare's sonnets? Even aspects of the sonnets that seem transcendent rather than timebound have a history, one that can be just as elusive to modern readers as the sonnets' names and dates. Many of the sonnets' apparently familiar ideas and experiences — homosexuality, heterosexuality, literature, love, marriage, ambition — had strikingly different meanings when Shakespeare wrote about them.

Certainly Shakespeare's sonnets continue to speak to us. But we can also learn to hear what the sonnets have to say that we no longer recognize or understand. Shakespeare praises the young man of the sonnets as the image of "what beauty was" (sonnet 68). But how did Shakespeare's ideas of beauty — literary and erotic — differ from today's? In the next section of this book I ask what it meant in the Renaissance to write a sonnet. In section two I consider what it meant for one man to write a sonnet to another. And in section three I ask what it meant to love a woman. Opinions about the sonnets have been equally timebound: section four describes the wide range of ways the sonnets have been read over the past nearly 400 years. And in the book's coda I ask why we should want to read the sonnets as chronicles of "what beauty was" in Renaissance England and after, rather than as timeless and universal works of art.

SECTION I

"This Powerful Rhyme"

1

Mirrors of Courtesy

The sonnet's history begins with the form's invention in thirteenth-century Italy and continues with its fruition in the fourteenth century at the hands of the Italian Francesco Petrarch. His sonnets to Laura would be much imitated throughout Europe, including in England, where the sonnet traveled in the early sixteenth century through Sir Thomas Wyatt and the Earl of Surrey. Surrey's role in this history is distinguished by his invention of the particular sonnet rhyme scheme, sometimes called the English sonnet, that Shakespeare also used. (The fame of the latter has trumped the invention of the former, since this form is also sometimes called, not very fairly to Surrey, the Shakespearean sonnet.) Literary forms don't really "travel" on their own, however. They have to attract talented writers. An important reason for the pull of the sonnet lies not in literary history, but in the history of manners.

We don't always think of manners as having a history, but they do, in ways brilliantly chronicled by the sociologist Norbert Elias. Here are some samples of advice, collected by Elias, from medieval guides to courtesy:

- Do not touch yourself under your clothes with your bare hands.
- It is unseemly to blow your nose into the tablecloth.
- May refined people be preserved from those who gnaw their bones and put them back in the dish.
- Do not spit into the basin when you wash your hands, but beside it.[1]

These precepts hardly sound like the height of good manners. Yet they were written for the elite of medieval society, its courtly class, and the good manners taught in these precepts helped to define this class's high status. Thus it is "refined people" who distinguish themselves by keeping gnawed bones out of the communal dish.[2] When we compare this advice to expectations for good manners today, it is plain how much ideas about manners have changed.

They were changing by Shakespeare's day. In his treatise on manners, the great Renaissance humanist Desiderius Erasmus has this to say about blowing the nose:

> To blow your nose on your hat or clothing is rustic, and to do so with the arm or elbow befits a tradesman; nor is it more polite to use the hand, if you immediately smear the snot on your garment. It is proper to wipe the nostrils with a handkerchief, and to do this while turning away, if more honorable people are present.[3]

The advice still seems crude. It goes on too long about nose blowing for modern taste and it advises to conceal blowing the nose only when "more honorable people are present"! But there are differences from medieval precept. The very detail of Erasmus's advice, however unpleasant to us, suggests greater subtlety in the contemplation of manners, a more careful effort to get them right. And Erasmus adds a refinement: the use of the handkerchief, a chic luxury item at the time he was writing.[4]

What drives these changes? Elias argued that increasing attention to manners did not emerge from an innate sense of good taste. If it did, one would have to explain why people in the medieval period lacked it. Rather, Elias found a cause for this emergence in what historians call the rise of royal absolutism. During the Renaissance, European monarchs increasingly claimed to have "absolute" power over their leading nobles and the affairs of the entire kingdom they ruled. Medieval kings had less power, both ideologically and practically. The monarch who perhaps represents the zenith of absolutist rule is France's Louis XIV, whose grandiloquent nickname "The Sun King" describes him as the height, center and source of all life. Elizabeth I's grandfather Henry VII is often considered the first of the absolutist English monarchs, while absolutist rule in England reaches its doomed height with Charles I, executed in 1649 by parliamentary revolutionaries.[5] Everything Shakespeare wrote came between these beginning and end points in the history of English royal absolutism. His art — and the great literary outpouring of the English Renaissance more generally — is shaped by the world that royal absolutism made.

To rule absolutely, Renaissance kings sought to blunt the power of their greatest nobles, who were also their greatest competitors for authority. In this struggle kings tended to discourage their nobles' involvement in war: a warrior nobility might not just fight for the monarchy but also threaten it. Moreover, war depleted the king's treasury and hence his ability to finance his rule. Changes in the nature of warfare, especially the growing importance of foot soldiers over horsemen, further discouraged noble involvement in wars. In England, three-quarters of the nobility had seen battle under the rule of Henry VIII. Only one-quarter had by 1576, under Henry's daughter Elizabeth. During the reign of King James, Elizabeth's even more war averse successor, the number of nobles who had seen military service decreased again, to one in five.[6] The Elizabethan poet Edmund Spenser registered these declines. A 1591 poem by Spenser complains that members of the nobility, having accomplished no great deeds of their own, live off the heroism of their ancestors. While Spenser's contemporaries boast of arms and ancestry, the "vertuous deeds, which did those Armes first giue / To their Grandsyres, they care not to atchiue."[7]

The military campaigns that the nobility did undertake were frequently disappointments. Queen Elizabeth sent the Earl of Leicester to bolster the Dutch in their rebellion against Spanish control of the Low Countries (roughly, the modern Netherlands). Leicester was hailed on his arrival to the Low Countries as a second King Arthur, but he lost battles with the Spanish at almost every turn. He left the Low Countries in less than two years later with Elizabeth looking to negotiate a peace with Spain. Robert Naunton, a younger contemporary of Leicester, suggested as the motto for the earl's lackluster military command *veni, vidi, redivi*: I came, I saw, I returned. To be sure, two years after Leicester's failure England triumphed over the Spanish Armada. But this was a battle at sea rather than the fight on land traditional to medieval chivalry.[8]

With diminishing opportunities for and skill in chivalric warfare, the Renaissance aristocrat required a new way of justifying his superiority.[9] Another remark of Naunton's about Leicester describes what the Renaissance noble or gentleman might do in these circumstances. The earl, Naunton writes, "had more of Mercury than of Mars."[10] No longer a god of war, the Renaissance aristocrat transformed himself into a master (like the messenger god Mercury) of the arts of peace. Elegant, fashionable and witty, he became a courtier — and sometimes a poet.

Baldesar Castiglione's hugely popular *The Book of the Courtier*, first published in England in 1561, defined the courtier's role.[11] The courtier, Castiglione writes, is "endowed by nature not only with talent and with beauty of countenance and person, but with that certain grace which we call an 'air,' which shall make him at first sight pleasing and lovable to all who see him."[12] Our word "courtesy" originally describes the graceful manners distinctively displayed by the aristocracy residing at court — only more recently has "courtesy" been democratized to mean the good graces expected of everyone.

In Shakespeare's England real-life adepts at the courtier's art were nobles and gentlemen such as the Earl of Leicester, the queen's long favorite. Leicester was renowned for his handsome body, fashionable clothing, and patronage of learned men. Leicester's nephew Sir Philip Sidney, a brilliant poet, provided another exemplar of the courtly style. Sir Walter Ralegh is famous for having tossed his fine cloak over a puddle in Queen Elizabeth's way. That story, first told about forty years after Ralegh's death, is probably false. But as legend it captures the glamorous sense of style that launched Ralegh from a younger brother and provincial gentleman to another of the queen's favorites.[13]

All these men were also known for their military exploits, even if their military experience was not always successful. But manners now had to supplement the aristocrat's warrior role. The courtier was indeed supposed to be an all-talented "Renaissance man," to possess, as Ophelia says of Hamlet, "the courtier's, soldier's, scholar's eye, tongue, sword."[14] For the accomplished Hamlets of this world, good manners required more than not blowing one's nose into a tablecloth.

Besides the mark of distinction they provided, deft manners helped the aristocrat adjust to the arena in which he now sought power, the royal court. While battle encourages aggression, the courtier's life required the elaborate and nuanced rules defined by good manners. At court the aristocrat depended on the absolutist monarch and on other courtiers, with whom he had to make alliances and arrange favors in order to move ahead in the court's hierarchy. He had to be politic (is this why Hamlet delays?), or, as Shakespeare's Kent unflatteringly puts it in *King Lear*, "superserviceable."[15]

Shakespeare's gruff medieval retainer Kent may not have liked courtly behavior, but in truth the aristocrat at court would not get far through mere violence (Kent himself is shortly to be put in the stocks for hitting the toadying courtier Oswald). Courtly manners thus helped to rein in aristocratic violence engrained by centuries of warfare.[16] Shakespeare has Touchstone, the clown in *As You Like It,* joke about the way the rules of courtesy deter aggression. Even the duel has its elaborate etiquette, provided by the gentleman's reading: "O sir, we quarrel in print, by the book, as you have books for good manners."[17] Touchstone slyly implies that the true reason for these bookish rules is to avoid real fighting.

What kept the courtier from feeling wholly captive to the rules and restraints of court life was the idea, emphasized by Castiglione, of courtly grace. True, the well mannered gentleman follows rules, but he follows them so effortlessly, cleverly and charmingly (think of Ralegh) that he appears charismatic rather than constrained. The stately court dance, with its exacting graces, epitomizes this mix of self-rule and self-expression.[18]

And so too does the sonnet. Philip Sidney is a master of the form:

Having this day my horse, my hand, my lance,
  Guided so well, that I obtained the prize,
  Both by the judgement of the English eyes,
And of some sent from that sweet enemy, France;
Horsemen my skill in horsemanship advance;
  Town-folks my strength; a daintier judge applies
  His praise to sleight, which from good use doth rise;
Some lucky wits impute it but to chance;
  Others, because of both sides I do take
My blood from them, who did excel in this,
Think nature me a man of arms did make.
How far they shoot awry! The true cause is,
  Stella looked on, and from her heavenly face
  Sent forth the beams, which made so fair my race.[19]

The sonnet's occasion is one of the chivalric pageants frequently staged at court in Shakespeare's time. This one was attended as well by ambassadors from France.[20] The "English eyes" viewing the tournament included not only the townsfolk Sidney refers to in the sonnet, but also other courtiers and Queen Elizabeth, all of whom view Sidney carry away the prize for his skill in horsemanship. Sidney's proud admirers find the cause for his victory in their own best qualities (horsemen credit good horsemanship, and so on). But, Sidney tells us, they are all wrong: it is the beauty of Stella, his beloved, that makes him great.

What a lovely thing to say. It's a clever one too, since it allows Sidney to praise his own abilities at length without seeming proud. Sidney gracefully concludes the sonnet by turning those praises to someone else. These are the pleasing manners of the courtier.

Why write a sonnet, with its demanding formal requirements in length, meter and rhyme? Sidney's sonnet offers one answer to this question. The sonnet displays Sidney's ability to follow the rules so well that doing so becomes a kind of grace. Just as humility balances pride in the story the sonnet tells, so the tight rules of the sonnet find a balance in the poet's creative exploitation of them. Balance is, in fact, the key idea in this sonnet: the balance of the nice compliment, the balance of the poet who maneuvers his way through the sonnet form, and the balance of the horseman that the sonnet celebrates.[21]

It is no coincidence that this sonnet describes Sidney's chivalric ability. The sonnet looks backward to the medieval warrior. Sidney longed to fight and, when he finally got his chance, died heroically in England's struggle against Spain. But the sonnet also reveals its present moment in the history of manners by twice confining the warrior: first to merely playing at fighting in the ornamental display of chivalry at court, and then to the narration of even this diminished court chivalry in the highly formal sonnet. The prize that Sidney finally wins from his admirers is given for his balance as a poet, not a horseman. But it was the balance of the poet — his tact, his grace, his way with words — that court life increasingly required.

Shakespeare is also a master of the form. Unlike Sidney he was not born into one of England's leading families, but by writing sonnets this commoner's son was emulating the courtier's social graces. His sonnet 62, for example, follows Sidney's deft transformation of pride into humility — though, perhaps because of Shakespeare's commoner origins, his sonnet is more edgy and introspective than Sidney's:

> Sin of self-love possesseth all mine eye,
> And all my soul, and all my every part;
> And for this sin there is no remedy,
> It is so grounded inward in my heart.
> Methinks no face so gracious is as mine,
> No shape so true, no truth of such account,
> And for myself mine own worth do define
> As I all other in all worths surmount.
> But when my glass shows me myself indeed,
> Beated and chapped with tanned antiquity,
> Mine own self-love quite contrary I read;
> Self so self-loving were iniquity.
>   'Tis thee, my self, that for myself I praise,
>   Painting my age with beauty of thy days.

The horse, the feats of chivalry, the French ambassadors, the crowd of admiring onlookers are gone, but the competitive self-display evoked by them in Sidney's sonnet remains discernible in Shakespeare's. Shakespeare's boast of grace in face and figure recalls Castiglione's ideal. His rivalrous comparisons of himself to others are not so far from Sidney's proud performance in the tiltyard, and recall the atmosphere of the Renaissance court, where the graces of body, gesture and word figure in struggles for attention and prestige.

Caught by self-love, Shakespeare praises his face and shape. But even more than for Sidney, Shakespeare's grace is with words. We can point especially to this sonnet's expert use of sound. For example, in the poem's second quatrain (a quatrain is a four-line unit of poetry) the sound of the word "gracious" echoes "face," "true" echoes "truth," "myself" echoes "mine," and "all," echoes, by repeating, "all." The poem everywhere exploits these kinds of sound effects, but they seem particularly pronounced in this quatrain. It is as if Shakespeare were marking his belief in his supreme physical grace with an equally supreme display of verbal graces.

Because the mirror-like symmetry of these verbal echoes begins to sound overwrought — their high artfulness giving the impression of someone trying too hard to be clever — we might further notice that the sonnet displays an excessive wish for physical grace by an excessive display of verbal graces. At the same time, this matching of style and subject makes for just the kind of proud performance that the poem condemns. If Shakespeare also means the mirroring of sounds in the second quatrain to provide a verbal equivalent to the mirror pictured in the third ("glass" is a Renaissance word for "mirror"), the sonnet's paradoxical effect of denying grace with an excess of it becomes more pronounced still.

Shakespeare's sonnet finally gracefully denies grace by changing the image in its mirror. Shakespeare's sonnet most obviously reminds us of Sidney's in the way it too avoids self-love by complimenting someone else. Just as Sidney finally praises Stella, so it is only by finally praising the young man, whom Shakespeare calls his other self ("'Tis thee, myself"), that Shakespeare can love himself without sin.

The subtle notes of Sidney's deft compliment play in the conclusion to Shakespeare's sonnet too. The sonnet manages to praise the young man, humble the writer and yet never wholly stop praising its writer either, since Shakespeare is elevated by his relationship to the young man, who becomes the right kind of mirror. The words of the sonnet also display Shakespeare's grace, even as these words declare that that grace belongs to another.

Dependent on others more powerful than himself, the courtier must assert his good qualities without appearing arrogant. He does so by lavishly praising his superior and hemming self-praise with humility. Good form, good manners: the art of the sonnet is the art of the courtier.

2

Educating the Courtier

Grace and good manners alone do not make a sonnet, however; it also requires considerable verbal dexterity. This the Renaissance aristocrat — or would-be aristocrat — got from the style of education in the Renaissance, which focused heavily on reading and writing. Meanwhile, the same political changes that encouraged the cultivation of courtly manners accelerated the drive to get these skills. Because royal absolutism increased the size of national government it put a new premium on literacy.

Looking back from the end of the sixteenth century, the earl of Essex complained of the ignorance of his forefathers: formerly "the nobility of England brought up their sons as they entered their whelps [i.e. trained their hounds], and thought them wise enough if they could chase their deer."[22] Essex's view was typical. The medieval aristocracy's reputation for brutish illiteracy extends from the sixteenth century into the present. This reputation has not been completely fair. Members of the later medieval nobility were often literate in their vernacular language and sometimes in Latin, even as some members of the English aristocracy remained illiterate well into the Renaissance. In 1536 one English gentleman defended himself against a charge of treason by claiming that he could neither have composed nor read the treasonous letter attributed to him, for he was unable to write more than his own name.[23] Nonetheless, the quest for a literary education among the aristocracy redoubled in the Renaissance, as the roles of the aristocrat changed in response to the development of more stable and war-averse absolutist rule.

Essex might sneer, but raising hounds and chasing deer were hunting skills fit for a warrior aristocracy. Under royal absolutism, however, power increasingly went through the instruments of a stronger national government, rather than through the sword. And this means power went through language: in legal and administrative records, in long-distance communication, in political persuasion, and in propaganda. The demand for sophisticated skills of reading and writing intensified in the bureaucratically complex national government. As the Renaissance aristocrat had fewer chances to fight in wars, moreover, a literary education became more attractive as a justification for his elite status. Again there was bet hedging: the stars of the Elizabethan court, "Renaissance men" like Sidney, Ralegh or Essex, cultivated literary, courtly and warrior personas all at once. The Renaissance noble or gentleman dashed off sonnets as well as dashing into combat.[24]

Lesser-born men like Shakespeare followed suit, emulating and often surpassing the literary accomplishments of their betters (whose high birth meant, after all, that they did not depend on their wits). Literary achievement by gentlemen like Sidney turned the writing of poetry into a mark of gentility. There was also the promise of a new audience for this writing: educated nobles and gentlemen who, even if they did not write themselves, could demonstrate their generosity and learning by favoring men who did.[25] Through this aristocratic patronage a literate commoner could hope to achieve not just monetary reward but also a place at court or in a noble household, which his sophisticated literacy showed him to be sufficiently qualified and cultivated to join — though hopes often outran the number of such places actually available.[26]

Renaissance absolutism intensified the demand for literate men. The style of education in the Renaissance shaped their skills — brilliantly. We have automobiles and automatic banking, but the Renaissance possessed a technology of language far superior to our own. Consider the "grammar school." This name for elementary school has fallen out of fashion because it equates education with the teaching of grammar. The modern unpopularity of the term is telling, for the name "grammar school" comes from medieval and Renaissance England, where lessons in grammar were considered the proper subject of a child's education.

The grammar taught to these eight to fourteen-year olds, moreover, was not English but Latin. During the long day — school typically went twelve hours — the child would be drilled in the mechanics of Latin and begin to write and translate the language. By the second half of a grammar school career the child — he was almost always a boy, and usually from the middling or upper classes — was expected to translate with ease from English to Latin or Latin to English. The boy honed his skills, and perhaps his literary sensibilities, on classical poets such as Ovid, Virgil and Horace, or on the much admired prose stylist Cicero. To develop his own Latin style the boy would be required to transform prose into poetry (or vice versa), to study the art of rhetoric and to write Latin compositions. He might also begin learning some Greek.[27]

Proliferating how-to manuals on speech and writing in the sixteenth century also spread instruction in the arts of language.[28] These books reveal — and often render into English for a broader reading audience — a dazzling rhetorical sophistication. Language in these books is to be shaped, twisted and transformed, by a reader whose relation to words is assumed to be remarkably easy and intimate. George Puttenham's *Arte of English Poesie*, published in 1589, provides a good example. A college-educated person today might be able to define a few basic figures of speech. Puttenham catalogues over 100 rhetorical terms. These include *hyperbaton* (an inversion of the expected word order), *traductio* (a repetition of different forms of a word), *metonymy* (naming something by one of its parts), *antitheton* (a use of opposing words or ideas), *merismus* (diving a whole into parts, in order to create a step-by-step account of some more general process), and *antenagoge* (compensating for a negative idea by following it with a positive one).[29] Strange-sounding to us, these terms were not exotic for the sixteenth century. Puttenham's sources for these figures were standard schoolboy fare.[30]

A favorite rhetorical art in the Renaissance was variation, or the rephrasing of the same idea in many different ways. Writers learned variation because it demonstrated their rhetorical skill. After a discussion of rhetorical devices, Erasmus in his *De duplici copia verborum ac rerum* [Foundations of the Abundant Style] provides a tour de force example of their use in the art of variation. How, Erasmus asks his reader, could we vary the sentence "Your letter pleased me mightily"? Erasmus's response — which runs to over 130 examples — is too long to quote in full. Here are some selected examples (even so, the reader is invited to skim):

From my dear Faustus' letter I derived much delight.
At your words a delight of no ordinary kind came over me....

Your missive was to me a very great delight.
Your epistle was an incredible joy to me.
How exceedingly agreeable did we find your epistle!...

Your letter was very sweet to me.
Your letter was the source of singular gladness.
Your letter made me positively jump for joy.
Your letter having arrived, I was transported with joy.
When your letter was delivered, I was filled with delight.
Once I had read your affectionate letter, I was carried away with a
    strange happiness.
On receipt of your letter, an incredible delight seized my spirits.

Your epistle poured the balm of happiness over me.
Your writing to me was the most delightful thing possible....

Good God, what a mighty joy proceeded from your epistle!
Heavens, what causes for joy did your letter provide!
Ye gods, what a power of joy did your missive supply!...

As I read the words you wrote me, a marvelous happiness stole over my mind.
As soon as I looked into your letter, a strange force of joy occupied my mind.
As my eye fell on your letter, an incredible tide of joy swelled in my breast.
When I received your most gracious letter, boundless happiness occupied every recess of my soul.
May I die the death if anything more delightful than your letter ever came my way.
May I perish if I ever met with anything in my whole life more agreeable than your letter.
As I aspire to the love of the Muses, nothing more gladsome than your letter has ever ere this befallen me.
Never believe that fortune could cast anything more delightful in my path than your letter....

Your pen sated me with delight....

Your epistle bedewed my spirit with an unfamiliar delight....

Can you imagine the tide of joy on which I rode as I perceived in your letter your affection for me?
When the messenger handed me your letter, my spirit immediately felt the motions of an inexpressible delight.
What need have I to tell you of the pleasure that stirred the soul of your Erasmus on the receipt of your letter?...

Whatever kind of a letter leaves your hand seems to me flowing with sweetness and honey.
I was most luxuriously refreshed at the sumptuous banquet of your letter.
What you wrote is sweeter to me than any ambrosia....

There is no pleasure, no delight, that I would willingly compare with your letter.
All else is utterly repellent compared with your letter....

The man who brought your letter brought a feast day.
A triumph came with the man who delivered your letter.
Nectar I would not prefer to a message from you.
Could I possibly compare Attic [i.e. Greek] honey with your dear letter!
Sugar is not sugar when set beside your letter.
The lotus tastes not as sweet to any mortal man as your letters do to me.
Your letters are to me like wine to a thirsty man.

Like clover to the bee, willow leaves to goats, honey to the bear, even so
are your letters to me.
Your highness's letter was to me more honeyed than any honey.
Once I had received your longed-for letter, you might have said Erasmus
was drunk with joy.
When your letter was delivered, you might have seen us tipsy with excess
of delight.
I love you as no one else, and I delight in your letters as in nothing else.

These examples may seem outrageous to modern readers, but *De copia* in the
Renaissance was an extremely popular book that served as a grammar school
textbook and as a source for the works of English rhetoricians.[32] It provides
a striking example of the rhetorical sophistication of Shakespeare's world. *De
copia* also suggests the relationship of that rhetorical sophistication to English
court life. Verbal pyrotechnics of the kind Erasmus sets off were valued because
they displayed the education and refinement expected of the gentleman — or
those who wanted to become gentlemen — in the Renaissance court.

In the introduction to *De copia* Erasmus extols Virgil and Homer. But
he does not claim that we should read these great poets of the Western literary tradition for any of the reasons that we might say we read them: to learn
about a past culture, to get insight into human nature, to learn moral values,
to discover ourselves, or even to appreciate, for our own pleasure, the beauties
of these poets' language. We are meant to experience these beauties, Erasmus
tells us, but as examples of socially prestigious skills of reading and writing.

For if we have to speak or write extemporaneously, a good literary style
and the ability to vary ideas will "prevent us from standing there stammering
and dumbfounded, or from disgracing ourselves by drying up in the middle."[33] Erasmus conjures a predicament with which many people could sym-
pathize. Nonetheless, this predicament particularly belongs to the ideal courtier,
who displayed his education, grace and wit — and never dried up in the middle. A courtier living in Shakespeare's day would find an example of this ideal
in no less a person than his formidable queen. Literate in several languages,
Elizabeth was famous for her ability to speak extemporaneously, as when her
spontaneous oration in Latin rebuking a foreign ambassador was triumphantly
copied in manuscript, referred to in private letters, reported in chronicles of
her reign, cited in one of her eulogies and even quoted by her successor King
James in the service of a rebuke (this time of parliament) of his own.[34]

The flattery of Erasmus's sentences was also useful for life at court,
where power in part depended on personal influence. The inward flow of
power to the absolutist court made social status more subject to the fortunes
of personal charm, as men whose social status was more fixed locally found
greater anonymity at the national court — like a person moving from a small

town to the city today. Strong writing and speaking skills helped courtiers and court followers to represent themselves effectively to others.[35] Flattering expressions of the kind Erasmus writes would be particularly suitable for men who were not aristocrats, but who traveled to court seeking aristocratic patronage. The spectacular verbal dexterity demonstrated by such flattery might also help direct the nature of the patron's help — tutor to the children in a noble's household, or perhaps appointment as some great man's secretary, an office of considerable consequence.

3

Love, or Literary Credential?

Where can we find Shakespeare's sonnets in this world of rhetorical skill and self-advancement? As with its display of courtly grace, the sonnet could provide a public rather than personal form of verbal expression. The stylistic challenges of the sonnet advertised possession of a prestigious and useful ability to write well. As with Erasmus's lesson in variation, the sonnet's flattering language also had a role in this self-promotion. Here's a man, the sonnet declared, who can write well and is devoted to you.

The most serious, moving and apparently heartfelt of sonnets can be seen to perform these public functions. Consider Shakespeare's sonnet 60, one of several in the sequence that laments the approach of death and vows fidelity to the young man's memory:

> Like as the waves make towards the pebbled shore,
> So do our minutes hasten to their end,
> Each changing place with that which goes before;
> In sequent toil all fowards do contend.
> Nativity, once in the main of light,
> Crawls to maturity, wherewith being crowned
> Crookèd eclipses 'gainst his glory fight,
> And time that gave does now his gift confound.
> Time doth transfix the flourish set on youth,
> And delves the parallels in beauty's brow;
> Feeds on the rarities of nature's truth,
> And nothing stands but for his scythe to mow.
>   And yet to times in hope my verse shall stand,
>   Praising thy worth despite his cruel hand.

This sonnet's expression of devotion and despair seems worlds away from the rules of rhetoric or pleas for advancement. The theme and imagery of the sonnet, however, closely follow lines from Ovid, whose poetry in Shakespeare's day was both a popular read and a school textbook.[36] And the strength of Shakespeare's own rendering of these lines owes much to the rhetorical education available to him. For example, the surprise of the sonnet lies in the way it varies through its length the idea that "time ends all things" until the sonnet's final heroic reversal: "And yet to times in hope my verse shall stand, / Praising thy worth despite his cruel hand." The young man's memory will stand, against time, in Shakespeare's verse. A moving conclusion: but the reversal is also quite stylized. The last two lines draw on the figure of speech that I've mentioned before and that Puttenham calls *antenagoge*, in which the writer deftly amends a negative idea with a positive one.

In fact, sonnet 60 provides instances of all the previously mentioned figures of speech defined in Puttenham's *Arte of English Poesie*. Take for example the repetition of like words, which Puttenham calls *traductio*. The use of this figure in the sonnet — in the word-pairs "gave"/"gift"; "time"/"times"; "stand"/"stands"— provides Shakespeare with an at once stylized and agile compression of opposites in which time both gives and takes, destroys but is defeated. Even the sound of these repeated words reinforces this vision. Just as waves replace one another, but ultimately create a sense of underlying continuity, so do the sonnet's sound-alike words.

The power of this sonnet cannot be separated from its figures of speech, including more familiar ones: the simile that compares the passage of time to the movement of waves, the personification of time mowing down what nature creates, or the use of alliteration (the repetition of initial consonant sounds, for example in "time doth transfix" and "beauty's brow") and of assonance (the repetition of internal vowel sounds, for example in "waves make").

If the power of this sonnet cannot be separated from its figures of speech, neither can the brilliance of its writer be separated from his education and experience in an intensely rhetorical age. Shakespeare, whose prosperous father could afford it, probably attended the local grammar school.[37] He did not continue on to university, but a grammar school education was rich enough. Readers have frequently regarded Shakespeare's verbal skill as the gift of his individual genius. Without denying Shakespeare's particular gifts, we can also see how much Shakespeare's genius owes to his age and its style of education. This education shaped and developed Shakespeare's powers as a writer, as it did for Shakespeare's contemporaries.

But suppose this sonnet, or others like it, is a collection of rhetorical devices, learned at a schoolboy's desk and perfected by the demands of writing for the commercial theater (and perhaps also by Shakespeare's time as a grammar school instructor, if biographical legend is correct).[38] Do not these rhetorical conventions just provide the tools for Shakespeare to express his own feelings, as sonnet 60 seems to do? What could be more personal than a reflection on death or a vow faithfully to preserve someone's memory?

Consider, however, Erasmus's second display, in *De copia*, of the art of variation. For this example, Erasmus rings changes on "Always, as long as I live, I shall remember you." This time Erasmus provides about 200 variations on the sentence, including

> You are consecrated in my heart in a monument that no passage of years can demolish, save only death to which every mortal thing must yield....
>
> So long as the breath of life shall govern these limbs, you shall never for one moment be absent from my thoughts....
>
> Without end shall I recall you.[39]

This exercise in variation is even more remarkable than Erasmus' first because it subjects to the calculations of rhetoric an idea that we might like to think was beyond that kind of artful speech. But especially following Erasmus's machine-like variation on "thank you for your letter" we can see this promise of devotion until death as a flattering rhetorical convention rather than heartfelt.

What then of Shakespeare's sonnet 60, which differs from the sentiment of Erasmus's rhetorical exercise only in its promise to preserve the beloved's memory even after death? There is, after all, something machine-like as well in the creation of sonnet after sonnet. We are usually encouraged to read the sonnets as expressions of personal feeling. We could instead read them as demonstrations of rhetorical accomplishment ("if you thought that sonnet was good....") and as conventional flattery, lavished on someone who could help Shakespeare on his way up.

4

In the Shadow of Abundance

Shakespeare was far from alone in composing sonnets. Sonnet sequences flowed like lovers' tears following the posthumous 1591 publication of Sidney's *Astrophil and Stella*: Samuel Daniel published *Delia* (1592), Henry Constable *Diana* (1592), Barnabe Barnes *Parthenophil and Parthenophe* (1593), Giles Fletcher *Licia* (1593), Thomas Lodge *Philis*, Michael Drayton *Idea* (1594), and Edmund Spenser *Amoretti* (1595), among many others.[40] Were all these men really crying? Falling in love may be universal and eternal, but the Renaissance sonnet was a fad, driven by men putting their talents on display.

On display for whom? Although the Renaissance sonnet frequently declares a man's passionate love for a woman, these sonnets were written not just — or even at all — for the beloved but for a different and broader audience. The private circulation of unpublished sonnets forged bonds among their writers and readers, bonds based on the sharing of secrets and the demonstration of exclusive courtly manners and literary education. The title-page of Fulke Greville's posthumously published sonnet sequence *Caelica* announces that the poems were written in "his youth and familiar exercise with Sir Philip Sidney."[41] It was this exchange of writing and exercise of talents with another aristocratic writer — not the praise of the woman, who might not even exist — that mattered.

Non-aristocratic writers would be even more likely to seek a wider (though potentially déclassé) audience by publishing their sonnets, and they often dedicated this book of poetry to a potential patron.[42] Spenser's *Amoretti* beautifully describes the poet's courtship of his future wife, whom Spenser insists is his poetry's sole audience: "Leaues, lines and rymes, seeke her to please alone, / whom if ye please, I care for other none."[43] Even so, Spenser published these sonnets.

In addition to displaying the writer's talents, as with the *Amoretti*, the sonnet's expressions of devotion could be turned directly toward a potential patron. Such devotion flattered the patron and declared the writer's promise of loyalty to him or her.[44] Spenser wrote this kind of sonnet as well, dedicating his epic romance *The Faerie Queene* by writing one sonnet each to no fewer than 17 courtiers and court ladies. So did the minor Elizabethan poets Barnabe Barnes and Gervase Markham, who both wrote sonnets to Shakespeare's patron the Earl of Southampton. Barnes' sonnet begins: "Receive, sweet lord, with thy thrise-sacred hand / Which sacred muses make their instrument, / These worthless leaves, which I to thee present."[45] Barnes published these lines in 1593, as part of the dedicatory verse for his sonnet sequence *Parthenophil and Parthenophe*. In the same year Shakespeare published his *Venus and Adonis*, which he too dedicated to Southampton. Did Shakespeare, like Barnes, write sonnets for the earl as well?

In the early 1590s Shakespeare was looking for literary patronage. A year after *Venus and Adonis* he followed with a second poem dedicated to Southampton, *The Rape of Lucrece*. The earl looked like a good prospect for literary men seeking glamour and fortune. He was young — about nineteen — handsome, urbane and wealthy. He traveled in aristocratic literary circles, had a reputation for supporting the arts, and, about to come into his inheritance, was expected to have plenty of money to do so.[46]

Shakespeare turned to Southampton when the London government closed the public theaters in the city for nearly two years, during 1592 to 1594, on account of plague. Shakespeare's career — and income — as a playwright came to a stop. With the theaters dark for so long Shakespeare may well have begun imagining new avenues for himself. He had already transformed himself from provincial nobody to London actor and then playwright. Why not from London playwright to court poet? After all, from Shakespeare's vantage point in the early 1590s it looked as if the theaters might never reopen. Nor did Shakespeare know that a great career as a dramatist lay before him.[47]

We do not know whether Southampton is the young man of the sonnets. But we can say that some of the sonnets' expressions of love, loyalty and praise for the young man recall the conventions of literary patronage. Sonnet 37, for example, depicts the young man as the source of all benefits to whom the needy writer must turn:

> As a decrepit father takes delight
> To see his active child do deeds of youth,
> So I, made lame by fortune's dearest spite,
> Take all my comfort of thy worth and truth;

> For whether beauty, birth, or wealth, or wit,
> Or any of these all, or all, or more,
> Entitled in thy parts do crownèd sit,
> I make my love engrafted to this store.
> So then I am not lame, poor, nor despised,
> Whilst that this shadow doth such substance give
> That I in thy abundance am sufficed
> And by a part of all thy glory live.
> > Look what is best, that best I wish in thee;
> > This wish I have, then ten times happy me.

The sonnet attributes to the young man virtues we might expect of an Elizabethan noble and that fit Southampton: beauty, birth, wealth and wit. Part of the richness of this sonnet lies, however, in its refusal to declare precisely which of these virtues belongs to the young man's store of worth: is it "any of these" or "all" or "more"? Perhaps the ambiguity implies that the young man is, finally, too good to describe completely. Or perhaps it implies, as the sonnets often do, that Shakespeare's love for the young man is so deep and true that it does not require these virtues, too commonly esteemed and too easily lost.

Shakespeare describes himself, on the other hand, in less ambiguous terms, as if undeserving of the rhetorical complication lavished on the young man. The writer of the sonnet is a humble suitor, lame, poor and despised. Or he will be without the aid of the young man. "I in thy abundance am sufficed / And by a part of all thy glory live." Of course, just as the sonnet never fixes the young man's worth absolutely, so does it refrain from a direct plea for patronage. Doing either would lack grace.

It is revealing though to compare this sonnet to *Venus and Adonis*'s dedication to the Earl of Southampton. Even if Southampton is not the young man of the sonnets, we remain struck by the similarity between this explicit appeal for patronage and the sonnets' language:

> Right Honourable, I know not how I shall offend in dedicating my unpolished lines to your lordship, nor how the world will censure me for choosing so strong a prop to support so weak a burden. Only, if your honour seem but pleased, I account myself highly praised.[48]

Like the lame suitor of sonnet 37, Shakespeare in this dedication characterizes himself and his writing as weak and in need of support. The "strong prop" that Shakespeare looks to is explicitly a noble, to whom Shakespeare, further along in the dedication, promises more work. As in sonnet 37 too, Shakespeare emphasizes his complete dependence on a greater man: "Only, if your honour seem but pleased, I account myself highly praised."

Nor are the sonnets' fervent avowals of love absent from Shakespeare's explicit appeals for patronage. Shakespeare's subsequent and still more impassioned dedication of *The Rape of Lucrece* to Southampton promises that "the love I dedicate to your lordship is without end.... What I have done is yours; what I have to do is yours, being part in all I have, devoted yours."[49] The style and sentiment of this devotion match the sonnets as well. How can I write of your worth, Shakespeare asks the recipient of sonnet 39, "when thou art all the better part of me?" As in the dedication to *The Rape of Lucrece*, Shakespeare plays on "part" and "all" to humbly disclaim any independent worth as a writer.

In some sonnets however Shakespeare is irreverent rather than humble — sonnet 20, for example, refers to the young man's androgyny (and penis, as we'll see in chapter 15) — while in others, such as 69 or 95, he is surprisingly critical.[50] How could you write like that to a patron? In her pointedly titled *The Art of Shakespeare's Sonnets* Helen Vendler argues along these lines that Shakespeare's chief interest in the sonnets was literary rather than social. Vendler suggests that Shakespeare is a "blasphemer" who borrows from a variety of Renaissance language conventions, patronage among them, but only to "interrogate" and "ironize" these conventions for his own distinctly literary project.[51]

But Renaissance authors — perhaps no more reasonable or timid than the rest of us — did write in ways that could antagonize their betters. When he fell out of favor Ralegh complained bitterly about Queen Elizabeth in his poem, "Ocean, to Cynthia." And Thomas Nashe wrote a tongue-in-cheek dedication to the Earl of Southampton for his work *The Unfortunate Traveler*, a dedication that did not appear in the second edition. Moreover, Vendler's notion of the sonnets takes the idea of "literature" for granted by assuming that it has always meant what it most often means to us today: a kind of writing that is playful or beautiful rather than written towards instrumental or material ends. To the extent that Shakespeare does transform actual appeals for patronage into more lovely or daring or ironic literary artworks, he is participating in the very creation of that modern idea. Disrespecting the conventions of patronage constitutes Shakespeare's declaration of independence as a poet from the social world in which poetry remained embedded.[52]

In a like manner, the sonnets may express sincere feeling rather than mere flattering words to a patron. But the realities of patronage remain an important horizon even for the sonnets that insist on the sincerity of the poet's feeling and reject any material interests. This is the case with sonnet 29, one of the most popular sonnets in the sequence. Wealth or status do not matter, Shakespeare writes, so long as he has the young man's love:

When, in disgrace with fortune and men's eyes,
I all alone beweep my outcast state,
And trouble deaf heaven with my bootless cries,
And look upon myself and curse my fate,
Wishing me like to one more rich in hope,
Featured like him, like him with friends possessed,
Desiring this man's art and that man's scope,
With what I most enjoy contented least:
Yet in these thoughts myself almost despising,
Haply I think on thee, and then my state,
Like to the lark at break of day arising
From sullen earth, sings hymns at heaven's gate;
    For thy sweet love remembered such wealth brings
    That then I scorn to change my state with kings'.

Particularly beautiful in this sonnet is the image of the "lark at break of day arising." Why is this image so striking — perhaps more so than the comparison to "kings" that follows? The lark rising up from the "sullen earth" represents a love that soars with the sun beyond worldly cares. Being a lark is better even than being a king, who is powerful but still of the earth.

This heaven-bound lark provides a glorious emblem for the poem's attractive, though admittedly common, sentiment. My love for you is more valuable to me than earthly wealth or position. "I don't care too much for money, money can't buy me love...."

Or so it seems at first glance. Yet it's worth noting how very frequently sonnet 29 refers to earthly possessions: "disgrace of fortune" can mean economic or social "fortunes," a possibility suggested because Shakespeare pairs it with a very public disgrace in "men's eyes."[53] So too Shakespeare complains about not being "more rich in hope," a phrase that can refer specifically to hopes of a fortune or inheritance, especially when coupled with the word "rich."[54] "State" may similarly refer to social status, rather than to an emotional state.

The word "friend" is especially important in this sonnet for what it implies about Shakespeare's relationship to the young man and about the intertwining of public and private in Renaissance culture. In Shakespeare's day "friend" had a double meaning it now barely possesses. (Actually, the word had a triple meaning, as "friend" could also mean "lover," a further possibility considered in chapter 10 of this book.) Though in the Renaissance a friend could be someone with whom one shares an emotional connection, a friend might also simply be a kinsman, a political ally or a connection at court. "A friend in court is worth a penny in the purse," runs a proverb of the day.[55] When Shakespeare envies those who have friends, he may be wishing for their access to patronage or "friends in high places" rather than for their popularity.

Thus many of the words that we might now understand only metaphor-ically — such as riches — or whose full implications we might miss — such as "friends" or "state" — when read in historical context begin to evoke a harsh world of social status and courtly favor from which the writer feels outcast. Shakespeare thought in particular that his career as an actor was a disgrace. But since he came to the city of London to make his fortune, like many young men of the time, this lark that's moving up from the sullen earth might not just be flying heavenward. It might also describe the quite worldly social tra-jectory that Shakespeare desires: "My state, / like to the lark."

Shakespeare may pursue this trajectory by elegantly complimenting the young man, who, if moved by the compliment, could provide him with patronage of some sort. Even the idea of the lark at "heaven's gate" draws on a more worldly practice, the customary distribution of charity by the Renaissance aristocrat at the gates of his home.[56] The metaphor implies that Shakespeare similarly comes as a beggar.

Sonnet 29 brings together two ideas we usually think of as opposites: the romantic love that scorns the world and the self-interested pursuit, per-haps through avowals of love, of worldly wealth and position. We may not hear this second aspect of the sonnet as much as the first, but that's in part because of its historical distance from us. It's also because Shakespeare him-self disavows interest in these things: "For thy sweet love remembered such wealth brings / That then I scorn to change my state with kings'." But these concerns remain even in Shakespeare's disavowal of them. Shakespeare can think of nothing better than wealth and the state of kings to compare to his friend's love. Moreover, if you were pursuing someone's favor, the compar-ison itself would be flattering. Here we can recall an example from Erasmus's *De copia.* "There is no pleasure, no delight, that I would willingly compare with your letter" — or in Shakespeare's case, with remembering "your love."

It might still seem that our first sense of this sonnet's meaning is cor-rect, that read without excessive skepticism the final lines of the poem mean what they say. Indeed, so much of this sonnet's power depends on the idea of putting love before the world that it would be a poor reading of the son-net that simply dismissed this idea as flattery — a point I'll return to at the end of this section of the book. But we also cannot fully appreciate the risk-taking of these lines, their closeness to the bone, if we fail to see that when Shakespeare declares indifference to wealth and position he is writing in a form associated with the pursuit of both. When Shakespeare claims not to care about these things, his first readers would have had good reason to assume that he did.[57]

5

Dedicated Words

The sonnets reveal Shakespeare's awareness that his love might sound hollow. Shakespeare is not just conscious of the poetry of patronage but intensely anxious about it. In sonnet 82, one of the eight complaining of a rival poet, we find Shakespeare angry that the young man seems to have shifted his favor to this rival and abandoned what Shakespeare calls his "Muse," that is, his poetry:

> I grant thou wert not married to my muse,
> And therefore mayst without attaint o'erlook
> The dedicated words which writers use
> Of their fair subject, blessing every book.
> Thou art as fair in knowledge as in hue,
> Finding thy worth a limit past my praise,
> And therefore art enforced to seek anew
> Some fresher stamp of these time-bettering days.
> And do so, love; yet when they have devised
> What strainèd touches rhetoric can lend,
> Thou, truly fair, wert truly sympathized
> In true plain words by thy true-telling friend:
>   And their gross painting might be better used
>   Where cheeks need blood: in thee it is abused.

Besides the young man's infidelity — his refusal to stay tied, as if in marriage, to only one poet — Shakespeare is annoyed by the young man's vanity. Shakespeare accuses him of favoring the rival poet because he believes himself greater than the praise Shakespeare has so far offered ("finding thy worth a limit past my praise").

Given the lavish praise offered the young man in Shakespeare's sonnets this would be vanity indeed. What's worse though is that the young man fails to recognize, in his vanity, that the rival poet's praise is conventional flattery, hammered out in a bid for patronage. These are the rival poet's "dedicated words." The phrase might first seem grudgingly positive toward the rival's expressions of love for the young man. Then we realize that "dedicated words" more subtly and contemptuously glances at the practice of dedicating books to potential patrons, as Shakespeare himself dedicated *Venus and Adonis* and *The Rape of Lucrece* to Southampton. Shakespeare mocks the formulaic quality of these dedications — at least those of other writers — which indiscriminately bless "every book."[58] Shakespeare's irony is sharp: "every" precisely undercuts "dedicated," which means bound to only one thing or person.

Indiscriminate praise finds another metaphor in the phrase "fresher stamp," which implies a mechanical quality, as if repeatedly stamped out by a machine, perhaps a printing press. (The computer's ability to personalize a letter by inserting a proper name into generic text merely facilitates a practice already known to the Renaissance.) A "fresher stamp" is another of the sonnet's precise and ironic opposites, since a stamp creates the same thing again and again, rather than afresh. The rival poet's praise may be in the newest, most currently fashionable style, but, as fashion, it cannot really be fresh. (The paradox in modern consumer culture whereby fashion promises a new and distinctive style for everyone was already known in the Renaissance.)

Shakespeare finally terms this fashionable but formulaic praise the "strainèd touches rhetoric can lend." We can identify this "strainèd" rhetoric — overly elaborate and overwrought — with the machine-like variation of Erasmus's *De copia*. It's as if Shakespeare is accusing the rival poet of writing by the prefabricated lines of Erasmus's book — or an education in the arts of rhetoric more generally. Shakespeare concludes sonnet 82 by insisting that his poetry, by contrast, is honest rather than flattering and formulaic. A "true-telling friend," Shakespeare speaks "true plain words."

Weighing the truthfulness of poetic language is a major concern of the sonnets, a problem that they share with the culture from which they come. Artful language in Renaissance England was seen not just as a thing of beauty and self-expression, but as an instrument of duplicity, used to persuade, cajole, evade and lie. In his *Arte of English Poesie* Puttenham observes that just as figures of speech are the "ornaments" of language, so are they its "abuses." Figures of speech "pass the ordinary limits of common utterance ... to deceive the ear and also the mind, drawing it from plainness and simplicity to a certain doubleness."[59] A metaphor is something like a lie, after all. A poet calls lips cherries or rubies when they are really just lips. "My mistress' eyes are nothing like the sun," Shakespeare declares in sonnet 130, reflecting on the capacity of the sonnet's metaphor to flatter and lie.

These anxieties about the honesty of literary language were prompted in part because poetry in the Renaissance was more connected to political life than it is today. Today poetry is often seen as a fine art, far removed from the sordid world of political power. The poet in the Renaissance *was* in power or sought it through the poetry of patronage. Even Queen Elizabeth wrote poetry. Thus there was no separate literary world — as we conceive of it today — that would make figures of speech safe, wall them off (as Vendler argues) within the confines of "literature." In Shakespeare's age one could not separate the craft that was part of the literary art of poetry from the craftiness that was part of the "real world" art of social advancement.[60]

Sonnet 125, the last regular sonnet in the group to the young man, makes these problems explicit. Its scene is a royal progress, in which the monarch parades through the streets to display royal magnificence, and courtiers bask in the honor of waiting on their sovereign. Most honored are those courtiers whose orbit takes them closest to the royal star, the ones who shade the monarch with a canopy lifted on poles:

> Were't aught to me I bore the canopy,
> With my extern the outward honouring,
> Or laid great bases for eternity
> Which proves more short than waste or ruining?
> Have I not seen dwellers on form and favour
> Lose all and more by paying too much rent,
> For compound sweet forgoing simple savour,
> Pitiful thrivers in their gazing spent?
> No, let me be obsequious in thy heart,
> And take thou my oblation, poor but free,
> Which is not mixed with seconds, knows no art
> But mutual render, only me for thee.
> > Hence, thou suborned informer! A true soul
> > When most impeached stands least in thy control.

The theme and even some of the imagery of this sonnet are similar to that of Shakespeare's more famous sonnet 55: "Not marble nor the gilded monuments / Of princes shall outlive this powerful rhyme." Both sonnets declare contempt for the public world of princes. Sonnet 55 calls the supposed grandeur of princely funeral monuments inferior to the memorialization of poetry and the experience of love. Sonnet 125 also evokes grandiose funeral monuments — the "the great bases" laid for eternity — as a metaphor for the ambitions of those who, carrying the prince's canopy, believe that they are laying the bases for their own political ambitions. In this sonnet, as in 55, Shakespeare protests that worldly ambition quickly ends in dust, proving "more short than waste or ruining."

While sonnets 55 and 125 share these themes, 125 affords a better view than 55 of the sonnets' roots in English Renaissance culture and politics. Sonnet 55 is so frequently encountered in poetry anthologies that we lose a sense of its place even in Shakespeare's sonnets, let alone in Renaissance England. And in any case, sonnet 55's triumphant praise of love and poetry overshadows its social content. Sonnet 125 lingers in more bitter detail on that social content, and never quite manages to get away from it (one reason why this sonnet, unlike 55, almost never makes it into anthologies[61]). The final couplet of 55 resoundingly expands love out to eternity: "So, till the judgement that yourself arise, / You live in this, and dwell in lovers' eyes." The final couplet of 125 narrows the poem to a specific and tawdry event, some rumor about Shakespeare spread by a "suborned informer."[62]

Leading up to this couplet, Shakespeare evokes a world of competitive courtly refinement and overloaded rhetoric. "Dwellers on form and favour" care only about superficial manners. Their over-fine protestations of love are suspect. Like a sour medicine disguised with sugary syrup, these vows of love taste of deceiving "compounds sweet" rather than of "simple savour." [63] Shakespeare again vows that he harbors no such disguise. Rejecting what is "extern" or "outward"— formal manners and language, lies that cover the truth, an obsession with social rank— he wants only to be "obsequious" in the young man's heart. The words "obsequious" and "oblation" come from a religious vocabulary: an "obsequy" is a ritual for the dead, and one who is "obsequious" lives up to the duty of performing this rite, while an "oblation" is a gift to God, often on the occasion of a mass, and sometimes refers to the offering of the Eucharist itself. This religious vocabulary seems to trump the merely secular ritual of the royal progress.[64] Likewise, Shakespeare's wish to be received in the young man's heart trumps the courtly ambition merely to stand close to the prince.

But as in other sonnets where Shakespeare rejects this world of courtly favor, these lines hint at a desire for what they deny. Though in Shakespeare's day "obsequious" can mean simply "dutiful" or "obedient," the word is already beginning to have its contemporary connotation of fawning servility.[65] And the wish to be carried in the aristocratic young man's heart intensifies as much as it opposes the rejected ambition to carry the prince's canopy.

Moreover, when Shakespeare claims in sonnet 125 that he "knows no art" can we believe it? How plain speaking can a sonnet really be? Certainly Shakespeare would know as much art as that outlined in an Elizabethan

English book on letter writing, whose author advises hitting on three points when writing a letter of praise. We must declare our wits unable to describe the "virtues, merits and praises" that belong to the man we are writing to, then we must declare one of his virtues, adding that he has so many virtues and graces that we are "scare able to recite them in many days"— and then, for the third point, that "it is no flattery nor adulation which we write, and etc." Are Shakespeare's sonnets different from such formulaic letters of praise? His sonnets echo each point in these instructions, including the advice to deny flattery.[66]

Or can we believe from sonnet 125 that Shakespeare is not also ambitious? He used some of the substantial wealth he earned in the theater to secure the coat of arms for his family that his father, because of financial setbacks, had failed to achieve. The coat of arms would establish his family's gentility. Shakespeare's effort was looked on with suspicion, however. His name was cited in a complaint about "based and ignoble persons" who had been granted arms. More humorously, the rather defensive motto of the Shakespeare arms, "non sanz droit" (not without right), was probably the target of some mocking by Shakespeare's friend and fellow playwright Ben Jonson. Jonson's play *Every Man Out of His Humour* features an ambitious fool who pays £30 for a coat of arms with a motto —"not without mustard"— that sends up Shakespearean pretension.[67]

6

He That Buys Must Sell

The sonnets' criticism of ambitious men reflects a very basic attitude in Renaissance England. The modern world embraces ambition. We are expected to be upwardly mobile, to achieve more than our parents. Not so in Shakespeare's England, where gentlemen were ideally born, not made.[68] (To recall John Houseman's puffery of Smith-Barney, the really old fashioned way to get money was to inherit it.[69]) Renaissance political theory valued the stability and cohesion that fixed social status was seen to promote. Its model was the human body, in which each organ and limb function together for the good of the whole. To ensure that good, each person has his or her own job: the foot must not seek to do the work of the head.

Ministers of the state-run Church of England regularly preached this doctrine in a sermon the crown supplied to them. According to this Homily on Obedience, God has prescribed to all people "their duty and order." Churchgoers (whose attendance at church was required by law) were warned that the hierarchies of prince and subject, noble and commoner, master and servant, and even rich and poor, are part of God's plan and necessary to good order. They were also warned that "where there is no right order there reigneth all abuse, carnal liberty, enormity, sin and Babylonical confusion."[70] In this worldview, ambition was in itself dishonest, a source of sin, crime ("enormity") and non–Christian, "Babylonical" chaos. To attempt to make oneself into a gentleman was to defy the divine plan, to make one's very identity a lie against God's truth. And a danger to this world. People who lived a lie most likely got ahead by lies, if not worse.

Political authorities were so fearful of social ambition (it leads to the disasters in every one of Shakespeare's four great tragedies) that, until the

48

end of the sixteenth century, even dress was minutely regulated by a series of sumptuary laws. People were forbidden to wear clothes considered too expensive for their rank. For example, only a man above the degree of knight might legally wear gowns of velvet or shirts embroidered with gold. Spelled out in obsessively status-conscious detail, these laws regulated Elizabethan glamour — purple silk, gold and silver embroidery, crimson velvets, scarlet cloths, enameled buttons, leopards' fur, silk nether stockings, gilded swords, silvered saddles, velvet slippers, taffeta gowns and satin doublets, among other fashions.[71]

Not surprisingly, people did not always behave as ministers exhorted and the law prescribed. Shakespeare's own life-story exemplifies the social mobility that occurred in Renaissance England. His great benefactor was finally not Southampton or any aristocratic patron, but the city of London. Its population grew fourfold from about 50,000 in 1500 to 200,000 in 1600, in large part because of migration from the country to the city. This was Shakespeare's experience. Like many of his contemporaries, Shakespeare was probably lured to London by the opportunities for wealth and social advancement its dynamic urban environment offered. Already the seat of government, London in the sixteenth century became a major European center for trade and fashion as well. The population and wealth of the city also sustained the permanent, commercial theater from which Shakespeare made his fortune.[72]

Shakespeare's sonnets register the clash between the ideal of social stasis and the reality of social change, especially as this change was experienced in commercial London. Consider sonnet 21, which begins as a satire of threadbare literary convention:

> So it is not with me as with that muse
> Stirred by a painted beauty to his verse,
> Who heaven itself for ornament doth use,
> And every fair with his fair doth rehearse,
> Making a couplement of proud compare
> With sun and moon, with earth, and sea's rich gems,
> With April's first-born flowers, and all things rare
> That heaven's air in this huge rondure hems.
> O let me, true in love, but truly write,
> And then believe me my love is as fair
> As any mother's child, though not so bright
> As those gold candles fixed in heaven's air.
> > Let them say more that like of hearsay well;
> > I will not praise that purpose not to sell.

Though less flippant than 130 ("My mistress' eyes are nothing like the sun"), sonnet 21 has a similar theme. Shakespeare will not exaggerate the virtues of the sonnet's recipient through elaborate — and false — metaphor. The other poet ("that muse") proudly compares the one he loves, "his fair," to all the fair things of heaven and earth: the sun, moon, April flowers, the sea's gems, every rare thing. Shakespeare, on the other hand, will not lie: "true in love" and therefore vowing to "truly write," he will only declare his love as fair as "any mother's child."

The most powerful idea in this sonnet comes last. "I will not praise that purpose not to sell." With the final line, really the final word, Shakespeare dramatically shifts direction, sending the poem from literary satire to social complaint. In part the line means that Shakespeare will not praise the young man as vendors exaggerate the quality of their goods in calls to passersby. The word "sell" suggests much more than just this verbal dishonesty, however. Rather, it makes an implicit comparison between an ideal of social relations as personal, permanent, and hierarchical, and the greater fluidity of a commercial society. In the idealized vision of Renaissance "good order" there is not just hierarchy but love. Another model for this order, besides the body, is the family, in which the father wields a loving and protective authority over his child (the other parent, the mother, is sometimes omitted here). As if a family, princes and subjects, landlords and tenants, masters and servants are bound together for life in ties of love, loyalty and service.

The relations engendered by modern commerce begin to dissolve these ties. In the marketplace change is rapid. Nothing lasting or trustworthy seems to bind men. People come together only for the moment of purchase and their relationships with one another are suspicious and self-interested. Each person seeks the best bargain.[73] "He that buys must sell," Thomas Nashe wrote in 1593, reflecting the imperatives of commercial London. This imperative, Nashe warns, draws every non-economic realm into its orbit. Charity, justice, even religion are threatened: "Shrewd alchemists there are risen up, that will pick a merchandise out of everything, and not spare to set up their shops of buying and selling even in the Temple."[74]

Inherited gentility is threatened too. Shakespeare was not alone in purchasing a coat of arms. Sir Thomas Smith, Queen Elizabeth's secretary of state, observed that men who had made enough money could easily pay to have a coat of arms invented for themselves, though no one would admit to the invention. Through some flexible tracing of lineage the man's family would be "found" ancient after all.[75] Under the reign of King James the honor of knighthood became a vehicle for financial speculation. A courtier received as a favor from the king the right to nominate a certain number knights. The courtier then sold that right to a speculator in knighthoods, who would make his profit from men who paid him to be made knights.[76] He who buys must sell.

Sonnet 21 suggests that patronage too — which in its ideal form implies a loyal master and servant relationship — has been distorted by market imperatives. When Shakespeare writes that his purpose is "not to sell" he is denying involvement in what Nashe sees as the market's buy-sell imperative: the canny but unprincipled pursuit of short-term gain over lasting relationships or values like love or honor. Shakespeare denies he is praising the young man in order to advance his own reputation, only to cast the young man off once he takes his profit in realized ambition. But the energies of the market and social change are so present and disturbing to Shakespeare and his contemporaries that Shakespeare need only invoke them in a single word — sell — uttered in sonnet 21 like a dangerous curse.

We see this thread of Shakespeare's social complaint more fully worked out in subsequent sonnets such as 67 and 68. Sonnet 67 accuses others of seeking to advance their social position by living, like parasites, off the young man:

> Ah, wherefore with infection should he live
> And with his presence grace impiety,
> That sin by him advantage should achieve
> And lace itself with his society?
> Why should false painting imitate his cheek,
> And steal dead seeming of his living hue?
> Why should poor beauty indirectly seek
> Roses of shadow, since his rose is true?
> Why should he live now nature bankrupt is,
> Beggared of blood to blush through lively veins,
> For she hath no exchequer now but his,
> And proud of many, lives upon his gains?
>   O, him she stores to show what wealth she had
>   In days long since, before these last so bad.

Why, Shakespeare asks, should the young man live only to "grace impiety" — that is, help bad people to look good? These people, whom Shakespeare so dislikes that he calls them "infection," hide their sins and even achieve "advantage" by clinging to the young man's "society."

But these people can achieve from the young man only "dead seeming," the looks but not the life of his beauty (and by implication his goodness). Their looks are "roses of shadow" — insubstantial, imitative, shady — while his "rose is true." Though focused on emulation of the young man and more highly metaphorical, the complaint in this sonnet recalls the anxiety about the emulation of betters that drove sixteenth-century sumptuary laws.

So too should the sonnet's lament that now nature is "beggared of blood to blush through lively veins" be read as a social complaint. Mentions of blood in Renaissance England frequently imply family and status: bloodlines. In the present, the sonnet complains, one can no longer tell natural nobility from those who seek to buy it. "Now nature bankrupt is" while money makes the world go round. Perhaps under the pressure of anxiety about social mobility, respect for the past becomes in this sonnet a panicked nostalgia for "days long since, before these last so bad." Only the young man shows nature's true wealth; he is the symbol and "store" of an idealized past. "Thus is his cheek the map of days outworn," Shakespeare begins the sonnet that follows.

Again, much that Shakespeare complains of in sonnet 67 might be said about Shakespeare himself. One wonders, in fact, if a source of the sonnet's rage lies in Shakespeare's need to distinguish himself from those very others whose infection he condemns. When Shakespeare in sonnet 67 condemns the "false painting" that imitates the young man's cheek he refers to a material artifice, the use of cosmetics (called "painting" in Shakespeare's day; we still refer to painted faces). These cosmetics create the rosy blush that the young man naturally displays. But Shakespeare also uses cosmetics as a metaphor for verbal artifice, the "strainèd touches" of rhetoric. Shakespeare, we may recall, concludes his condemnation of the rival poet in sonnet 82 with this metaphor: "And their gross painting might be better used / Where cheeks need blood: in thee it is abused."

Yet any description of the young man paints him, including Shakespeare's verbal art. Shakespeare has to add a negative adjective — "false" or "gross" — to the painting of others, to distinguish their writing from his own. Is Shakespeare's art or its motives so different?

7

Thy True-telling Friend

The prospect of Shakespeare condemning in others his own flattery and ambition challenges a frequently held idea of him as a guide to morality. Yet Shakespeare, like many of his contemporaries, knew skepticism of human claims and motives. He is after all the creator of "honest Iago." And though "To thine own self be true" is often quoted as Shakespearean wisdom, we should recall that the line is spoken by the obtuse Polonius, whose speeches are strings of well worn sayings (including that one) and whose actions and advice in *Hamlet* usually involve deceit.[77]

Nonetheless, Shakespeare's protestations of honesty in the sonnets ultimately reflect neither the calculating Machiavellianism of Iago nor the ignorant self-blindness of Polonius. Rather, the sonnets are most compelling in the very way that they struggle with the wish to speak true during an age that did dwell, a lot, on form and favor. This struggle appears in two striking qualities of the sonnets: their unexpected tendency toward satire and their relative emphasis on the writer's inward experience. These qualities of the sonnets have important implications for the pursuit of ambition that engages and appalls their author.

First, satire: though the sonnets usually lavish praise on the young man, at times they bare an unexpectedly critical edge. Some of the more openly critical sonnets, such as numbers 33–35 and 92–93, deal with particular wrongdoings on the young man's part. In 92–93 (and more obliquely in 33–35) this wrongdoing involves the young man's infidelity to Shakespeare. Sonnet 92 declares Shakespeare's joy at possessing the young man's love, but then concludes: "What's so blessèd fair that fears no blot? / Thou mayst be false, and yet I know it not." Several sonnets that follow emphasize the idea that the young man merely appears good. His secret thoughts or deeds suggest otherwise.

At the beginning of sonnet 95 Shakespeare likens the young man's ill-behavior to a "canker," a worm that eats and destroys the buds of roses:[78]

> How sweet and lovely dost thou make the shame
> Which, like a canker in the fragrant rose,
> Doth spot the beauty of thy budding name!
> O, in what sweets dost thou thy sins enclose!

From the beginning of the sequence Shakespeare has identified the young man with the rose. In this sonnet Shakespeare takes a closer look at this rose and finds disease. Sonnet 67's "infection" came from the faults of others, the young man being the source of all perfection. In this sonnet the young man's own faults ("thy sins") cause it.

The literary critic Arthur Marotti has incisively suggested that these accusatory moments in the sonnets bear out Shakespeare's promise to be "thy true-telling friend" rather than a flatterer like the rival poet. Just as Cordelia in *King Lear* proves that she truly loves her father the king by refusing to flatter him, so moments of criticism in the sonnets give the impression of a more genuinely sincere speaker, one who struggles against the glib and oily art of pursuing aristocratic favor.

The nature of the relationship described in the sonnets contributes to this sense of truth as well. In contrast to many Renaissance sonnet sequences, Shakespeare's sonnets describe an ongoing relationship rather than a courtship. The lover in pursuit tends to idealize the beloved; an actual relationship necessarily produces more conflicted emotions. One is now engaging with a real person rather than a fantasy. The possibility that the young man has flaws — for example, he might be unfaithful — leads Shakespeare to chart a range of feelings about the young man, rather than monotonously declaring his desire for him, as courting poets do for their "cruel fair." [79] The sonnets' range of feeling and unexpectedly sharp edges, at least as much as their words of love, contribute to our sense of the poet's genuineness.

These qualities of the sonnets also have political implications. They express, as Marotti argues, Shakespeare's wish to escape a poetics of patronage that obligates him, as a social subordinate, to mindlessly praise the young nobleman.[80] In fact, Shakespeare verges on challenging not just one nobleman's undeserved reputation, but the Renaissance idea of inherited social status altogether. The sonnets' focus on the difference between the young man's superficially beautiful appearance and his inward faults draws on a line of thought in Renaissance England that was critical of nobility justified by nothing deeper than birth, rather than virtuous character.[81] In *King Lear*, the Earl of Gloucester's illegitimate son Edmund gives voice to a similar critique of nobility defined by birth rather than character. Edmund asks why he should be treated differently than his brother Edward simply because he was born out of wedlock, especially if his mind and body are at least as good as his brother's: "why brand they us / With base? with baseness? bastardy?"[82]

Edmund's questions echo in the sonnets. "The summer's flower is to the summer sweet," Shakespeare advises the young man, "but if that flower with base infection meet / The basest weed outbraves his dignity" (94). This warning, which again revises the sonnet's language of flowers, provides another example of Shakespeare's more assertive tone with the young man. It also implies the class politics that underlies this tone. The word "base" in these lines first seems to refer to low morals. The next appearance of the word, in its superlative form ("basest"), gives these lines a social dimension as well, since when paired with "dignity" the word must also refer to social rank. Even "base" men surpass in dignity a noble who acts irresponsibly.

The exploitation in this line of words with double meanings reinforces (and perhaps also nervously obscures) this idea. While Shakespeare's metaphor refers primarily to flowers and weeds it contains secondary references to clothing. "Outbrave" in Renaissance English can mean "to outdo in fine apparel." This meaning is especially present when coupled with the word "weed," which could also mean clothing.[83] As we have seen, social rank determined what one could legally wear in Renaissance England. In this light, the lines contain an even more class-specific warning. If those whose rank confers high dignity do not also act virtuously, then no sumptuary law will preserve respect for them. Clothes will not make the man. Even those who wear the basest weeds (that is, clothes) will outdo the noble in true dignity.

Literary form and political statement have an interesting relationship here. The most common arrangement of the English Renaissance sonnet facilitates this kind of unexpectedly sharp statement. While the rhyme schemes of the Italian sonnet usually emphasized a split between the sonnet's first eight lines and its last six, English sonneteers most commonly employed a rhyme scheme that broke the sonnet's fourteen lines into three quatrains and a final rhyming couplet. There were practical reasons for this. It is harder to find words that rhyme in English than in Romance languages like Italian, French and Spanish, so dividing the sonnet into quatrains alleviated the need to carry two rhymes through eight lines.[84]

Left over from the sonnets' three quatrains was the final rhyming couplet, which had its own attractions. The pithiness of the couplet lends itself to providing a sudden solution to the problem explored in the previous twelve lines. The couplet can also be treated as the two-line poem called an

epigram. Traditionally, an epigram is an especially witty, pointed or satirical rhyming couplet. These epigrammatic endings ally the sonnet, frequently
a vehicle for the expression of love and praise, with a literary form associated with the quite different values of wit and satire. And indeed, many of
the sonnets' "true-telling" critical punches arrive in their epigrammatic final
lines. As in sonnet 93: "How like Eve's apple doth thy beauty grow / If thy
sweet virtue answer not thy show!" Or in sonnet 94: "For sweetest things
turn sourest by their deeds: / Lilies that fester smell far worse than weeds."[85]

With his own stake in the class hierarchies of his time, however, Shakespeare tends to pull these punches or limit them to occasional gestures and
particular sonnets. Take, for example, the couplet that ends sonnet 96. In
this sonnet, Shakespeare writes that the young man is so attractive that if he
chose to he could easily deceive and betray his many admirers. Because he
makes even his "faults graces," the young man's "errors" could easily be "to
truths translated and for true things deemed." To this possibility of easy
deception the final couplet answers: "But do not so: I love thee in such sort
/ As, thou being mine, mine is thy good report." Shakespeare apparently liked
these lines: he used them twice, in this sonnet and at the end of sonnet 36.

Perhaps he liked their ambiguity. The last line may be interpreted in a
number of different ways. "Thou being mine" means "you being my love,"
but what about the consequence of Shakespeare's claim on the young man,
"mine is thy good report"? Especially because it succeeds the satiric epigrams
of 92–95, this couplet might express Shakespeare's power as a poet to make
or break the young man's reputation. Not only is the young man's love "mine"
but so is the "report," via the sonnets, of the young man's virtue or vice.

The line allows another interpretation, however, that stresses Shakespeare's dependence on rather than power over the young man. The line
could mean that if the young man achieves through his behavior a good
report, then so too will Shakespeare, who is associated with the young man
("Thou being mine"). The glamour and credibility of the sonnets depend
on the idea that this young man really is worth the praises his poet heaps on
him. Shakespeare is unwilling to abandon or even too much darken the glory
by which he lives.

In fact, the sonnets that follow 96 return to singing the young man's
praises, though they also refer to a hiatus during which Shakespeare stopped
writing sonnets, perhaps hesitating about what to do.[86] Sonnets following
96 also turn their sharper edges back on the writer. Reversing the accusations of earlier sonnets they apologize for *Shakespeare's* betrayal of the young
man's love. These sonnets also emphasize Shakespeare's class insecurity that
he is merely an actor.[87]

One might argue that Shakespeare, unable fully to criticize the noble young man, turns the anger of that criticism back on himself. He also acknowledges his need for the socially prominent young man's love and protection: "Your love and pity doth th'impression fill / Which vulgar scandal stamped upon my brow" (sonnet 112). Marotti, on the other hand, finds in the last poem to the young man a more aggressive stance. In this twelve-line send off, which recalls a number of sonnets in the sequence that lament the passage of time, Shakespeare warns the young man that he cannot escape death.

Rather than understanding this poem as an example of sympathetic grief for the beloved's mortality, Marotti reads it with a nicely bracing cynicism as Shakespeare's closing death threat against the unreliable and undeserving noble young man.[88] In truth, the sonnets do not tell a complete enough story for us finally to say how they end and what conclusions we should draw from them. But if *King Lear* may shed light on the sonnets' class politics then we can observe this: despite what seem moments of sympathy for Edmund's social complaint, Shakespeare made the illegitimately born son a bastard in every sense.

8

From Form to Feeling

Another quality of the sonnets that persuades us of their truth is the frequency with which Shakespeare uses them as vehicles of self-reflection, often of a very painful kind. The sonnets turn not just outward to the depiction of their subject but inward toward the writer's mind and experiences. In the final couplet of sonnet 29, for example — "For thy sweet love remembered such wealth brings / That then I scorn to change my state with kings'" — Shakespeare does not say that the young man's love brings wealth, but that the *memory* of it does. The sonnet subtly shifts our attention from an objective event to its recollection in the poet's mind.[89] Like shadows in a painting, these moments create a sense of depth. We experience the writer as a more fully realized character, not a praise machine.

Frequently this self-consciousness extends through an entire sonnet, as in 27, which recounts the writer lying in bed recalling his beloved ("then begins a journey in my head"). Even more striking are the sonnets that subject their writer to extended self-criticism. We have already considered sonnet 62, which expresses Shakespeare's guilt at his "sin of self-love." We would hardly expect to find the expression of guilt in a sonnet simply designed to flatter a patron and assure him or her of the writer's worthiness. Shakespeare's sense of guilt makes the sonnets seem more real. We feel we have access to an actual mind, struggling and uncertain.

More subtle verbal and literary qualities of the sonnets also encourage our sense that the sonnets reflect true feeling rather than the pursuit of "form and favor." For example, while the sonnets point to a client-patron relationship between Shakespeare and a young nobleman, they never declare outright or even clearly hint at the name of the nobleman concerned.[90] Nor are the sonnets' appeals for patronage explicit. By relatively obscuring the public identities of client and patron, the sonnets give the impression of a private relationship between individuals, an affair of the heart.[91] The sonnets likewise encourage this impression in the way they refer to social status. These references are equivocal, ambiguously referring either to the young man's rank or his individual character. "O, how thy worth with manners may I sing," Shakespeare asks in sonnet 39. The word "worth" in Renaissance England may refer to social rank or individual merit. Shakespeare leaves unsaid in what that worth consists. The ambiguity is typical. Without failing to suggest the young man's social status the sonnets allow public and private identities to blur together. Worth in rank becomes worth in character or love.

Perhaps most importantly from a literary point of view, the sonnets communicate intimacy by their muting of rhetorical invention. The sonnets are, as we have seen, by no means untouched by the rhetorical culture of the Renaissance. We should not take Shakespeare at his word when he promises "plain speech" (sonnet 82). But Shakespeare does contrive a plainer speech, especially by using relatively simple words and toning down the elaborate and extended metaphors, called "conceits," that frequently color Renaissance sonnets.

We see this effect in one of the sequence's most conceit-filled sonnets, number 44. In this brilliant sonnet about the young man's absence, Shakespeare plays on the Renaissance belief that all matter was composed of a combination of four elements: earth, water, air and fire.

> If the dull substance of my flesh were thought,
> Injurious distance should not stop my way;
> For then, despite of space, I would be brought
> From limits far remote where thou dost stay.
> No matter then although my foot did stand,
> Upon the farthest earth removed from thee;
> For nimble thought can jump both sea and land
> As soon as think the place where he would be.
> But ah, thought kills me that I am not thought,
> To leap large lengths of miles when thou art gone,
> But that, so much of earth and water wrought,
> I must attend time's leisure with my moan,
>> Receiving naught by elements so slow
>> But heavy tears, badges of either's woe.

First Shakespeare wishes he were immaterial thought so that he could immediately bridge the physical distance between himself and the young man by merely imagining himself to be with him. In line 9, however, Shakespeare concedes that he is "not thought" but matter. Indeed, he is made of earth and water, the two heaviest of the four elements. Hence he must "attend time's leisure," that is, wait for the slow passage of time to return him to his beloved.

The different metaphors for Shakespeare's body make up the sonnet's conceit. But these metaphors heighten rather than overshadow the feelings expressed in the sonnet. There are a number of reasons for this effect. First, Shakespeare avoids the temptation to play in one sonnet on all four elements; he saves air and fire for the sonnet following. Had he included all four elements in one sonnet he would have been led to a more mannered working out the conceit — how his feelings are like each one of those elements. Freed from an overly mechanical schema, Shakespeare instead is able to express more complex feelings and attitudes.

Thus the turn of feelings from hope to despair at line nine: "But ah, thought kills me that I am not thought." Besides shifting the emotional direction of the sonnet, this line strikingly transforms the original metaphor of the poem by making it less metaphorical and more suggestive of real feeling. "Thought kills me that I am not thought" might seem a perplexing statement — if Shakespeare is not thought, how does his thought kill him? — until we realize that Shakespeare is brilliantly distinguishing his real thought from the poem's initial, and more fanciful, conceit: "If the dull substance of my flesh were thought."

Real thought painfully understands the limits of "thought" used as a metaphor (writing "I am thought" does not really give one magical wings to fly). Shakespeare does not abandon the association of himself with thought but — wary of false compare — he transforms it, making it more psychological, more realistic, less facile than the conceit of the first eight lines. The metaphor that follows in the sonnet — that the writer is made of earth and water — is indeed more down to earth. Shakespeare's association of earth and water with his tears also gives this metaphor an inward, psychological turn.[92]

We can get a good sense of Shakespeare's effectiveness at muting the sonnet's rhetorical excess by turning to another sonnet about the lover's wish to be near his beloved, this one by Barnabe Barnes:

> Jove for Europa's love took shape of bull,
>   And for Calisto played Diana's part,
>   And in a golden shower, he filled full
>   The lap of Danae with celestial art.
> Would I were changed but to my mistress' gloves
>   That those white lovely fingers I might hide,
>   That I might kiss those hands, which mine heart loves,
>   Or else that chain of pearls, her neck's vain pride,

Made proud with her neck's veins, that I might fold
   About that lovely neck, and her paps [breasts] tickle,
   Or her to compass like a belt of gold.
Or that sweet wine, which down her throat doth trickle,
   To kiss her lips, and lie next at her heart,
   Run though her veins, and pass by pleasure's part.[93]

In Barnes's sonnet, as in the first eight lines of Shakespeare's, metaphor is magic. It can transform you into whatever you need to get close to your beloved. But where Shakespeare deepens his poem and turns it inward by rethinking the easy magic of metaphor, Barnes's poem is — or at least at first seems — wholly driven by its conceits.

Initially the sonnet moves forward by repeating a list of magical transformations Jove underwent in order to have sex with women. Then it invents a list of things — glove, pearls, belt, wine — into which the poem's speaker would like to be transformed in order to be near his mistress. With all those lists there's not much room for actual feeling and thought, nor does the fancifulness of the transformations seem conducive to expressing the speaker's actual experience.

When Barnes happily concludes that if he were his mistress' wine he would eventually be urinated and have the privilege of passing by "pleasure's part," I assume that Barnes thinks these metaphors are silly too. Barnes, like Shakespeare, finally does draw back from overly mechanical rhetoric. The way that he does so however, through ironizing humor, also fails to suggest genuine feeling for the beloved.

Yet we should not regard Shakespeare's sonnets in contrast as direct cries from the heart. The renunciation of literary convention is *itself* a convention of the sonnet form.[94] And Shakespeare's muting of the figural language of his sonnets might be said to make them even more deviously artful. The flatterer you don't recognize is more dangerous than the one you do. Thus, for example, even as the line "But ah, thought kills me that I am not thought" disclaims the fanciful metaphor that Shakespeare's body was the stuff of imagination, it makes use of another figure of speech — *epanalepsis*, the repetition at the end of a clause of a word used at its beginning (Puttenham calls it "resumptio").[95]

Moreover, the thought that *kills* Shakespeare is finally no less a figure of speech than the thought that would give him wings to fly. Thoughts, after all, do not literally kill. The idea is a personification and a hyperbole. As Shakespeare's own character Rosalind says to Orlando when he professes to die with longing for her, "men have died from time to time, and worms have eaten them, but not for love."[96] In other moods Shakespeare, like Rosalind, might have preferred Barnes's comic skepticism.

It is too simple to choose between seeing the sonnets as sincere in their love or seeing them as a product of Renaissance rhetorical convention. For the kind of rhetorical training encouraged by an elite Renaissance education must have also helped to encourage the exploration and expression of the writer's personal feelings, as we usually think of poetry as doing. This means that a sophisticated tool for the refinement and exploration of feeling was during the period also a sophisticated tool for social competition and deception — for hiding feeling. A powerful means of expressing the self was also a powerful means to misrepresent the self.

Moreover, expression and misrepresentation do not just exist together in the sonnets like two inert chemicals held in suspension. It is rather their reaction that gives the sonnets their tense energy: Shakespeare struggles to express true feelings in a form suspected of rhetorical convention and flattery. But he also draws a greater rhetorical force from that very struggle. The protestations of truth and the muted style of the sonnets make more believable the conventions of sonnet praise. The impulse toward sincerity in the sonnets both challenges *and* serves their impulse toward flattery.[97]

There is similarly no reason to believe that love and self-interest were, for Shakespeare, separate drives, that the expressions of love for the young man have to be considered either true feelings or fawning attempts to secure a nobleman's patronage. Shakespeare may have been attracted both to the young man *and* his exalted station, attracted to the young man because of that station. Sex and power need not be opposed. Power can be sexy. Shakespeare's praises for the young man may have been both self-interested and passionately felt.

We may also wish to know more about that passion, which has embarrassed some readers of the sonnets. What does it mean in Renaissance England for one man to declare his love for another? The book's next section considers this question.

Section II

"A Man Right Fair"

9

Before Homosexuality

"Not marble nor the gilded monuments / Of princes shall outlive this powerful rhyme." Shakespeare's famous promise in sonnet 55 to preserve the memory of his beloved echoes in sonnet 63: "His beauty shall in these black lines be seen / And they shall live, and he in them still green." But sonnet 63 makes clear the beloved's sex: "His beauty." Many people remain unaware that the first 126 of Shakespeare's 154 sonnets pay tribute to his love for a man. Contemporary representations of the sonnets often encourage this misapprehension.[1]

The difference between poetry and perception is especially great because readers usually prize the sonnets written for the man rather than for the woman. The group of sonnets written for the man celebrates a romantic love that resists change in time, fortune, or heart. This is Shakespeare as we like him: "Shall I compare thee to a summer's day" (sonnet 18), "You live in this, and dwell in lovers' eyes" (sonnet 55); "Let me not to the marriage of true minds / Admit impediments" (sonnet 116). The sonnets written about a woman are different and less quotable — if one's aim is endearment. Love in these sonnets is cynical, even disgusted. Has any lover ever sent a carefully handwritten copy of sonnet 129 ("Th'expense of spirit in a waste of shame / Is lust in action") along with a dozen roses? Has any wedding service ever included a reading of sonnet 138: "When my love swears that she is made of truth / I do believe her though I know she lies"?

On learning that many of the sonnets commemorate Shakespeare's love for a man people frequently wonder whether Shakespeare was gay. And largely because of the sonnets Shakespeare's name sometimes appears in lists of famous gay authors or historical figures.[2] There is something to be said for these autobiographical readings. Imagining the sonnets as the place where Shakespeare reveals his gay identity (as well as his adulterous, cross-class and, as we shall see, possibly cross-racial loves) provides a tonic to bland characterizations of Shakespeare as an icon of cultural conservativism.

Still, reading the sonnets as autobiography has its problems. We cannot with certainty identify the young man or black mistress, or the degree of physical intimacy Shakespeare had with either. The sonnets to the black mistress sound more sexual than the sonnets to the young man. But the language of love to the young man hardly rules out sex, just as the sexual language about the black mistress cannot prove that Shakespeare really had sex with her.

More importantly, autobiographical readings of the sonnets are limiting. The focus on Shakespeare the man may short-circuit the difference of culture and treat Shakespeare as if he were our contemporary. We need rather a sense of the cultural differences between ideas of sexuality in Shakespeare's time and in our own. Identifying Shakespeare as gay from an autobiographical reading of the sonnets is particularly misleading, since the term evokes a contemporary idea of fixed sexual identity that the Renaissance did not share. The term "gay" (or "homosexual") has other limitations as well. It reduces the same-sex love in the sonnets to a modern, personal category rather than recognizing its importance to the world of patronage and social status recounted in the previous section of this book. And it implies that same-sex love was viewed in the English Renaissance, as it often is today, as subversive or transgressive of orthodox morality. As we will see, it was just the opposite.

Rather than treating the sonnets in narrowly biographical terms I frame my discussion of Shakespeare's relationship to the young man around the different understandings of love between men in the Renaissance and today. Nor do I focus only on whether the sonnets reveal a sexual relationship with the young man — a topic frequently debated in discussions of these sonnets — though in the final chapter of this section I do consider the matter. The question of whether two people had sex is usually interesting, but so too is the historically different experience of love and desire expressed in Shakespeare's relationship to the young man.

As the fight over gay marriage in the U.S. and elsewhere intensifies, the stakes in this history are high. Objecting to gay marriage, social and religious conservatives invoke a traditional conception of marriage as between one man and one woman. These traditionalists, as Katha Pollitt observes, ignore the wide variety of marriage traditions in the past five thousand years of western history.[3] Enter Shakespeare's sonnets, which neglect all the way to adultery Shakespeare's legal and child-bearing marriage to Anne Hathaway, while celebrating a marriage between men based on the love they share. These aspects of the sonnet story become more important if they are seen not as biography, as clues to Shakespeare's particular emotional and sexual life, but as evidence of the changing historical understandings of love and marriage. "Let me not to the marriage of true minds / Admit impediments" may not be Shakespeare's bumper-sticker take on the debate over gay marriage.[4] But the history reflected in the sonnets should be part of that debate.

The sonnets, which never define themselves as "homosexual" poetry, suggest the variability of our conceptions of same-sex desire. To start with, there were no "homosexuals" in Renaissance England — and no "heterosexuals" either. Both these terms date from the late nineteenth century. Why didn't these words (or similar ones) exist earlier, since they now seem so indispensable for categorizing people and dividing up sexual desire? Historians have argued that not just the words "homosexual" and "heterosexual" are missing, but the kinds of people they describe.

Of course, people of the same sex had sexual relations before the invention of the term "homosexual." But they understood and experienced those relations differently. The word often used to describe sex between men was "sodomy," which meant something substantially different than the later category of the homosexual. In his *History of Sexuality* the influential historian Michel Foucault made a crucial distinction between these two terms:

> As defined by the ancient civil or canonical codes, sodomy was a category of forbidden acts; their perpetrator was nothing more than the juridical subject of them. The nineteenth-century homosexual became a personage, a past, a case history, and a childhood, in addition to being a type of life, a life form, and a morphology.... Nothing that went into his total composition was unaffected by his sexuality.[5]

There was, in other words, nothing special about the person accused of sodomy except that he or she had committed a crime (and hence became a "juridical subject," that is, a person now under the law's purview). What mattered was the act, not the identity. With the advent of psychoanalysis, the science of biology and the Linnaean classification of species (as well as related pseudosciences such as phrenology), something changed. The identity of the person who committed what was once the sodomitical act became a fixed and knowable type, definable by scientific analysis. Just as one could classify mammals and marsupials, one could identify people as gay or straight.

This shift from sexual act to sexual identity implies something more than the past's failure to see what was there all along. It's not the case, Foucault argued, that before the nineteenth century doctors or judges or the accused themselves didn't look carefully enough within the "juridical subject" of sodomy laws to discover the homosexual person. Foucault argued the more radical point that this identity did not exist.

To imagine this different way of understanding sexual experience, we could think of same-sex sexuality before the category of homosexuality as something like we see adultery today. We usually consider adultery wrong, but we don't usually divide people sexually into adulterers or non-adulterers as we do hetero- or homosexual. And though we may associate adultery with moral or psychological qualities such as selfishness or lechery, we don't usually see adultery as integral to identity the way we do hetero- or homosexuality. We compare homosexuality to other kinds of group identities such as race or religion. Many people would hear "I am gay" and "I am Jewish" as similar types of statements. It's harder to imagine someone saying "I am an adulterer" in the same way. One is Jewish — and happens to commit adultery. Or one is a doctor — and happens to commit adultery. Adultery is something one does, not who one is.

Not so with the modern concept of homosexuality, which most often describes something more than committing particular sexual acts. Homosexuality has come to be seen, Foucault suggests, as one of the deepest sources of self, a crucial and usually fixed definition of who one is and who one has been.[6] The divide between hetero- and homosexual identity now frequently seems so natural that many people believe it must be as genetically determined as eye color or sex. One hears of the search for the gay gene, but not for the gene that causes adultery.

It is worth repeating that in saying there was a time when homosexuality did not exist Foucault is not saying homosexual *acts* did not exist. This would be as absurd as saying adulterous acts did not exist. Rather, Foucault is saying that in the past same-sex desire was not seen as limited to a minority group of persons with a distinct homosexual psychology. Since there was no notion of a fixed sexual identity — gay or straight — *anyone* might feel, and act on, same-sex desire.[7] Tellingly, the term sodomy encompassed more than sex between men. It included bestiality and sometimes illicit heterosexual sex, rather than defining a specific, narrowly defined "homosexual" desire.[8]

The implications of Foucault's argument for Renaissance society and culture have been ably explored in recent years by the historian Alan Bray and the literary critic Bruce R. Smith, among others. They have argued that a person living in the Renaissance, rather than dividing the sexual universe into homo- and heterosexual, would see it as peopled by the chaste and the unchaste, the pure and the sinful.[9] Is sex confined to marriage, or does it take place outside of it? Do you like a little sex, or a lot? Men who liked a lot of sex might be just as likely to sin with men as with women, or with men and women both.[10]

The poet John Wilmot, Earl of Rochester, proudly celebrated these expansive lusts. In Rochester's poem "The Disabled Debauchee" the title figure looks back fondly on his former sexual exploits:

> Nor shall our love-fits, *Chloris*, be forgot,
>   When each the well-look'd Linkboy strove t'enjoy
> And the best kiss was the deciding lot
>   Whether the boy fuck'd you, or I the boy.[11]

These lines celebrate sex with a handsome "linkboy" (a servant torchbearer) but Rochester is remembering a debauched life, not a homosexual one. His sexual nostalgia has room for his mistress Chloris, and it's only the chance of a kissing game that decides whether the linkboy will have sex with a woman or a man.

Nor is Rochester's debauchee bisexual in the modern sense of having a distinctive minority sexual orientation. Every man in the Renaissance was thought liable to the unchaste desires that Rochester's debauchee wickedly indulges. Sodomy, according to the Protestant theologian John Rainolds, was a result of "men's natural corruption and viciousness." Rainolds, who later became one of the translators of the King James Bible, wrote those words in an attack on the immorality of plays, a frequently made connection between sodomy and the theater especially relevant to Shakespeare. In fact, sodomy was sometimes associated not with particular sexual desires at all, but with persons given to irreligious behaviors and immoderate appetites. The English jurist Edward Coke deemed it the product of "pride, excess of diet, idleness, and contempt of the poor."[12] Like Rainolds, Coke understood sodomy not as the desire of a distinctive homosexual identity, but as one of any number of moral failings or sinful acts.

Sodomy in the Renaissance was considered morally wrong and it was illegal. Conviction of sodomy was punishable by death. But evidence from court records indicates that homosexual sex was rarely punished or even prosecuted during the period. Moralists and laws said one thing. What people did and what happened to them was another.[13]

This contradiction reflects the fact that in any society the meanings and morality attributed to sexual acts vary widely, and English Renaissance society was no exception to this rule. On the one hand, since in the Renaissance all sex outside marriage was sinful — even sex within marriage was not clearly free of sin — homosexual sex could be viewed as one sexual transgression among many. It was wrong, but so was fornication — heterosexual sex outside of marriage. Practically speaking, fornication in fact presented more of a problem than homosexual sex. Authorities were more worried about sex that would result in illegitimate children, for which the community would have to provide.[14]

On the other hand, sodomy could be singled out for special condemnation. It was declared monstrous, a treason against God and country, akin to witchcraft and sorcery. Often in such cases it was associated with persons felt to threaten established order, such as Catholics or foreigners. Yet these condemnations may also have created a break between this official morality and ordinary sexual practice.[15] Did such terrible offenses, committed by dangerous men, have anything to do with a little messing around among friends? According to a 1991 study, about 60% of contemporary U.S. college students did not define engaging in oral sex as having "had sex"; for various kinds of foreplay the percentage is much lower still.[16] Likewise, "ordinary" (or privileged) men in Renaissance England could engage in sexual activity with one another and not see themselves, or find themselves prosecuted as, monstrous sodomites. Even English Renaissance legal authorities did not view most same-sex sexual relations as prosecutable sodomy. Coke recommended prosecution only for the rape of a minor.[17]

The recognition of these historical differences in the legal and moral treatment of homosexuality has significant consequences. When in the 2003 U.S. Supreme Court case *Lawrence v. Texas* the 6–3 majority declared antisodomy laws unconstitutional, its decision relied in part on the historical insight that such laws did not have the long tradition a previous Supreme Court decision asserted. The court recognized in *Lawrence* that English Renaissance and U.S. colonial anti-sodomy laws — not rooted in the modern divide between hetero- and homosexuality — covered a wider range of sexual offenses, sometimes including heterosexual ones. One could not maintain therefore that there was a tradition of legislation against specifically homosexual sodomy. To keep to precedent anti-sodomy laws would have to make illegal all kinds of non-procreative sex engaged in by both same- and heterosex couples. And the justices were not going to do that. The court majority in *Lawrence* also recognized that same-sex sex between consenting adults was usually not prosecuted in the Renaissance. Modern anti-sodomy laws, by contrast, *more restrictively* sought to regulate sexual activity even where there was adult consent.[18]

Traveling through Ireland in 1602 to 1603, Josias Bodley awoke to find that some of the men with whom he was traveling "greeted their companions the back way." Bodley did not think this practice "decent" but he noted that some said it was "good for the loins." And, he concluded, "nothing is amiss which is not taken amiss."[19] Bodley did not see homosexuals or even sodomites but men enjoying themselves (and perhaps looking after their health) in a way that, if he did not like, he could casually ignore. Nothing was amiss if not taken amiss.

10

The King Loved Him Well

Men having sex with one another in Shakespeare's day would not have tried to puzzle out whether they were gay. Nor would they usually have feared prosecution. To these contexts for Shakespeare's sonnets to the young man we can add the most important of all: Renaissance English culture placed a high value on the love between men.

Male same-sex love in the English Renaissance was not marginal or subversive. It was integral to some of the most cherished aspects of English cultural life, and to England's most important political institutions. Just as the sin of sodomy was not seen as the expression of a distinct sexual identity, neither was the celebrated virtue of male love. This love, rather, was part of a man's place in particular cultural and social worlds, where it affirmed his public, social or political bonds with another man.

First, there was the bond between lord and vassal. Medieval warrior culture celebrated the ardent love between men who fought together. We read in the early medieval poem *Beowulf* how, upon Beowulf's departure, King Hrothgar (whose kingdom Beowulf has saved) "might not restrain his breast's welling, for fixed in his heartstrings a deep-felt longing for the beloved man burned in his blood." Another early medieval poem, *The Battle of Maldon*, similarly celebrates the love of vassal and lord, especially when they risk their lives together: "Ever may he lament who now thinks to turn from warplay. I am old of life; from here I will not turn, but by my lord's side, by the man I loved, I intend to lie." There are late medieval examples of this love as well. In Sir Thomas Malory's fifteenth-century *Morte D'Arthur*, Arthur overlooks Lancelot's adultery with Queen Guenever "for Sir Launcelot had done so much for him and the queen so many times, that wit ye well [know you well] the king loved him passingly well."[20] Him, not her: it is Lancelot's loss Arthur fears. Shakespeare looked back with admiration on this medieval ideal. In *King Lear*, the loyal Kent expects to follow the king his master into death.

In Shakespeare's day the warrior culture that gave rise to such relationships between lord and vassal was disappearing.[21] But classical ideals began to replace knightly ones. With the recovery of the literature of Greece and Rome — the very hallmark of "the Renaissance" — came an admiration of cultures in which male-male sex was considered perfectly normal and in some cases preferred to male-female sex.[22] This literature, much of which every schoolboy knew, provided a way of seeing same-sex desire outside of its condemnation by Christianity.

Ovid's male gods carry on affairs with boys as well as girls. Plutarch treats the respective worth of marriage and male erotic relationships as a matter for genteel discussion. Virgil's pastorals include a poem much admired and imitated during the Renaissance in which the shepherd Corydon complains of his unrequited love for the youth Alexis.[23] The interpretation of this poem by the internationally renowned humanist scholar Erasmus emphasized the differences between the shepherd and his love: Corydon is older, ugly and of low social status, Alexis younger, handsome, and a courtier.[24] It is not difficult to hear Corydon's longing for Alexis echoing in Shakespeare's desire for the aristocratic young man.

These medieval and classical traditions of male love were evocative to their Renaissance readers because they mirrored realities of their own lives.[25] Renaissance England was often a man's world, and key institutions in it created close male relationships. At all-male schools and universities students developed a shared identity and formed strong and sometimes socially advantageous attachments with one another. The atmosphere at these schools was — as with any grouping of adolescent boys — sexually charged.[26] Men were also joined together as master and servant. The Renaissance household often included more than just immediate family. Middle-class and aristocratic households had servants too, and these servants — male as well as female — were subject to the commands, and sexual predations, of their masters or other men in positions of authority.[27] Even at the highest level of society and government, just about every male in Renaissance England was someone's else's "man." Kings had favorites, noblemen retainers, courtiers followers, patrons clients. Men in these relationships proudly declared their ardent love for one another.[28]

The meanings of the word "friend" in Renaissance England reflect this combination of personal and political ties. As we saw earlier, friendship was not just a private concern. Like Renaissance marriage, friendship was a public matter, binding together through private affections men's social or political interests. A tradition of sworn "friendship" or "brotherhood," dating from the eleventh century to the seventeenth, united men and their families in a manner that resembled and often complemented marriage alliances. Vows of friendship or brotherhood, in fact, were sometimes themselves called "weddings" (the word "wed" originally refers to the making of a pledge) and taken before a church. Men bonded in friendship were also sometimes buried together in the manner of husband and wife. The epitaph of a seventeenth-century church monument celebrating the friendship of Thomas Legge and John Gostlin declares "iunxit amor vivos sic iungat terra sepultos / Gostlini reliquum cor tibi Leggus habes" [Love joined them living. So may the earth join them in their burial. O Legge, Gostlin's heart you still have with you].[29]

As Legge and Gostlin's epitaph suggests, friendship could involve an ardent emotional relationship as well as a practical one. In fact, "friend" in the Renaissance could also mean "lover." We sometimes use "friend" in this way but the usage was more frequent in the Renaissance, and did not carry a sense of concealment. In *Measure for Measure* it is reported of Claudio that "he hath got his friend with child" (1.4.29), while in *A Midsummer Night's Dream* Hermia addresses the man she is eloping with as "sweet friend" (2.2.66). Likewise, the word "lover" could mean friend. In *Julius Caesar* Brutus after participating in the assassination of Caesar asserts his good intentions by publicly declaring "I slew my best lover for the good of Rome" (3.2.41–42).[30] This blurring of the words friend and lover suggests that Renaissance England did not make a strong distinction between the emotions involved in male-female relationships and in same-sex ones, or between friendship and love. In Shakespeare's day there was no saying: "we're just friends."

One of the places men pursued their friendships — both public and passionate — was in their letters to one another. Erasmus's examples of variation, as we have seen, included imagined responses to a friend's letter — responses we would consider appropriate for a lover: "What need have I to tell you of the pleasure that stirred in the soul of your Erasmus on the receipt of your letter?"; "I love you as no one else, and I delight in your letters as in nothing else"; "Your pen sated me with delight."[31] Erasmus was offering models. But these protestations of love between men were common in real Renaissance letter-writing. The Dutch humanist Hubert Languet, who for awhile was the intellectual and political mentor of Sir Philip Sidney, wrote to Sidney after they had parted, "What care and anxiety, nay, what fear had you spared me, if you had written to me only once or twice on your journey!" Sidney accepted the intensity of Languet's feelings for him: "I am well aware how that 'love is full of anxious fear,'" he writes. "You tacitly charge me with some slackening of the affection with which I have regarded and ever shall regard you and all your noble qualities."[32]

Viewing this relationship with modern eyes we might suppose that Languet was the pursuer and Sidney the pursued because Sidney, who was 19 to Languet's 55, had youth on his side. This view would emphasize the private, emotional aspects of the relationship. But its social and political dynamics are important too. Sidney is a gentleman, courtier and possible heir to the Earl of Leicester. Languet was looking to Sidney as a friend in high places in the English court who could advocate a Protestant English-Dutch alliance against Spain.[33] Likewise, when Shakespeare wrote of his love for Southampton he was also pursuing the earl's patronage. The social or political aspects of these relationships need not imply, however, that the love men expressed for one another was not real. Men who depended on one another for patronage or alliance often felt and relied upon their strong emotional ties.[34]

Another place men pursued relationships with one another was in bed, which they regularly shared — tutors and students, masters and servants, friend and friend. Bed-sharing was partly a practical matter — there weren't so many beds to go around — but it also had social and political implications. If the man with whom you shared your bed — "your bedfellow" — was of higher social status, then having such a bedfellow would be a sign of honor. Moreover, one could use the intimacy of the bed to advance social or political interests. The bed is a place where, as the historian Alan Bray remarked, one "talks as well as sleeps." The intimacy of the bed suggests that one's bedfellow will be receptive to what was said. Bray cites as an example of concern about the abuse of this intimacy a letter from the Countess of Oxford, in which she complains about the friendship of a John Hunt with her son: "Hunt has impudently presumed to be his bedfellow and otherwise used him most unrespectively [disrespectfully]."[35]

Shakespeare's contemporary and fellow dramatist Christopher Marlowe provides another example of this concern in his play *Edward II*. In the play, the king's nobles are enraged by Edward's love for Piers Gaveston not because the love is homosexual ("the mightiest kings have had their minions," one noble observes), but because the nobles consider Gaveston a social upstart who is gaining too much political advantage on account of the king's love.[36]

Of course, the intimacy of the bed need not have included sexual acts, though it did in the story that Bodley tells. Bed-sharing was generally taken for granted, without the supposition of sexual sin. But the bed was not free from sexual suspicion. In a debate in *The Courtier* about remarkable feats of sexual self-control, Socrates' spiritual love for Alcibiades (the very origin of "Platonic love") comes under fire: "Bed and night were indeed a strange place and time for the contemplation of that pure beauty which Socrates is said to have loved without any impure desires."[37]

More generally male friendships were not free from allegations of "impure desire." The inhabitants of Francis Bacon's *New Atlantis* (published in 1627) are said to be without "unlawful lust" or "masculine love," and yet "there are not so faithful and inviolate friendships in the world" as in that land.[38] We are to wonder that the New Atlanteans manage to keep sinful "masculine love" out of their faithful friendships. But the New Atlantis is a Utopia, and so implies that in Bacon's real England "masculine love" and friendship sometimes mix.

Though sex between men in Renaissance England was frequently ignored, men's relationships with one another might come under special scrutiny when there was hay to be made — as with political sex scandals today. Perhaps the gap in social status between the two friends was inappropriately large or perhaps one of the men involved had enemies who could use the relationship against him. Might the socially lower bedfellow be trading sex for favor? Might not the nobleman who engaged in such trade be revealing his depravity? Francis Bacon was himself a victim of this kind of accusation.[39]

We also have an example at the highest level of affectionate language and physical intimacy between men — as well as the accusation of sexual sin by political enemies — in the correspondence between King James I and one of his favorites, George Villiers, Duke of Buckingham.[40] Letters that quickly became public knowledge or were even read publicly at James' court affirmed the closeness of the king to the duke in erotic terms. When Buckingham's return from an important diplomatic trip was delayed — Buckingham was in Spain helping to negotiate a marriage between the king's son Charles and the Spanish king's daughter — James wrote to Buckingham and Charles that "I now repent me sore that ever I suffered you to go away. I care for match nor nothing, so I may once have you in my arms again. God grant it! God grant it! Amen, amen, amen." For his part Buckingham promised before leaving Spain that "when he once gets hold of your bedpost again, never to quit it."[41]

On the occasion of marriage negotiations conducted by one man for the other man's son, this erotic language between men might sound strange to modern ears. The exchange between Buckingham and his king, however, well expresses some of the dynamics of the love between men in Renaissance England. In this case not only do heterosexual marriage bonds and male master-servant bonds co-exist with rather than oppose one another, but the real affection lies in the bonds between men.

The plan to marry Charles to the Spanish princess was an instrument of English foreign policy. No affection between the parties to be married would have been necessary, although Charles claimed to have fallen for the princess, based on her picture.[42] There was a political bond between James and Buckingham as well, that between king and favorite. But this bond also involved what we might expect from heterosexual marriage: love.

11

Marriages and Men

The making of bonds between men through the arrangement of a marriage returns us to Shakespeare's sonnets, which begin with a marriage too. Not the marriage of true minds made famous in sonnet 116, but the marriage for economic or political advantage that, like the one proposed for James I's son, shaped many marriages in Renaissance England, especially among elites. The parties to the marriage negotiation in the sonnets are Shakespeare and the young aristocratic man to whom he writes.

The first seventeen sonnets lament the young man's disregard for his family name and masculine duty in refusing to marry. So Shakespeare argues in the sonnet that begins this group and the sonnets as a whole:

> From fairest creatures we desire increase,
> That thereby beauty's rose might never die,
> But as the riper should by time decease,
> His tender heir might bear his memory;
> But thou, contracted to thine own bright eyes,
> Feed'st thy light's flame with self-substantial fuel,
> Making a famine where abundance lies,
> Thyself thy foe, to thy sweet self too cruel.
> Thou that art now the world's fresh ornament
> And only herald to the gaudy spring
> Within thine own bud buriest thy content,
> And, tender churl, mak'st waste in niggarding.
>   Pity the world, or else this glutton be:
>   To eat the world's due, by the grave and thee.

Shakespeare transforms sonnet convention. Writers of sonnets often beg their beloveds to have sex with them. The sex Shakespeare urges in this sonnet,

however, is not with the sonnet's author. Nor is it adulterous, as the sonneteer's courtly love traditionally was. Sir Philip Sidney, whose *Astrophil and
Stella* helped create the Elizabethan vogue for sonnets, wrote for the already
married Lady Penelope Rich.[43] Even in Renaissance sonnet sequences in
which the relationship is not explicitly adulterous, marriage — much less children — rarely enters their poets' verse. Against this sonnet tradition, Shakespeare urges the young man to have sex with a woman in marriage.

For it is through marriage and children that the fair young man will
preserve his beauty from decay (a beauty, the sonnet suggests, now being
wasted on self-love), by passing it on to the child who will bear his "memory." The young man's child will be "tender," Shakespeare puns, in every
sense: young, loving and, as heir, the father's repayment for the beauty and
life he owes the world (the "world's due"), since "tender" is also, in legal terms,
something offered to discharge a debt.[44]

English Renaissance culture considered the emotional and legal relationship between father and son, contained in that word "tender," to be all-
important, another form of the bonds between men. Not only should
children care for and respect their parents but the child also carries on the
family's name, status and wealth into the next generation. The identity of
the Renaissance child is absorbed into that of the family — in contrast to the
modern celebration of the child's development of an independent self.

Especially for fathers and sons: if the status of the family is to remain
unchanged, then the transfer of the family's head from father to son should
be seamless. The son should be, as a painter rendered the identically posed
Sir Walter Ralegh and his son, a replica in miniature of the father.[45] Shakespeare reflects this identification of father and son in his plays. In *The Winter's Tale* King Leontes must be assured that his son is an exact replica of
himself: "Although the print be little, [the son is] the whole matter / And
copy of the father" (2.3.99–100).

Perhaps because of worry that sons are not always just like their fathers
(even biologically — sons have mothers too), these lines from *The Winter's
Tale* transform sexual reproduction into the more identical reproduction of
the printing press. Shakespeare uses the same metaphor in sonnet 11, where
he advises the young man that before getting old he should "print more" of
himself by having a son.

In urging the married sexuality that produces an heir over the unmar-
ried or adulterous sex that disturbs inheritance, Shakespeare flouts literary
convention. But in doing so he aligns his sonnets with much more important social convention. His adaptation of the sonnet is like the corporate
advertising that uses the rebellious music of the late twentieth century to sell
the mainstream consumer goods of the twenty first. Shakespeare's originality

lies in the way he takes a literary form associated with sexy and adulterous courtly love and turns it to the art of persuading the young man to fulfill his familial and social obligations. Sonnet 1 is so far from the romantic desires we usually associate with sonnets that no woman is even mentioned in it.

But while there is no woman in this sonnet it is not the case that there is no desire. On the contrary, Shakespeare continually expresses his desire for the young man whom he calls "beauty's rose" and who, he warns, must like a rose reproduce himself. The intimacy of Shakespeare's protective admiration for the young man replaces the courtly love sonnet's seductive address of the woman.

Readers of the sonnets have sometimes considered the fact that Shakespeare urges the young man to marry evidence that he has no homosexual desire for him.[46] This idea is mistaken because it confuses modern ideas of married love with the utilitarian purpose of marriage in the Renaissance. If marriage is for conducting diplomacy, allying prominent families, or producing heirs then love between the partners is unnecessary. This is why courtly love was traditionally adulterous: because men and women marry for practical reasons, romantic desire occurs not within but outside of marriage. Of course, people did marry for love in Renaissance England, and even the partners in an arranged marriage were, ideally, supposed to develop an affection for one another. Yet the sonnets in the marriage group do not emphasize spousal love as a reason for marriage.[47]

We should not, however, reach the opposite conclusion that Shakespeare lacks enthusiasm for married love because he is "homosexual." A utilitarian conception of marriage is ordinary for Shakespeare's time, not the psychology of a particular sexual identity. Nor is Shakespeare's emphasis on his own relationship to the young man in the marriage sonnets evidence of homosexuality in the modern sense. Again, this is ordinary. If a marriage forges economic, social or political relationships, it is not surprising that it should bind not just the marriage partners but the parties — frequently men — who benefit from those relationships.[48]

Shakespeare portrays men's bonding with one another through marriage in his play *The Taming of the Shrew*. The play aligns the romantic courtship of the beautiful Bianca with a second courtship of her father Baptista. To marry Bianca it is necessary to win the approval of her father too, to court both "him and her" (1.2.221). Winning the father's approval, moreover, requires still more men to rely on one another. Friend helps friend: Petruchio must first be recruited by Bianca's suitors to marry the shrew Katherine (in the plotline we most often recall from the play) before Bianca's father will allow Bianca to marry. And servant helps master: in order to carry on the courtships of Bianca and her father at once, the servant of Bianca's main suitor disguises himself as his master. The disguised servant woos the father while his master woos the daughter.

The plot of *Taming of the Shrew* nicely suggests the web of male-male as well as male-female relationships that Renaissance marriage might create. So extensive is that web and so public an affair is marriage that Shakespeare in sonnet 1 calls the young man's obligation to marry and have children nothing less than the "world's due," the young man's duty not to a woman but to the world.

Unlike *The Taming of the Shrew*, however, which features the heterosexual romance plot common to Renaissance comedy, the sonnets make marriage almost wholly an affair between men, one that affirms men's love for one another. The word "tender" in sonnet 1, as we have seen, expresses the relationship between the young man and his future son. When Shakespeare uses that word a second time in the same sonnet (in line 12) it expresses the relationship between Shakespeare and the young man. Shakespeare calls the young man "tender" as well, a reference to the beloved's youth and a term of endearment, made even more personal by calling the young man a "tender churl"—which means something like "sweet jerk"—a friendly insult of the sort one might expect among intimates.

Sonnet 10 provides another example of how the prospect of marriage facilitates Shakespeare's expression of love for the young man. In this sonnet Shakespeare again accuses the young man of failing himself and those who love him by refusing to marry.

> For shame deny that thou bear'st love to any,
> Who for thyself art so unprovident.
> Grant, if thou wilt, thou art beloved of many,
> But that thou none lov'st is most evident;
> For thou art so possessed with murd'rous hate,
> That 'gainst thyself thou stick'st not to conspire,
> Seeking that beauteous roof to ruinate
> Which to repair should be thy chief desire.
> O, change thy thought, that I may change my mind!
> Shall hate be fairer lodged than gentle love?
> Be as thy presence is, gracious and kind,
> Or to thyself at least kind-hearted prove.
>> Make thee another self for love of me,
>> That beauty still may live in thine or thee.

Marriage in this sonnet again means family preservation. The "beauteous roof" is Shakespeare's metaphor for the young man himself, particularly his body. But the metaphor also calls to mind the family estate, which will fall to ruin if the young man does not produce an heir.

This prospect is the young man's "shame" and an outrage to all who love him — to none more, it seems, than Shakespeare himself. "O, change thy thought, that I may change my mind!" Shakespeare exclaims: change your mind about marrying, so I may change my mind about you. By refusing to marry, the young man not only reveals his "hate" for those who worry about the future of his family line, but even more cruelly denies his admirers another him, preserved in a son.

The sonnet imagines even the momentous event of having a child in terms of its effect not on husband and wife, but on Shakespeare and the young man: "Make thee another self for love of me." "For love of me" in this line can mean "out of respect for my love," "on my behalf" or even "because you love me." The young man should have a child in recognition of Shakespeare's own tender regard for him. Marriage in this group of sonnets is an affair between men — between the young man and his future son or the young man and Shakespeare. Far from celebrating romantic love and marriage between a man and a woman, the young man's wife appears in the sonnets as "some mother" (sonnet 3). So long as she bears the young man a child, any woman will do.

12

"Eternal Lines":
Marriage or Poetry?

In the next section of this book, I discuss the way the black mistress sonnets exemplify and challenge the sonnets' initial misogynistic attitude toward women and marriage. For now I continue to focus on Shakespeare's relationship to the young man. In doing so I follow the course of the sonnets themselves. After the initial seventeen marriage sonnets, mention of a woman drops out of the great majority of the next 100 or so sonnets altogether and the story of the relationship between Shakespeare and the young man deepens and becomes more complex. The sonnets turn strikingly in this direction at number 15:

> When I consider every thing that grows
> Holds in perfection but a little moment,
> That this huge stage presenteth naught but shows
> Whereon the stars in secret influence comment;
> When I perceive that men as plants increase,
> Cheerèd and checked even by the selfsame sky;
> Vaunt in their youthful sap, at height decrease,
> And wear their brave state out of memory:
> Then the conceit of this inconstant stay
> Sets you most rich in youth before my sight,
> Where wasteful Time debateth with decay
> To change your day of youth to sullied night;
>   And all in war with time for love of you,
>   As he takes from you, I ingraft you new.

This sonnet with its wonderful first two lines continues the theme begun in sonnet 1: the danger to the young man of passing time. Fearing the effects of time on the young man, whose "day of youth" will last only so long, Shakespeare finds himself again "at war with time" because of his love for him ("for love of you").

In sonnet 15 Shakespeare's means of fighting that war have changed, however. The young man's preservation will no longer come through the birth of a son, but through Shakespeare himself, who promises to preserve the young man's memory in his poetry. As time takes from the young man, the sonnet concludes, "I ingraft you new."[49] "Ingrafting" is a kind of reproduction, but no longer a simply natural one. The verb means to "implant" or "incorporate" and, picking up on this sonnet's plant metaphors, comes from the language of horticulture: "grafting" refers to the joining of a stem from one kind of plant to the stock of another. Buried in the etymology of the word "ingraft" lies the means by which Shakespeare will accomplish this distinctive form of reproduction. The Greek root "graph" means "pencil" or "stylus," which the stem of the graft was thought to resemble.[50]

Shakespeare again makes this promise to preserve the young man's memory — a convention of the Renaissance sonnet — in sonnet 18, the triumphant "Shall I compare thee to a summer's day?":

> Shall I compare thee to a summer's day?
> Thou art more lovely and more temperate.
> Rough winds do shake darling buds of May,
> And summer's lease hath all too short a date.
> Sometime too hot the eye of heaven shines,
> And often is his gold complexion dimmed,
> And every fair from fair sometime declines,
> By chance or nature's changing course untrimmed;
> But thy eternal summer shall not fade,
> Nor lose possession of that fair thou ow'st,
> Nor shall death brag thou wander'st in his shade
> When in eternal lines to time thou grow'st.
> So long as men can breathe or eyes can see,
> So long lives this, and this gives life to thee.

The final two lines of this sonnet are among the most famous of the sequence. Their familiarity, however, should not keep us from recognizing how decisive a turn they make in the sequence or how forward Shakespeare's promise to sustain his beloved's memory could be.

The "eternal lines" that will preserve the young man past death are those of Shakespeare's sonnets. They recall — only to replace — the family line, the inheritance from father to son that Shakespeare has been celebrating in most of the previous sonnets. By making reproduction a matter of poetry rather than sex, of ingrafting rather than childbirth, Shakespeare now takes (steals?) the place of two members of the young man's future family: the son who will reproduce the young man and the wife who will be responsible for that reproduction. The "print" metaphor of sonnet 11 gets literalized: not the child as print, but printing itself will preserve the young man.

To modern readers, the sonnets' transformation of family lines into lines of poetry feels right. *We* remember Shakespeare's sonnets, not the family of the young man. Nor do we usually now regard lineage as a primary source of a person's identity and status. But these perceptions are contemporary. While Shakespeare in his day was a popular poet and playwright, his works were not yet "Literature." Playwriting and poetry, in fact, were on the social and cultural margins in Renaissance England. A playwright wrote what was then considered ephemeral entertainment for a popular audience. The seventeenth-century founder of Oxford's Bodleian library refused to accept English plays for the library: he called them "baggage [trashy] books" that would bring the library "scandal." Poets claimed a higher vocation than playwrights. Still, commoners like Shakespeare wrote their poems to men and women whose birth made them patrons. And though poetry might suggest the writer's usefulness or social belonging, writing poetry was also viewed as an idle, youthful indulgence. The latter was especially true of love poetry.[51] The promise Shakespeare makes in sonnet 18 to preserve the man's memory through his poetry is so iconic, and so confident about a literary achievement not yet achieved, that we forget it derives from and substitutes for the family line which in Shakespeare's England counted for much more than the poet's.

Shakespeare confronts this substitution in the last of the marriage sonnets, number 17, which directly compares family and poetic lines. In this sonnet Shakespeare worries that his praises of the young man will *fail* to live up to the young man's true worth or preserve his memory:

> Who will believe my verse in time to come
> If it were filled with your most high deserts?—
> Though yet, heaven knows, it is but as a tomb
> Which hides your life, and shows not half your parts.
> If I could write the beauty of your eyes
> And in fresh numbers number all your graces,
> The age to come would say 'This poet lies;
> Such heavenly touches ne'er touched earthly faces.'
> So should my papers, yellowed with their age,
> Be scorned, like old men of less truth than tongue,
> And your true rights be termed a poet's rage
> And stretchèd metre of an antique song.

> But were some child of yours alive that time,
> You should live twice: in it, and in my rhyme.

Read as extravagant flattery, "less truth than tongue" or a "poet's rage," Shakespeare's sonnets, far from keeping alive the memory of their recipient, will find themselves subject to decay and disbelief. They will not provide the young man the more fitting tomb boldly promised in sonnet 55 ("Not marble nor the gilded monuments"), but entomb him in their yellowing pages, burying his memory. The sonnet closes more optimistically, however, with a comparison between poem and child: "But were some child of yours alive that time, / You should live twice: in it and in my rhyme."

This conclusion is tentative compared to Shakespeare's confident boasts of the power of poetry elsewhere in the sequence. But even this sonnet is moving toward that idea. Though the sonnet's final two lines associate children and poetry as sources of memory, Shakespeare's subtle crafting of the sonnets' final couplet leads us to recall not the bland word "it," which refers back to the supposedly all-important "child," but the concluding music of "time" and "rhyme." It is not surprising that the sonnet following this one is "Shall I compare thee." But sonnet 17 reminds us of what 18 has left behind: the child Shakespeare so vehemently urged the young man to produce in the first group of sonnets.

13

"Being Your Slave"

In the procreation sonnets Shakespeare declares his love for the young man by urging him to have a child. In the sonnets that follow Shakespeare intensifies that love by making himself responsible, through poetry, for the young man's reproduction. Shakespeare no longer just advises the young man but puts himself in the place of the young man's family by promising that he rather than wife or child will preserve his beloved's memory.

This relationship is striking because Shakespeare celebrates his personal bond with the young man and his skills as a writer over the Renaissance belief in family as the source of identity, status and alliance. His claims on the young man's love violate the class difference that was as central to life in Renaissance England as the differences perceived between men and women are to us. For Shakespeare, the young man's higher status makes him both desirable and quite possibly unavailable. To the young man, the sonnets' assertions of a close friendship might have appeared intrusive, even embarrassing, like the unwanted attentions of a celebrity-obsessed fan.

As Shakespeare more frankly makes himself the object of the man's attentions and preserver of his memory, he returns to the most traditional idea in the history of the sonnet. While in the first seventeen sonnets Shakespeare alters sonnet convention to discuss marriage, in later sonnets he sounds the familiar language of courtly love.

The social distance between Shakespeare and the young man prompts this return, since courtly love was often forbidden not only because it was adulterous, but also because it often involved an aristocratic woman and a socially lower male writer, admirer and (sometimes) seeker of patronage. Because of his lower status, the writer of courtly love poetry typically expresses a distant and humbled desire for the impossible object of his affections.

Shakespeare found in courtly love poetry a useful language for his own difficult attraction to the socially superior young man. He needed only to change the more usual aristocratic female recipient to an aristocratic male, as in sonnet 26:

> Lord of my love, to whom in vassalage
> Thy merit hath my duty strongly knit,
> To thee I send this written embassage
> To witness duty, not to show my wit;
> Duty so great which wit so poor as mine
> May make seem bare in wanting words to show it,
> But that I hope some good conceit of thine
> In thy soul's thought, all naked, will bestow it,
> Till whatsoever star that guides my moving
> Points on me graciously with fair aspect,
> And puts apparel on my tattered loving
> To show me worthy of thy sweet respect.
> > Then may I dare to boast how I do love thee;
> > Till then, not show my head where thou mayst prove me.

As in sonnet 17, Shakespeare fears that his poetry will inadequately honor his beloved, fears that his "wit so poor" will fail the great duty he owes the man he calls "lord of my love." So humbled is Shakespeare that he calls his own words merely "bare" and "naked" expressions that require improvement, or sufferance, through the young man's "good conceit" ("conceit" in this sonnet means "understanding," not "pride"). Only if some star exercises a more "gracious" influence over his life may Shakespeare more confidently "boast" that he loves the young man.

Variously melancholy or celebratory descriptions of the distance between writer and recipient run through the sonnets. The metaphor of sonnet 26 especially suggests the social distance between Shakespeare and the young man. The young man is a lord and Shakespeare his vassal. The metaphor reminds us of the bonds between medieval warriors, and provides an idealized image of devoted service and its reward — one that exactly opposes the modern "selling" invoked in sonnet 21 (discussed in chapter 6).

Though in that sonnet Shakespeare denies trading on the young man's love, in sonnet 26 he hopes instead for an older and more aristocratic form of exchange: the gift between lord and vassal. In return for Shakespeare's "wit so poor," the young man might generously improve the words that Shakespeare offers to him. The sonnet insinuates Shakespeare's wish for more gifts as well, while politely making "whatsoever star" rather than the young man the gracious influence that would raise him up. Nonetheless, Shakespeare connects star and young man: each provide clothing for Shakespeare's "naked" or "tattered" loving. Shakespeare's wish for this metaphorical "apparel" implies social aspiration. As noted in chapter 6, in Renaissance England clothing signified rank (or was supposed to). Moreover, a man who served a great lord received clothes from him, called livery, as a uniform or badge of his service. The poem indirectly calls on this custom as part of the exchange of duty and support between lord and vassal.

Shakespeare sounds in this sonnet like a poet seeking aristocratic patronage, but this is love poetry too.[52] A potential noble patron would have been glamorously attractive, a fantasy figure. As we saw in chapter 1, the English Renaissance aristocrat increasingly expressed his status through looks and charm.[53] These are the nobles and gentlemen portrayed in late Elizabethan portraiture, such as Nicholas Hilliard's *Young Man among the Roses*. Hilliard emphasizes the young man's expensive clothing and lithe body, especially the curly hair and long and shapely legs provocatively set off by his peascod doublet. Shakespeare's sonnets similarly celebrate *his* young man's physical beauty: he is "beauty's rose" (sonnet 1), "beauty's pattern" (sonnet 19), one on whom "every eye doth dwell" (sonnet 5).[54]

Many of the sonnets suggest, moreover, that the young man's superior social status added to his allure. The more Shakespeare is humbled, the more fierce is his desire for this "lord of my love." The class difference between Shakespeare and the young man creates idealizing fantasies about how fulfilling it would be to enjoy the young man's "sweet respect." And Shakespeare experiences his love for the young man with a masochistic intensity: "Being your slave," Shakespeare asks in sonnet 57, "what should I do but tend / Upon the hours and times of your desire?" This is the pleasing pain of the courtly lover.

Since we usually think of courtly love poetry as written by men to women, the courtly love expressed in sonnets such as 57 might seem to reflect Shakespeare's homosexuality. Again, however, the love Shakespeare avows for the young man reflects a Renaissance cultural norm, not the minority sexual orientation implied by the modern notion of the homosexual. Even the language of male/female courtly love, as developed by the medieval troubadours, drew on earlier descriptions of the love and loyalty between a lord and the vassals who served him. The medieval inventors of courtly love adopted this language by transforming master into mistress.[55] Shakespeare turns the mistress back into a master. In doing so he was being inventive — and conventional. For the bonds between men that helped to shape the courtly love tradition remained compelling in Shakespeare's time.

Consider one of the most famous and most beautiful of English Renaissance sonnets, Thomas Wyatt's "The Long Love That in My Thought Doth Harbor":

> The long love that in my thought doth harbour
> And in mine heart doth keep his residence
> Into my face presseth with bold pretense
> And therein campeth, spreading his banner.
> She that me learneth to love and suffer
> And will that my trust and lust's negligence
> Be reined by reason, shame, and reverence
> With his hardiness taketh displeasure.
> Wherewithal unto the heart's forest he fleeth,
> Leaving his enterprise with pain and cry,
> And there him hideth and not appeareth.
> What may I do when my master feareth,
> But in the field with him to live and die?
> For good is the life ending faithfully.

By Shakespeare's time Wyatt was already renowned as an originator of the sonnet in England. This sonnet, written in the 1520s or 30s, is a free translation of one of Petrarch's *Rime Sparse*. In the metaphor of the sonnet the lover/knight spreads his banner, revealing his love to the mistress, perhaps simply by blushing.[56] The sign of affection is mild, but to the tortured courtly lover it is "bold pretense." His mistress' displeasure at it makes him flee "his enterprise with pain and cry" and return to his hiding place in the "heart's forest"— that is, the innermost feelings of the poem's writer, who once again must conceal his too presumptuous love.

While Wyatt's sonnet records anguished desire for an unattainable woman, the poem's metaphor of lord and vassal reminds us of the importance and intensity of relationships between men in the Renaissance. The sonnet ends with an avowal of the devotion, even to the death, between men at arms: "For good is the life ending faithfully." In the metaphor of the sonnet this vow means that the writer will devotedly serve the female beloved, even if she continues to rebuke him. The metaphor which renders this vow, however, refers to one man's loyalty to another man in war. The best thing Wyatt can promise to a woman is, "I will love you as I would love a man." Shakespeare's sonnet 26, which in its metaphor of devoted vassalage recalls Wyatt's sonnet, reflects in the gender of its beloved the same centrality of male relationships. It returns courtly love to its roots in them.

The male beloved in Shakespeare's sonnets reflects as well another influence on the courtly love sonnet, a Neoplatonic strain of Petrarchanism that seeks to spiritualize the lover's desire by insisting, as Plato does in the *Symposium*, that the beloved's external beauty points the way to a higher love.

Both the classical origins of this idea and continuing strains of medieval and Renaissance misogyny made a male rather than female beloved a natural conduit for this higher love. This is the kind of love that Michelangelo professes to the male beloveds to whom he writes in his sonnets. He calls the most important of these men, the aristocrat Tomasso de' Cavalieri, "signor mio," as Shakespeare refers in sonnet 26 to the young man as "lord of my love." Just as the purity of Socrates' love for Alcibiades is questioned in *The Courtier*, however, so Michelangelo has to protest the purity of his love, in a context in which male-male sex was an established, if also criminalized, part of Florentine culture. And as with Shakespeare's sonnets, Michelangelo's "he" was rewritten into a "she," in a seventeenth-century edition of the sonnets created by Michelangelo's great-nephew. This edition remained the established text of his poetry for over 200 years.[57]

Moreover, while there is only one other sequence of sonnets in the English Renaissance explicitly written to a man — by Shakespeare's contemporary Richard Barnfield — many male poets wrote individual sonnets to male patrons, or men they hoped would become their patrons. Barnes and Markham, as we have seen, both wrote sonnets to Southampton. Of the seventeen dedicatory sonnets prefacing Spenser' great poem *The Faerie Queene*, fourteen were to male nobles and gentlemen. Genres are fluid. Patronage poetry could share the language of courtly love (Barnes refers to Southampton's eyes as "heavenly lamps"), courtly love poetry the language of patronage (Spenser's promise to two of his male dedicatees to make their memory eternal in his verse is familiar from the period's love poetry as well, including Spenser's own sonnet sequence *Amoretti*, or Shakespeare's sonnets).[58] And imitation and innovation were both part of the sonnet tradition: Shakespeare may well have seen his writing of sonnets to a socially superior male, and his intensification of the amount and eroticism of this writing, as a natural product of the already existing amalgam of patronage and love poetry. He could not know, as we do, that same-sex sonnet sequences would remain the exception, rather than become a new rule.

Finally, even Renaissance sonnets addressed to women are, in effect, often addressed to men. These sonnets, as we saw in section two of this book, were often written by men for a broader audience than their supposed female recipients. This audience included other men, either friends with whom one could share one's wit, or patrons to whom one could display one's skills as a writer. As in the stereotypical male locker room, sexual gossip about women helped to unite the men. The conventional aloofness of the female beloved in courtly love poetry facilitated these exchanges. Her unavailability meant that no real relationship with a woman would interfere with the male writer's focus on himself— or with the friendships that the circulation of his poetry helped to sustain.[59] In this respect too the gender of the beloved in Shakespeare's sonnets is not idiosyncratic. Rather it reflects male attachments formed through the sharing of courtly love poetry. Shakespeare eliminates the "middlewoman" to write his poems directly to another man.

14

Friendship and Its Flatteries

Besides the initial group of sonnets advising the young man to marry, further instances of Shakespeare bonding with the young man by way of a woman emerge in a set of six sonnets (40–42, 133–134, and 144) in which Shakespeare describes how the young man has betrayed him by sleeping with his mistress. These are important sonnets in the sequence, though not as it might first seem because their story sounds so idiosyncratically personal. Rather, this is a story told and retold in Renaissance literature.[60] Its hold on the Renaissance imagination lay in its fantastic idealization of— and expression of deep anxiety about — male friendship. In the sonnets, the story also provides a wonderfully compressed and culturally resonant instance of the way men's relationships with one another significantly underpin the male-female courtly love tradition.

Sonnet 42 is one of the sonnets that describe the love triangle involving Shakespeare, his friend and the mistress:

> That thou hast her, it is not all my grief,
> And yet it may be said I loved her dearly;
> That she hath thee is of my wailing chief,
> A loss in love that touches me more nearly.
> Loving offenders, thus I will excuse ye:
> Thou dost love her because thou know'st I love her,
> And for my sake even so doth she abuse me,
> Suff'ring my friend for my sake to approve her.
> If I lose thee, my loss is my love's gain,
> And losing her, my friend hath found that loss:
> Both find each other, and I lose both twain,

> And both for my sake lay on me this cross.
> But here's the joy: my friend and I are one.
> Sweet flattery! Then she loves but me alone.

Now that Shakespeare's friend and mistress are sleeping together, it is his friend, Shakespeare tells us, whose loss "is of my wailing chief, / A loss in love that touches me more nearly." Shakespeare's more powerful emotional commitment to the young man recalls Wyatt's sonnet, where the highest compliment Wyatt can pay his female beloved is the promise that he will be as faithful to her as he would be to a male military companion.

This sonnet's witty defense of the friend's sexual betrayal — "thou dost love her because thou know'st I love her" — likewise contains a serious insight into the creation of male attachments through the sharing of courtly love poetry. Men's interest in the female beloved is often driven by their interest in one another. Sonnet 42 makes this point with algebraic concision: you love her because I love her (and you love me).[61]

The equally witty conclusion to the sonnet, "But here's the joy: my friend and I are one. / Sweet flattery! Then she loves but me alone," further suggests this twining of male-female relationships with relationships between men. Shakespeare finds solace for the loss of his mistress in the Renaissance ideal of male friendship. So perfectly — or improbably — close are the two friends that in loving the young man the mistress really loves Shakespeare since "my friend and I are one."

The motives Shakespeare ascribes to friend and mistress throughout this sonnet likewise confuse objects of affection and confound lines of desire. Earlier in the sonnet we encounter the surprising idea that the mistress' "abuse" of Shakespeare's trust by having sex with the young man is actually a favor to Shakespeare. How could this be a favor? By having sex with the young man she allows him to pay Shakespeare the greater favor still of "approving" the poet's mistress: "And for my sake even so doth she abuse me / Suff'ring my friend for my sake to approve her." The friend "approve[s]" Shakespeare's mistress in two senses. He approves of Shakespeare's choice in women, and in doing so honors him. And since "approve" can also mean "try out sexually," the friend is said to be confirming his respect for Shakespeare's choice in women by having sex with the mistress himself. This is really conducting relationships between men through a woman!

Given Shakespeare's subordination of his love for the mistress to his love for the young man it is not surprising that the mistress remains a shadowy character, or that following sonnet 42 a woman no longer appears in the sonnets until the final ones devoted to the black mistress. The next rival for the young man's affection is not a woman but another male poet with whom Shakespeare competes for the young man's attention and patronage.

Sonnet 42's improbable ascription of charitable motives to the young man's infidelity is a joke. But the joke is only funny because it plays on the wishful way male friendship was conceived in Shakespeare's world. Such friendship was shaped not just by the everyday realities of male friendships but also by the conventions that idealized them, in a manner not unlike the idealizing romantic conventions of heterosex love. This celebration of idealized friendship — we have already seen some examples of its conventions in chapter 10 — appears especially in the work of Renaissance English humanists, who drew the ideal from classical writers such as Cicero. Following Cicero's *De amicitia* [Of Friendship], these humanists emphasized the faithfulness and especially the equality of the friends.[62] George Wither's emblem of perfect friendship (figure 1), with its two identical clasping hands, symbolizes this equality, while the emblem's verse suggests the friends' faithfulness to one another: "That's Friendship, and true-love, indeed, / Which firme abides, in time of need."[63] Shakespeare's "My friend and I are one" likewise suggests perfect equality and trust.

Shakespeare finds in this idea of male friendship a better alternative to the submissive yearning of the courtly lover. After all, despite his social inferiority Shakespeare asserts — however tentatively or guiltily — a claim on the young man's love. He also, as we saw in chapter 7, weighs the value of good character against good birth, in a way that humanist scholars found attractive. By praising the bonds formed over internal qualities such as intelligence, these humanists justified their intimacies with the social superiors whom they served (often as client of a patron or

Figure 1: Two identical hands grasping a single heart symbolize the perfect equality and identity of the friends, like the "mutual render" of sonnet 125. (The English Emblem Book Project, *http://emblem.libraries.psu.edu/withetoc.htm.)*

again mirror one another, but there's no reciprocity this time. Shakespeare will not "remove" from his love; nor will he allow *himself* to "be removed." If his friend should do the removing, Shakespeare will hang on like grim death.

Likewise, the resonant lines of 116, "love is not love / Which alters when it alteration finds, / Or bends with the remover to remove," sound like they're celebrating mutuality and reciprocity. Hence the popularity of this sonnet for marriages. But what's actually happening in these lines is more one-sided. If the beloved tries to "alter" or "remove" himself from the relationship, Shakespeare promises that he will not, nevertheless, remove or alter himself. This promise could be viewed as one of admirable fidelity. But it could also be creepy and obsessive — as well as bespeak a lack of faith in what the friend might do.[69]

Stories of perfect friendship in the English Renaissance are frequently shadowed by stories of friendship's betrayal. Even the sonnets that celebrate friendship admit that the likeness and commitment of the friends might be illusory — as conventional and idealizing as anything in courtly love. Again the love triangle that Shakespeare describes in sonnet 42 is culturally exemplary. It and the other sonnets on this theme closely echo a common motif in the literature of friendship, in which two male friends fall in love with the same woman. The motif emphasizes both the glories of Renaissance friendship and its "sweet flatteries."

The humanist Sir Thomas Elyot, for example, tells the story of Titus and Gisippus, two friends so alike that it seemed "when their names were declared ... that they had only changed their places, issuing ... out of one body, and entering into the other." Titus is so like Gisippus that he falls in love with Sophonia, whom Gisippus is to marry. Though Gisippus loves Sophonia too, out of his love for his friend he secretly allows Titus to marry her. (In a reversal of the Shakespearean bed trick, Titus who also looks just like his friend sneaks in place of Gisippus into Sophonia's bed on her wedding night.) When the marriage is revealed Gisippus is exiled for the deception. Distraught at the mistaken belief that his now wealthy and happily married friend Titus has forgotten him, Gisippus suicidally allows himself to be framed for a murder. As Gisippus is about to be put to death for the crime, however, Titus recognizes him and claims to have committed the murder instead. Gisippus, newly confident of Titus's friendship, insists that he is the murderer, until the real murderer, inspired by this display of friendship, confesses to the crime.[70] Shakespeare would echo this story in what is likely his first play, *The Two Gentlemen of Verona*, in which Proteus attempts to steal and nearly rapes Sylvia, beloved by Proteus's friend Valentine. When Proteus apologizes for these sins to Valentine the latter is so moved he offers Sylvia to his friend anyway.

Other writers recount similar love triangles but are less optimistic. In John Lyly's prose story *Euphues, the Anatomy of Wit*, the friends Euphues and Philautus "used not only one board but one bed, one book." Euphues, however, falls in love with Philautus's fiancée Lucilla, whom he seduces. Subsequent revelation of the affair between Lucilla and Euphues destroys the latter's friendship with Philautus. The two friends are reunited only when Lucilla rejects Euphues in turn for another man. In Thomas Heywood's play *A Woman Killed with Kindness*, the gentleman Frankford all but foists his wife Anne on his impoverished friend Wendoll. Frankford wills Wendoll "to make bold in his absence and command / Even as himself were present in the house; / For you must keep his table, use his servants, / And be a present Frankford in his absence." Wendoll makes bold by seducing Anne.[71] Related stories of friendship and betrayal drive two of Shakespeare's great tragedies, *Othello*, where the betrayal by Cassio of Othello turns out to be false, and *Hamlet*, where the men are brothers rather than friends, but the betrayal is true.

These popular stories of one friend stealing the other friend's mistress/wife captured at once a number of different cultural anxieties. They expressed men's fears about their control over women through the idea of the wife or mistress who abandons one friend for another. They also put in competition two forms of desire and alliance. Should the friend be more upset at the breach of male friendship or heterosex love? And these stories provided a way of airing tensions in male relationships. If men bonded with one another through an exchange of women — a daughter given in marriage, a mistress praised in a poem — then conflicts in that exchange could express stresses in those bonds. Stories of female sexual betrayal might as much reveal men's fears about the honesty of other men as their fears about the honesty of women.

For all their idealizing language of friendship, the sonnets similarly chronicle breaches or suspected breaches of faith by both Shakespeare and the young man. Sonnet 61 gives us Shakespeare alone and awake at night thinking about the young man, who is himself awake but — worryingly — in the company of others: "For thee watch I whilst thou dost wake elsewhere, / From me far off, with others all too near." The overtones of the word "wake" intensify the sonnet's impression of the young man's faith-breaking promiscuity. Especially in the Renaissance the word can refer to festival revelry, drinking and sex, an interpretation encouraged by the unseemly occurrence of these wakes at night.

In sonnet 110, Shakespeare will apologize for the same sort of crime. He promises that "mine appetite I never more will grind / On newer proof to try an older friend, / A god in love, to whom I am confined." The "newer proof" is a new love, or more precisely, "appetite," that tests the faith of Shakespeare's "older friend," the young man. These lines render Shakespeare's faith-breaking shockingly hyperbolic in their echo of the Old Testament. The young man is a "god in love" to whom Shakespeare promises from now on to remain faithful. It is as if Shakespeare has followed the course of the biblical Jews by worshipping new, false idols, but now recognizes his need to keep faith by returning to his one, true god, the young man. Perhaps too the young man is a jealous and angry god, or so the more ominous overtones of the word "confined" suggest.

15

But Did They Have Sex?

I have suggested so far that the class difference between Shakespeare and the young man helps create these feelings of mistrust and guilt. Should we not, however, also read the sonnets' betrayals as literally sexual? More broadly, is the friendship between Shakespeare and the young man sexual? To ask these questions is not to leave behind the sonnets' social drama, but rather to seek in it the familiar connections of sex and power.

Of course, no sonnets, no words at all, can tell us for certain whether Shakespeare and the young man had sex. And there's no hope for ocular proof. Words such as sonnet 110's "appetite," however, certainly suggest sexual desire. Or consider the sweet eroticism of sonnet 99. In this sonnet Shakespeare draws on the courtly love tradition of the *blazon*, in which the poet compliments the beloved's body part-by-part, usually a woman's body but in this case the young man's:

> The forward violet thus did I chide:
> Sweet thief, whence didst thou steal thy sweet that smells,
> If not from my love's breath? The purple pride
> Which on thy soft cheek for complexion dwells
> In my love's veins thou hast too grossly dyed.
> The lily I condemnèd for thy hand,
> And buds of marjoram had stol'n thy hair;
> The roses fearfully on thorns did stand,
> One blushing shame, another white despair;
> A third, nor red nor white, had stol'n of both,
> And to his robb'ry had annexed thy breath;
> But for his theft in pride of all his growth

A vengeful canker ate him up to death.
More flowers I noted, yet I none could see
But sweet or colour it had stol'n from thee.

Shakespeare cleverly rewrites comparisons traditional to the blazon by restating them as thefts: it's not that you are like flowers, but that flowers have stolen their colors and fragrances from you. This turn on the traditional compliment heightens the sonnet's praise by making the man rather than the flowers the genuine source of "sweet" and "colour."

Shakespeare retains, however, the usual sensuality of the blazon, as he celebrates his lover's body. He lingers over the young man's breath, hand, hair and cheeks (the last implicitly: the poem refers to the violet's "soft cheek" but since cheeks are personifications we tend to associate them with the person addressed, the young man). Shakespeare's connection to the young man sounds intimate and erotic. He knows the smell of his breath, the whiteness of his hand. Perhaps Shakespeare feels guilt over this intimacy as well — hence the appearance of a worm (the "vengeful canker") in this otherwise pleasant garden. Can we see in the "forward violet" the aspiring poet himself, swelling with sinful pride over his closeness to the aristocratic young man and stealing his beauty for these sonnets?[72]

In other sonnets too Shakespeare describes the male friend as a lover and object of sexual desire, such as in the apologetic sonnet 110, where Shakespeare calls the friend a "god in love," or in 104, another sonnet in which Shakespeare contemplates the physical attractiveness of the sonnets' addressee: "To me, fair friend, you never can be old; / For as you were when first your eye I eyed / Such seems your beauty still." Shakespeare's compliment casts the young man as an ever-youthful beauty and a memory of first physical attraction. These lines' emphasis on eyes seeing and seen, and on the young man's enduring good looks, hardly support assertions that Shakespeare in the sonnets pays tribute to the young man's spiritual rather than physical beauty.[73]

Nor is the language of the sonnets limited to a non-sexual appreciation of the friend's good looks. The literary critic Joseph Pequigney has identified in the sonnets a host of bawdy puns that delineate Shakespeare's interest in particular sexual parts and acts. Consider, for example, the sexual suggestiveness of sonnet 52:

So am I as the rich whose blessèd key
Can bring him to his sweet up-lockèd treasure,
The which he will not ev'ry hour survey,
For blunting the fine point of seldom pleasure.
Therefore are feasts so solemn and so rare
Since, seldom coming, in the long year set
Like stones of worth they thinly placèd are,

> Or captain jewels in the carcanet.
> So is the time that keeps you as my chest,
> Or as the wardrobe which the robe doth hide,
> To make some special instant special blest
> By new unfolding his imprisoned pride.
>> Blessèd are you whose worthiness gives scope,
>> Being had, to triumph; being lacked, to hope.

Shakespeare compares the young man to feasts, jewels, and fine clothing (a special "robe" usually hidden in a "wardrobe" or closet). These are objects of sensory pleasure — especially sight and taste — that because of their rareness are even more desirable. The first comparison in the sonnet, of the young man to "up-lockèd treasure," is the most sexual of all. Though "treasure" has less immediate physical appeal than a robe or a feast, the words that describes this "treasure" render it a sensual and, through a set of double entendres, sexual pleasure. The key opening up a lock is a familiar image of sexual penetration, an interpretation supported by the adjective "sweet" to describe the treasure achieved. One does not usually think of treasure as "sweet," but in the Renaissance, as now, "sweet" can mean "filled with sexual pleasure" (as in "sweet kisses").

The following lines, which describe how the rareness of visiting this treasure increases its pleasure, suggest the build up of sexual desire. Because Shakespeare does not visit this sweet treasure "ev'ry hour," the "fine point" of his pleasure is not "blunted." The imagery suggests the erect penis.

Also both intimate and sexual is the final comparison of the young man to a robe kept in a wardrobe for some "special instant." The comparison sounds as if Shakespeare were thinking about the secret contents of the young man's closet. Moreover, the personified description of the "wardrobe" suddenly revealing its "robe" sounds a lot like disrobing, especially since Shakespeare refers to this moment as an "unfolding." What's unfolded — "his imprisoned pride" — extends the sexual suggestion of disrobing, since the word "pride" in Renaissance England can refer to an erect penis. The final couplet concludes the sonnet with similar sexual suggestion. "Had" in the Renaissance as well as today can mean "possess sexually." When Shakespeare has "had" the young man, he triumphs; when he lacks him, he hopes.[74]

Two objections might be made to interpretations of the sonnets that emphasize their sexual suggestiveness. The first objection is that the sonnets' language, which sounds erotic to us, was conventional for the time. This was how friends wrote to another. The conventionality of this language does not render its eroticism meaningless, however. Conventions are not the opposite of real feelings. On the contrary, conventions reflect and help shape real feelings. We do not believe in the literal truth of every love song's broken heart or every movie's romantic fantasy. But love songs and movie romance nonetheless affect us because, despite their conventionality, we can imagine their relevance to our lives, and they give us something to dream about. Similarly, the conventional language of Renaissance sonnets or of Renaissance friendship need not have always been literally true to have felt true or to have represented real desires.

What do the conventions of Renaissance friendship tell us about the feelings and experiences to which those conventions appealed? Most contemporary love stories assume heterosexuality — as do popular representations of Shakespeare's love sonnets. Shakespeare's sonnets and the friendship conventions they draw on, however, do not give priority to heterosex relationships. Their fantasy is not Hollywood's heterosexual romance, but humanism's perfect friendship.

For the bonds between men were politically, socially and culturally central to this world. Thus when we read Shakespeare's sonnets to the young man we should ask not "was Shakespeare gay?" but "what was it like to live in a culture in which love between men was perfectly conventional"? Or: "what was it like to live in a culture in which all men were gay?" — if "gay" is taken to mean not the expression of a minority sexual identity, but rather the assumed potential for any man to love and desire another man.

A second objection might be made to interpretations that find the expression of sexual desire in the sonnets. One might argue that descriptions of the young man's beauty are diffusely appreciative but that they do not express sexual desire. Of the evidence of sexual wordplay in the sonnets (as in the analyses above) one might further argue that motivated readers can always find sexual references and double entendres by looking hard — pun intended? — enough.

Were these sonnets addressed to a woman, however, it is unlikely that their sexually suggestive language would be dismissed. In fact, when people assume the sonnets are addressed to a women they also assume that the writer and his recipient are lovers. Why should words that when addressed to a woman imply sexual desire not imply the same desire when addressed to a man? The answer can't be that the same words are sexual only when said to a woman. That answer would beg the question, because it presumes the non-sexual quality of the male-male relationship that the sexually evocative language put in doubt in the first place.

Why then should there be a double standard regarding the linguistic evidence of sexual desire? Contemporary homophobia plays a role. Some readers may refuse to admit the existence of male-male sexual desire, especially in a figure of such cultural authority as Shakespeare. There may also be a more subtle reason. In contemporary culture the language between men and women is more volatile, more likely to be examined for hints of sexual attraction, because it is assumed that such attraction might always exist. The language used between men, on the other hand, is usually protected from this volatility by the assumption that homosexuality is the sexual expression of a minority group only (though homophobia evidences men's continued anxiety about the potentially sexual aspect of their relationships with other men). Hence readers may be unused to having the same kind ear for flirtation in the language between men that they do for language between men and women.[75]

In the Renaissance, however, the status of male-male erotic language is more ambiguous. On the one hand, official moral and legal prohibitions against male-male sex make it safer for men to speak to one another in erotic terms. Men can speak love because they aren't allowed to have sex. Yet the period's assumption that homosexual desire was universal — rather than restricted to a minority population — would have made it possible nonetheless to interpret men's claims of love for one another sexually. Men's words to one another — even their lofty expressions of friendship — could be searched for hints of sexual interest just as men's and women's words to one another today.[76]

In sonnet 20, a flirtatious sonnet if there ever was one, the reader need not search very far:

> A woman's face with nature's own hand painted
> Hast thou, the master-mistress of my passion;
> A woman's gentle heart, but not acquainted
> With shifting change as is false women's fashion;
> An eye more bright than theirs, less false in rolling,
> Gilding the object whereupon it gazeth;
> A man in hue, all hues in his controlling,
> Which steals men's eyes and women's souls amazeth.
> And for a woman wert thou first created,
> Till nature as she wrought thee fell a-doting,
> And by addition me of thee defeated
> By adding one thing to my purpose nothing.
>   But since she pricked thee out for women's pleasure,
>   Mine be thy love and thy love's use their treasure.

Shakespeare seems at first to deny the possibility of a physical relationship with the young man. In the story that he tells, which seems influenced by the convention of cross-dressing on the Renaissance stage, Nature originally intended the young man to be a woman: "For a woman wert thou first created."[77] Nature, however, in a love that glances at female same-sex desire, becomes enamored with her creation, and so gives the young man a penis instead (thus also giving new meaning to the young man being created "for a woman"). In Shakespeare's witty pun nature "pricked thee out for women's pleasure." To "prick" in the Renaissance meant to choose, but the word was also slang, then as today, for penis. Nature thus apparently defeats Shakespeare's desires by "adding one thing to my purpose nothing."

Yet Shakespeare does not so easily admit defeat. And the playfulness of this sonnet points to the flexibility of Renaissance sexual desire and the ambiguities of Renaissance friendship. For though the sonnet in line 12 claims defeat, there's no evidence of it elsewhere in the poem. On the contrary, Shakespeare calls the young man his "master-mistress," both the master who takes the place of a mistress in courtship, and Shakespeare's best (master) mistress. The rest of the poem emphasizes this irrelevance of gender to desire: the young man contains the beauty of both men and women, and both men and women desire him.

The admission of defeat in the final lines of the sonnet sounds then like a nervous joke, a last minute reinstatement of a gender difference the significance of which (for both men and women) the sonnet has already denied. Given Shakespeare's love for the young man's entire body and being in this and other sonnets, the decisiveness of the penis in these lines is improbable, especially since the penis need not be the only source of the young man's sexual attraction.[78] The sense of the word "love" in the final line also remains unclear. Shakespeare apparently contrasts an emotional "love" to a sexual "love's use" by women (the sonnet has often been read this way), but his repetition of the word "love" in the final line also blurs the distinction. Does Shakespeare want the young man's "love" and allow women to use it too? When Led Zeppelin sang "I'm gonna' give you every inch of my love," it was not measuring emotional commitment alone.[79]

Sonnet 20 remains ambiguous about Shakespeare's desires. But the wit of the sonnet, the fame of its author and the cultural stakes in its interpretation often prevent us from recognizing how ordinary these ambiguities are. What happens when friendship becomes tinged with sexual desire? When does one begin to recognize these feelings? How does one broach them with the friend without risking rejection?[80] These are the ordinary dilemmas of this sonnet and its protective equivocations.

The complex experience of male friendship in Renaissance England, however, would have made Shakespeare's navigation of its ambiguities even more difficult. On the one hand, friendship for Shakespeare and his contemporaries was much less distinguished from sexual desire. Male friends publicly and proudly expressed their physical intimacy; friend, as we have seen, was already another word for lover. On the other hand, sex between men, though often ignored, remained a sin — like most other kinds of sex in Renaissance England. Moreover, an explicit accusation of sodomy might be triggered not by the crossing of a line between a permissible eroticism and forbidden sexual acts, but by the expression of a desire that crossed social boundaries, as it would have in a love between Shakespeare and the young man. It should not surprise us then that in the otherwise pleasant garden of sonnet 99 lurks a growing pride (and vengeful worm) that suggests sin, sexual excitement, and social overreaching all at once.

Nor should it be surprising that the sonnets to the young man are evasive, that they speak of love but not sex or, as in sonnet 20, speak of sex in deniable ways. The sonnets to the black mistress are much more frankly sexual. Their more overt sexuality might lead us to make a distinction after all between Shakespeare's affection for the man and his sexual desire for the woman. In the next section we'll see why this distinction would be wrong, and consider the broader implications, for Renaissance ideas of women, of the more obviously sexual language of the black mistress sonnets.

Section III

"A Woman Coloured Ill"

16

Gynerasty

Shakespeare finds the black mistress by means of his penis: "Flesh stays no farther reason, / But rising at thy name doth point out thee / As his triumphant prize" (sonnet 151). Bawdy lines such as these have led many readers of the sonnets to conclude that while Shakespeare loves the young man spiritually he loves the black mistress sexually. This distinction is common in modern introductions to the sonnets, which, in characterizing the poems for a new readership, seek to preserve Shakespeare from the presumed taint of homosexual desire.

In his introduction to the sonnets in the *Riverside Shakespeare* Hallett Smith writes that "the attitude of the poet toward the friend is one of love and admiration, deference and possessiveness, but it is not at all a sexual passion." The attitude toward the black mistress, however, is "frankly lustful."[1] Douglas Bush's introduction to the Penguin edition of the sonnets cautions against mistaking friendship for homosexual desire:

> Since modern readers are unused to such ardor in masculine friendship and are likely to leap at the notion of homosexuality (a notion sufficiently refuted by the sonnets themselves), we may remember that such an ideal — often exalted above the love of women — could exist in real life ... and was conspicuous in Renaissance literature.[2]

As we have seen, however, the ardor of Renaissance friendship was not clearly distinguished from sexual desire, an ambiguity reflected in the sonnets. When Bush suggests with nervous bravado that the notion of homosexuality is "sufficiently refuted by the sonnets themselves," he is probably referring to "A woman's face with nature's own hand painted" (sonnet 20) — a sonnet more flirtation than refutation.

Both writers may also have in mind that the sonnets to the young man are usually less sexual than those to the black mistress. Yet the sexual frankness of Shakespeare's sonnets to the black mistress does not necessarily express his more intensely physical desire for her, in contrast to his spiritual love for the young man. People do not always speak what they feel — especially about sex. Writers have even more opportunity to shape the expression of their feelings. Who is being addressed, when and where the address takes place, cultural convention — all play a role in the ways sexual desire is openly, or not so openly, declared. We understand that when newlyweds celebrate their "marriage of true minds" on their wedding day it doesn't mean they won't have sex on their wedding night. It's just that the language of love is more encompassing, more respectful, more romantic. And some sexual expression — for example, sexual obscenities — has little to do with sexual desire.

Shakespeare's more sexually frank sonnets to the black mistress have everything to do not with the relative strength of his homo- or heterosexual desires but with the relative status of men and women in the Renaissance. The focus on sex in the sonnets to the black mistress reflects the way Renaissance women were often defined by their sexual being. Or reduced to it: the potential misogyny of Smith's distinction between love for the man and lust for the woman is fully celebrated in Bush's remark that the ideal of male friendship in the Renaissance was "often exalted above the love of women." Shakespeare may want to have sex with the black mistress but he doesn't love her, these critics suggest, as he loves the young man. Smith even notes that at times Shakespeare expresses "revulsion" toward her.[3] Though Smith and Bush wish to save Shakespeare and his sonnets for heterosexuality, the version of heterosexuality they offer — lust and revulsion reserved for women, love reserved for men — is hardly appealing.

This modern view of the sonnets echoes a view of men, women and sex current in Shakespeare's day. In the following passage a contemporary of Shakespeare's confronts the same problem as Bush and Smith: what to make of the expression of one man's love for another. The writer, known only by the initials "E.K.," provided interpretive notes for Edmund Spenser's 1579 *The Shepherdes Calender*. In this pastoral poem the shepherd Colin tells how he is loved by a shepherd named Hobbinol, even though he himself loves a girl named Rosalind. E.K. writes about these lines:

> In this place [passage of *The Shepherdes Calender*] seemeth to be some savor of disorderly love, which the learned call pederasty: but it is gathered beside his meaning. For who that hath read Plato his dialogue called Alcibiades ... may easily perceive, that such love is much to be allowed and liked of, specially so meant, as Socrates used it: who sayth, that in deed he loved Alcibiades extremely, yet not Alcibiades' person, but his soul.... And so is pederasty

much to be preferred before gynerasty, that is the love which enflameth men with lust toward woman kind. But yet let no man think, that herein I stand with Lucian or his devilish disciple Unico Arentino, in defence of execrable and horrible sin of forbidden and unlawful fleshiness.[4]

According to E.K. there are two kinds of pederasty, one "forbidden and unlawful" because fleshly, the other "much to be allowed, and liked" because spiritual: it involves love not of the "person" but the "soul." This second kind of pederasty is "much to be preferred" over what E.K. calls "gynerasty," the "lust toward woman kind." Unlike "pederasty," however, E.K. assigns "gynerasty" no second kind of desire, directed toward the woman's soul. Perhaps this was because women had no souls — a proposition offered for mock debate by Renaissance intellectuals, and a common saying during the period.[5]

In this section of the book I consider how Shakespeare portrays his black mistress through the lens of negative Renaissance stereotypes about women. These stereotypes particularly involve the narrowing of female identity to sexual identity. When modern critics agree that Shakespeare sexually desires the black mistress without loving her they evoke these stereotypes no less than does E.K.'s definition of gynerasty: lust inflamed for a body without a soul. E.K. denounces the inflaming lusts of gynerasty, moreover, in the course of disavowing lust in the ennobling world of male friendship. Does Shakespeare similarly encumber a woman with the desires — and fears — that he cannot so readily express to a man? Does the magnificent fairness of Shakespeare's young man depend on locating anything that's black somewhere else — in the mistress?

17

Saucy Jacks

Sexual speech is not necessarily a measure of love. It may be an insult. We can see this possibility in the comparison of two sonnets, one to the young man, the other to the black mistress. The sonnets share the same theme: jealousy. Here is sonnet 57 to the young man:

> Being your slave, what should I do but tend
> Upon the hours and times of your desire?
> I have no precious time at all to spend,
> Nor services to do, till you require:
> Nor dare I chide the world-without-end hour
> Whilst I, my sovereign, watch the clock for you,
> Nor think the bitterness of absence sour
> When you have bid your servant once adieu.
> Nor dare I question with my jealous thought
> Where you may be, or your affairs suppose,
> But like a sad slave stay and think of naught
> Save, where you are, how happy you make those.
> > So true a fool is love that in your will,
> > Though you do anything, he thinks no ill.

There is no question of Shakespeare's passion here. We have already en-countered this sonnet, in which Shakespeare declares himself the young man's "slave." As such, Shakespeare declares he can do nothing — he has no "services to do" — until the young man calls. He can only wait, "watch the clock." He has no right to think "the bitterness of absence sour." He may not even "dare" with "jealous thought" to wonder what the young man is doing, where he is, or "how happy" he is making those with whom he is.

Whatever the young man does, Shakespeare vows that he "thinks no ill" of him. The sonnet intimates that Shakespeare has reason for his jealousy, but loves the young man anyway. Hence the motto: "so true a fool is love." Shakespeare's love is true and truly foolish.

Now here is sonnet 128, to the black mistress. Shakespeare in this sonnet names the black mistress "my music," and pictures her playing a harpsichord-like instrument called a virginal:

> How oft, when thou, my music, music play'st
> Upon that blessèd wood whose motion sounds
> With thy sweet fingers when thou gently sway'st
> The wiry concord that mine ear confounds,
> Do I envy those jacks that nimble leap
> To kiss the tender inward of thy hand
> Whilst my poor lips, which should that harvest reap,
> At the wood's boldness by thee blushing stand!
> To be so tickled they would change their state
> And situation with those dancing chips
> O'er whom thy fingers walk with gentle gait,
> Making dead wood more blessed than living lips.
>> Since saucy jacks so happy are in this,
>> Give them thy fingers, me thy lips to kiss.

Jacks are pieces of wood with quills attached. When the finger strikes a key, the jack moves up and the quill plucks a string. Shakespeare jealously complains that the jacks — mere wood — get to kiss the black mistress' hand when she plays the virginal, while he stands blushing by. (In fact, this jealousy at the jack's contact with the mistress' hand overwhelms the conceit of the sonnet, since really the keys rather than jacks of the virginal touch the player's hand.[6])

Shakespeare wishes he could change places with the jacks, so that he could be "tickled" by the black mistress' fingers. Or better, Shakespeare concludes, let the jacks have her fingers, so long as he gets her lips. In the Renaissance "jack" is also a nickname for a lower class, uncouth or disreputable man ("a regular Joe," though not as negative, has something of this sense).[7] So Shakespeare is jealous not only of the inanimate virginal, but also, in the punning language of the sonnet, of other, less worthy men — "jacks" — who seem to have the physical contact with the black mistress that Shakespeare wants.

Shakespeare notably portrays himself in both sonnets as a wallflower who can only jealously "watch the clock" for the young man or "blushing stand" by the black mistress. The sonnet to the black mistress differs from the sonnet to the young man, however, in its specifically sexual jealousy. Only in the black mistress sonnet does Shakespeare wish for a specifically physical act: "thy lips to kiss." Moreover, Shakespeare's language seems noticeably physical throughout this sonnet. Indeed, readers who usually encounter Shakespeare's sonnets in anthologies, which tend to select for inclusion his more genteel sonnets to the young man, may be surprised at the salaciousness of many of Shakespeare's sonnets to the black mistress.

Sonnet 128, for example, casts a titillating look at the movement of the black mistress' hands. The jacks "kiss the tender inward" of her hand; Shakespeare wishes that he, like the virginal, could be "tickled" by the black mistress' fingers. A set of obvious double entendres turns kissing and tickling into masturbation. The "jacks that nimble leap" as they are kissed by the "tender inward" of the black mistress' hand clearly suggest an erection — in fact "jack" was also slang for an erect penis.[8] The "chips" (that is, keys of the virginal) that dance as the black mistress' "fingers walk" over them provides a similar image. This walk with "gentle gait" makes "dead wood" blessed — another phrase suggesting an erection (as in the modern slang "a woody").

Sonnet 57 is arguably fraught with Shakespeare's jealous imaginings of the young man's sexual exploits.[9] Nonetheless, the meaning of sonnet 57 does not depend on bawdy sexual puns as does sonnet 128, nor does it ever express a direct wish for sexual satisfaction, as Shakespeare does in sonnet 128 when he asks for "thy lips to kiss."

Penis at the fore, Shakespeare more loudly announces his sexual desires in the black mistress sonnets. On this basis critics such as Smith and Bush suggest that only Shakespeare's love for the black mistress is sexual. But this idea depends on the shaky assumption that people explicitly express their sexual desires, especially in public or semi-public arenas (as Shakespeare sonnets, circulated among his "private friends," seem to be). Shakespeare's sexual directness in the sonnets to the black mistress may have less to do with his relative sexual interest in men or women than with the relative status of men and women in the Renaissance. Shakespeare wouldn't talk to a man, especially an aristocratic man, the way he would talk to a woman.

He especially wouldn't talk sexually to the young man in the way he talks to the black mistress. The language of sonnet 128 isn't just sexual; it's sexually forward. This forwardness could be considered flirtation. The sonnet's combination of racy puns and erotic compliment might be read as sexual teasing between intimates. Perhaps the word in sonnet 128 that expresses this experience of the sonnet is "tickled": playful and amorous at once.

At the same time, however, Shakespeare admits in the sonnet that he is not yet an intimate of the black mistress. So it is not clear that the sexual teasing would be welcome. Moreover, Shakespeare's teasing tends to slide from playful eroticism to insult. The sonnet, after all, pictures through its double entendres the black mistress masturbating other men — an aggressive sexual exposure of her apparent promiscuity, luridly exaggerated with the idea of rows of "jacks" over which the black mistress' "fingers walk."

Nor does the company Shakespeare implies that the black mistress keeps — disreputable "jacks" — seem complimentary. These insinuations of the black mistress' low and loose sexuality make the sonnet's tone less ticklish and more like the attitude suggested by another of the sonnet's words: "saucy." An impudent Shakespeare wants to compete with other "saucy jacks" for the sexual favors of the black mistress. And he doesn't mind loudly announcing this.

This reading of sonnet 128 might seem to overemphasize its sexual aggression. But consider how much more than sonnet 57 this sonnet takes liberties — even playful liberties — with its subject. The humbled Shakespeare of sonnet 57 does not dare speak to the young man with the sexual frankness with which a far more saucy Shakespeare addresses the black mistress in sonnet 128. Consider too that sonnet 128 is one of the most complimentary of what is conventionally called the "dark lady group," so called because of the "dark" (and more often, "black") vision of its subject — her character as well as her appearance. Even sonnet 128, though, contains hints of the black mistress' unworthiness and promiscuity. Shakespeare fully develops these hints in other sonnets. In 137 the black mistress is no longer "my music" but, with obviously crude sexual meaning, "the bay where all men ride."

18

Weaker Vessels

Whether lustily or angrily, Shakespeare thinks of the black mistress in terms of sex, whereas the young man evokes a broader set of responses. This difference corresponds to the way women's identities in the Renaissance significantly depended on their sexual identity, in a way that men's identities did not. When Shakespeare focuses on the black mistress' sexuality he is already describing her in culturally conventional ways. To understand more fully Shakespeare's feelings about the black mistress then, we need better to understand English Renaissance ideas and stereotypes of women.

Juan Luis Vives' *The Instruction of a Christian Woman* went through nine editions between the late 1520s and 1592. The counsel he offers women in this advice book provides a dramatic example of the centrality of a woman's sexual identity in the Renaissance. "Many things are required of a man," Vives writes, such "as wisdom, eloquence, knowledge of political affairs, talent, memory, some trade to live by, justice, liberality, magnanimity, and other qualities that it would take a long time to rehearse." But, Vives continues, "in woman, no one requires eloquence or talent or wisdom or professional skills, or administration of the republic, or justice or generosity; no one asks anything of her but chastity. If that one thing is missing, it is as if all were lacking to a man." While Vives is recognized in the history of education for advocating the education of women, he views this education chiefly as a means to preserve women's chastity, not to prepare her for the male privilege of speaking outside the home.[10] Of course, many women did not fit the mold Vives offers them. But Vives' limiting of the lives of women to their sexual being does reflect the idea, if not always the reality, that in Renaissance England women's primary roles were wife and mother. Thus according to a Renaissance guide to laws in England affecting women, all women are considered either "married or to be married."[11]

In addition to keeping herself chaste on the way to and in marriage, the ideal woman of the Renaissance was expected to yield to her husband's authority. This subordination was grounded in the Bible's description of woman as "the weaker vessel" (1 Peter 3:7) and enshrined in official ideology. The Church of England's official marriage ceremony enjoined women (in words that remain familiar) to "love, cherish and to obey" their husbands, while husbands were enjoined only to "love and to cherish" their wives.[12]

Following the marriage ceremony, the minister might preach to the newly married couple and the assembled congregation the "Homily of the State of Matrimony," one of a number of sermons pre-written by the state-run church. The "Homily" enjoined female obedience and male forbearance. Wives had to obey their husbands and men had to forbear wives because, the homily declared, the woman is "a weak creature.... more prone to all weak affections and dispositions of mind than men be, and lighter they be, and more vain in their fantasies and opinions." Classical philosophy and medicine, which similarly held women to be guided by emotion and men by reason, provided another rationale for male authority. Aristotle, for example, thought that women, like children, required a reasonable male head.[13]

These rigid ideas about female chastity and obedience inevitably generated fears about women's failure to conform to them. Prominent among these fears — and a staple of Renaissance drama, including Shakespeare's — was the wife's adultery, which violated her chastity and obedience to her husband at once. Joseph Swetnam's notorious antifeminist pamphlet *The Arraignment of Lewd, Idle, Froward and Unconstant Women* (1615) warns women that their behavior will be constantly scrutinized for signs of sexual infidelity:

> It behooveth every woman to have a great regard to her behavior, and to keep herself out of the fire, knowing that a woman of suspected chastity liveth but in a miserable case, for there is but small difference by being naught [in being "naughty"] and being thought naught, and when she heareth other women ill spoken of, let her think in her mind what may be spoken of her.[14]

There is small difference between "being naught and being thought naught." This is the plot of *Othello*. Everyday life in Renaissance England reflected Swetnam's warning about the importance of female chastity and its dependence, fairly or not, on the opinions of others. Someone who wanted to insult a woman during the period would likely call her a "whore" — what Othello calls Desdemona. The insult did not usually mean the woman was a prostitute, but that she was sexually licentious, or otherwise difficult or dishonorable. Laura Gowing, a historian who has studied the substantial increase in lawsuits for sexual slander in Renaissance England, writes that "whatever made a good reputation [for women], sexual discredit could threaten it." Gowing notes as well the telling difference between sexual insults directed at women and men. Men were not called "whores" but "cuckolds"—this is what Othello fears himself to be—an insult that meant a man's wife had been sexually unfaithful to him.[15]

A woman who committed adultery threatened her husband by asserting her independence from him, sexual or otherwise, as well as by jeopardizing the succession from father to son (that succession, we recall, is the reason Shakespeare counsels the young man to marry). A sexually unchaste wife could raise doubts about the legitimacy of the son's right to inherit his father's wealth and status—a fear Shakespeare dramatizes in *The Winter's Tale*.[16]

And there was another reason for Renaissance fears about female sexual license. Though required to be chaste and obedient, women during Shakespeare's day were also frequently held to be more sexual than men, both in desire and performance. "Though they be the weaker vessels, yet they will overcome 2, 3, or 4 men in the satisfying of their carnal appetites," wrote the Elizabethan musician Thomas Whythorne. This sexual voraciousness, which Whythorne reported as a kind of common knowledge about women, rebuts the Renaissance idea of female submission: Whythorne describes sex as a struggle in which the "weaker vessel" sexually overcomes her male challengers.[17]

Men expressed fears about losing control over women through the stereotype of female deceitfulness. These stereotypes especially focused on women's use of cosmetics and wearing of fancy clothing. Evoking these stereotypes, the controversialist Thomas Nashe warned women that "however you disguise your bodies, you lay not on your colors [makeup] so thick that they sink into your souls." Make sure, he continued, "that your skins being too white without, your souls be not all black within." In similar terms he asked, "how will you attire yourselves, what gown, what head-tire will you put on, when you shall live in Hell amongst Hags and devils?"[18] God will have to punish the women that men cannot, since these women disguise "black" and hellish deeds with "white" appearances and beautiful clothing. Beautiful clothes in particular could proclaim the wife's manipulative control over her husband's wealth. For this reason, part of Katherine's "taming" in *The Taming of the Shrew* involves denying her fashionable new apparel. Expensive clothes could even raise fears that the woman was living beyond her husband's means by becoming a kept woman. That was the sin her beautiful clothes concealed.[19]

But these stereotypes are about more than literal female deception. They express deeper male fears that arise from a central contradiction in Renaissance thought about women and desire. Men and women were supposed to love one another, even to become "one flesh" in marriage. But how did that closeness relate to an ideology of male superiority? In misogynist polemics, men who loved a being inferior to themselves could only be deceived. Consider Swetnam's warning about female deceit, which extends beyond the use of makeup. Observing that men lay "their nets to catch a pretty woman," Swetnam warns these men that

> he which getteth such a prize gains nothing by his adventure, but shame to, the body and danger to the soul, for the heat of the young blood of these wantons, leads many unto destruction for this world's pleasure. It chants [enchants] your minds, and enfeebleth your bodies with diseases; it also scandleth your good names, but most of all it endagereth your souls.[20]

Men who think to trap a desirable woman find themselves entrapped by her, their minds enchanted and bodies enfeebled. If a man desires a woman, how can one explain this desire of a superior for an inferior? It must be male weakness caused by female deceit.

The deceit of female beauty, moreover, is nothing less than soul killing. Like the cosmetics and fancy clothing that enhance it, female beauty is deceitful because it involves a blinded love for "this world's pleasure" rather than for spiritual things.[21] When Hamlet finds a symbol of mortality in the skull of the jester Yorick, he thinks about the deceiving beauty of women: "Let her paint an inch thick, to this favour she must come."[22] No amount of cosmetics ("painting") can hide the reminder of death underneath, the skull that is the woman's true, and final, appearance (that is, "favour"). Deceived by a woman's beauty a man may believe he is falling in love with something heavenly. He does not realize he is falling in love with dangerously irrational passion, the mortal body and sin. "The beauty of women," Swetnam writes, "hath been the bane of many a man."[23]

A discussion in Baldesar Castiglione's *The Courtier* presents a troubling idea of how a man might feel degraded by sex with the woman he once desired. The participants in the discussion are debating the thesis that women are less perfect beings than men. One of the courtiers in the discussion — the misogynist Gasparo — offers women's and men's presumed different experiences of their first sexual encounter as proof of female imperfection. Gasparo recalls the following questions from Aristotle, and explains the philosopher's answers to them:

> 'Why is it that a woman always naturally loves the man to whom she first gave herself? And why, on the contrary, does a man hate the woman he first enjoyed?' And, in giving the reason, he affirms that this is because in such an act the woman takes on perfection from the man, and the man imperfection

from the woman; and that everyone naturally loves that which makes him perfect, and hates that which makes him imperfect.[24]

By having sex with women men diminish themselves, by taking on women's imperfection. When Shakespeare's Romeo cries "O sweet Juliet, / Thy beauty hath made me effeminate," he is responding to more than his failure to protect Mercutio from Tybalt. The idea that in loving women men became dangerously effeminate — that is more like women — was common in the Renaissance.[25] And no matter how romantic *Romeo and Juliet* seems, this play too affirms the deadliness of desire.

Renaissance physiology likewise assumed the danger of sex to men: every emission of semen was thought to shorten a man's life. In Renaissance slang "to die" meant to have an orgasm. Even the woman "chaste and fair," the inaccessible, idealized beloved of many a Renaissance sonnet, in her own way confirmed that there was something sinful or dangerous about the woman as a sexual being. Female perfection and female inferiority were two sides of the same delusory coin, especially because the failure of the woman to live up to chaste perfection (or the frustration when she did) easily led to misogynist denunciation.[26]

Gasparo's question, echoing Aristotle's, certainly does not speak for the sexual understanding of all Renaissance men. Nonetheless, it is of a piece with the popular Renaissance proverb that women were "necessary evils."[27] Gasparo's question also accords, as we'll see, with Shakespeare's simultaneous feelings of lust and revulsion for the black mistress.

19

A Reproach of Their Own

Misogynist views of women in the English Renaissance did not go unchallenged. *The Courtier's* Gasparo, for example, is a straw man, his misogyny defeated by representatives of a more gracious courtly ethos. Antifeminist pamphlets such as Swetnam's also produced forceful responses, including a number of refutations either written by women or purported to be written by them.[28] Like Swetnam's *The Arraignment of Lewd, Idle, Froward and Unconstant Women*, these pamphlets carried sensational titles: *Jane Anger her Protection for Women*, *A Muzzle for Melastomus* ("Melastomus" means "black mouth"), *Ester hath hang'd Haman*, *The Worming of a Mad Dog*, and *The Women's Sharp Revenge*.[29] There was even an anonymous play, *Swetnam the Woman-Hater, Arraigned by Women*, in which a group of women try, convict and punish the notorious misogynist for his offenses against them.[30]

One of the male offenses these writers point to is the sexual double standard. Men are everywhere concerned with women's chastity, but what about their own sexual sins? In *Ester hath Hang'd Haman* Ester Sowerman writes: "If a man abuse a maid and get her with child, no matter is made of it — but as a trick of youth; but it is made so heinous an offence in the maid that she is disparaged and utterly undone by it."[31] And just as women bear inordinate blame for sexual transgression, so, these writers point out, do they bear inordinate blame for inciting sexual desire in the first place. This point is made by Jane Anger, the earliest of these pamphleteers: "We have 'rolling eyes' and they railing tongues: our eyes cause them to look lasciviously, and why? because they are given to lechery."[32] Men rail at women for having "rolling eyes" — or as we might say now, "wandering eyes." But it is men's eyes that wander. Men who look "lasciviously" at women should blame their own "lechery" rather than the incitement of women, writes Anger, whose name is probably an apt pseudonym. Sowerman, whose name is likewise probably pseudonymous, makes a similar point in her response to Swetnam: "Our adversary bringeth many examples of men which have been overthrown by women. It is answered before: the fault is their own."[33] Sowerman argues that men are the guilty ones, seducing women, and then blaming them for their own sexual guilt: "What care if they make a thousand oaths and commit ten thousand perjuries, so they may deceive a woman? When they have done all and gotten their purpose, then they discover all the woman's shame."[34]

These writers find male misogyny particularly hypocritical because the Renaissance norm of heterosexual marriage should oblige men to love and respect women. Responding to the proverb that women are "necessary evils," Anger writes, "they confess we are necessary but would likewise have us evil." Sowerman specifically invokes the social expectation for a loving marriage: "There can be no love betwixt man and wife but where there is respective estimate the one towards the other. How could you love — nay, how could you loathe such a monster to whom Joseph Swetnam pointeth?"[35]

Sowerman's identification of the contradiction between the norm of heterosexual marriage and the ideology of female inferiority was especially powerful because the Protestant reformation elevated the status of marriage in England. Where Catholicism praised celibacy as the highest state, Protestants celebrated wedded love.[36] "Marriage is a merri-age, and this world's Paradise where there is mutual love," Rachel Speght writes. "The single man is by marriage changed from a bachelor to a husband, a far more excellent title: from a solitary life unto a joyful union and conjunction with such a creature as God hath made meet for man."[37] Speght was echoing official church teaching. Though the "Homily of Matrimony" assumed the wife's inferiority to the husband, it also warned husbands about abusing their authority and maltreating their wives, to whom they owed their respect.[38] The defense of women as good wives was limited because it insistently saw women through the lens of marriage.[39] But this defense was also powerful because it drew on official ideology.

Finally, these responses to Renaissance antifeminism emphasize that men are able to get away with their easy criticism of women because it is men whose views typically see print, not women's. As Anger points out, women make easy targets since men think women "will not write to reprove their lying lips."[40] Authoritative texts in the Renaissance are overwhelmingly written by men — recall, for example, Gasparo's invocation of Aristotle — and are shot through with male bias. "I would," Anger writes, "that ancient writers would as well have busied their heads about deciphering the deceits of their own sex as they have about setting down our follies."[41] Sowerman too suggests that when men, seized by sexual guilt, blame their faults on a woman, they find a ready storehouse of misogynist commonplaces in authors such as Swetnam "to rail upon her and the whole sex."[42] "Anger" and "Sowerman" are not only pseudonyms, but pseudonyms for writers who were actually men, we have a further, and ironic, example of the degree to which men dictated the portrayals of women in print — even sympathetic ones.

20

The Black Mistress: A Renaissance Common Place?

How much does Shakespeare draw on the tradition of Renaissance misogyny that Sowerman complains about? Shakespeare writes in sonnet 137 that his heart has believed the black mistress a "several plot" when he knows she is a "common place." "Several" in the Renaissance meant "single," while a "common place" was a plot of land not owned by one person, but available for "common" or public grazing.[43] Though Shakespeare wishes to believe the black mistress is singly his, he knows she has been held in "common." In the language of Renaissance sexual insult, the black mistress is a "whore."

The very familiarity of the insult suggests another sense in which the black mistress is a "common place." "Common places" are also familiar proverbs or beliefs, as in the Renaissance "commonplace" book, which contained sayings, stories, proverbs, ideas, poetry and the like, recorded by the person who kept the book. It is difficult to believe that Shakespeare did not hear this second meaning of the word.[44] For the sonnets' portrayal of the black mistress is a compendium of Renaissance misogynist commonplaces. The black mistress is unchaste, deceitful in her beauty, and a dangerous source of physical and spiritual disease.

The very instrument that the black mistress plays in sonnet 128 — the virginal — emphasizes the black mistress' sexuality while mocking her evident failure to conform to the Renaissance sexual ideal for women. The woman playing the virginal is sexually promiscuous, the accusation as well of sonnet 137. In sonnet 152 Shakespeare charges that she has "in act thy bed-vow broke," so she may, according to Shakespeare, be guilty of adultery as well — depending on whether the "bed-vow" implies marriage, or a vow to another lover.[45]

In sonnet 135 Shakespeare links the black mistress' unchastity to her failure to submit to male authority. This sonnet, one of the most sexually obscene in the group, exploits multiple senses of the word "will": wish, desire, sexual desire, penis and vagina (in Renaissance slang), Shakespeare's first name, and, some have speculated, the first name of the young man or of the black mistress' husband.[46] The word "Will" was capitalized in the quarto edition of the sonnets, presumably to emphasize its relationship to Shakespeare's name, as well perhaps as its wealth of meanings:

> Whoever hath her wish, thou hast thy Will,
> And Will to boot, and Will in overplus.
> More than enough am I that vex thee still,
> To thy sweet will making addition thus.
> Wilt thou, whose will is large and spacious,
> Not once vouchsafe to hide my will in thine?
> Shall will in others seem right gracious,
> And in my will no fair acceptance shine?
> The sea, all water, yet receives rain still,
> And in abundance addeth to his store,
> So thou, being rich in Will, add to thy Will
> One will of mine to make thy large Will more.
>> Let no unkind no fair beseechers kill,
>> Think all but one, and me in that one Will.

Shakespeare's puns comically draw on the Renaissance tie between a woman's sexual infidelity and her failure more generally to conform to the period's idea of the "good" woman, who is subject to male authority. The black mistress' great "will" — "Will to boot, and Will in overplus" — refers at once to her willfulness rather than passivity, her strong sexual desire, and her vagina.

Recalling the Renaissance stereotype of the sexually voracious woman, Shakespeare suggests that the black mistress' "will" is "large and spacious" because it has admitted so many other wills ("will in others"), that is, penises. The meanings of "will" that refer to the black mistress' willfulness remain active as well. For the black mistress has a great will, has wishes and desires. In the marriage sonnets, the wife is anonymous. As long as she produces a baby, it doesn't matter who she is ("some vial" — pun intended — is how Shakespeare refers to this woman in sonnet 6). In fact, if the woman is to remain chaste and obedient, it is better if she lacks a strong identity. In the sonnets to the black mistress, however, men become anonymous: one "will" after another.[47] Shakespeare makes this sexual promiscuity the basis for his own plea for sex with the black mistress: just as the sea continues to add more rain to its store, "So thou, being rich in Will, add to thy Will / One Will of mine to make thy large Will more."

The abundance of "wills" in this sonnet makes it confusing to read. These confusions match the black mistress' confusion of gender norms, but they are also funny. Shakespeare in sonnet 135 seems mainly to enjoy the black mistress' willfulness. His riotous punning reflects, almost celebrates, her wild behavior. Though more bawdy, the tone of this sonnet recalls the good naturedly way Shakespearean comedy treats women who are willful — sexually or otherwise. In these comedies, however, the woman's willfulness can be a laughing matter because at the play's end order is restored: the woman is married (as in *The Taming of the Shrew*) or she is known to have been sexually faithful to her husband all along (as in *The Merry Wives of Windsor*).

No return to order is suggested in this sonnet. Rather, Shakespeare enjoys the black mistress' "will" exactly because he imagines that he too will enjoy her — in the sexual sense: "Let no unkind no fair beseechers kill; / Think all but one, and me in that one Will." Shakespeare switches to the high tone of courtly love. The black mistress' sexual partners are comically — because suddenly and incongruently — transformed into courtly "fair beseechers" whom the black mistress can kill with an unkind word. But don't kill me, Shakespeare begs. Instead, "think all but one, and me in that one Will." That is, consider one "will" (penis, or man named Will) to be as good as any other, and consider me to be that "Will."

As we have seen, Shakespeare does not always react to the black mistress' sexual promiscuity with good natured humor. Perhaps Shakespeare treats the black mistress' sexual infidelities more happily in sonnet 135 because he wittily invents another of the sonnets' "sweet flatteries": that the black mistress will consider him her "one Will." In sonnet 137, on the other hand, Shakespeare confronts the prospect of other men being equally accepted by the black mistress. The humor of sonnet 135 (besides blunting the insult to the black mistress) also protects Shakespeare's ego. The sonnet's wit and ironic detachment preserve Shakespeare from expressing a too passionate desire for an imperfect, effeminizing or unruly woman.

In other sonnets, which lack this comic distance, Shakespeare sounds more panicked about his desire for the black mistress. His panic echoes misogynist warnings about the dangers women present to men.[48] In sonnet 147 Shakespeare all but wails.

> My love is as a fever, longing still
> For that which nurseth the disease,
> Feeding on that which doth preserve the ill,
> Th'uncertain sickly appetite to please.
> My reason, the physician to my love,

Angry that his prescriptions are not kept,
Hath left me, and I desperate now approve
Desire is death, which physic did except.
Past cure I am, now reason is past care,
And frantic mad with evermore unrest.
My thoughts and discourse as madmen's are,
At random from the truth vainly expressed;
> For I have sworn thee fair, and thought thee bright
> Who art as black as hell, as dark as night.

Swetnam warns that women burn men's blood, enfeeble their bodies, and enchant their minds; Shakespeare describes his desire for the black mistress as fever, disease and madness. The black mistress is as deceptive a beauty as misogynist sensationalism would have women. She is Nashe's fair woman, who lives among "hags and devils," but hides her soul "all black within" with whitening cosmetics and brilliant attire: "For I have sworn thee fair, and thought thee bright / Who art as black as hell, as dark as night."

Shakespeare's spiritual health is as threatened by the black mistress' false attractions as his mental and physical health. "Love is my sin, and thy dear virtue hate, / Hate of my sin grounded on sinful loving," Shakespeare begins sonnet 142. Because Shakespeare's love for the black mistress is sinful, her best virtue would be to hate him.

Though sonnet 146 does not mention the black mistress, its presence among the black mistress group underscores culturally resonant connections between women and sin. "Poor soul, the centre of my sinful earth," the sonnet begins "Why dost thou pine within and suffer dearth, / Painting thy outward walls so costly gay?" Shakespeare's black mistress, her depiction shaped by misogynist stereotypes of painted women, lurks behind these lines. The black mistress leads Shakespeare to betray his soul to his body (the soul's "outward walls") because she herself is a deceivingly beautiful body that conceals inward sin.

Besides associating the black mistress with disease, deceit, madness, sin and death, Shakespeare in a culturally resonant manner regards his love for the black mistress as a mistake both strange and terrible. His desire for her raises the misogynist question, how can men love a being inferior to themselves, except by a mysterious, and probably malign, enchantment? "O, from what power hast thou this powerful might / With insufficiency my heart to sway," Shakespeare asks at the beginning of sonnet 150. Shakespeare personifies the black mistress as "insufficiency" and later in the sonnet asks why his desire for her "worst" exceeds "all best."

Shakespeare regards his desire for the black mistress with the same kind of regret that *The Courtier*'s Gasparo claims a man feels after he has slept with a woman. He laments that he has felt (or, more complexly, continues to feel?) love for an unworthy object:

> O me, what eyes hath love put in my head,
> Which have no correspondence with true sight!
> Of if they have, where is my judgement fled,
> That censures falsely what they see aright?
> If that be fair whereon my false eyes dote,
> What means the world to say it is not so?
> If it be not, then love doth well denote
> Love's eye is not so true as all men's. No,
> How can it, O, how can love's eye be true,
> That is so vexed with watching and with tears?
> No marvel then though I mistake my view:
> The sun itself sees not till heaven clears.
>   O cunning love, with tears thou keep'st me blind
>   Lest eyes, well seeing, thy foul faults should find!
>   [sonnet 148]

This sonnet *almost* sounds like a testament to romantic passion, in which the lover defies conventional beliefs about the worthiness of his beloved (think of the movie *Pretty Woman*, or its novelistic predecessor *Jane Eyre*). But Shakespeare does not quite write this plot. Instead, he agrees with the world's disapproval of his love and judgment. His only defense is that, as in *A Midsummer Night's Dream*, the eyes of lovers ("love's eye") "have no correspondence with true sight." Shakespeare metaphorically suggests that were his eyes not clouded with desire — "The sun itself sees not till heaven clears" — he would readily find the black mistress' "foul faults."

Shakespeare writes in this sonnet with a peculiar combination of anger and abstraction. He never refers directly to the black mistress until the last line's "thy faults." And even "thy" could refer to "love" rather than to the black mistress.[49] While abstraction and anger might not seem to mix, in this case Shakespeare's more abstract language underscores his complaint about the black mistress, by combining it with a broader complaint about love for women in general. We see this effect in the grammar of lines 5 and 6, where Shakespeare replaces the expected personal pronoun "she" with the impersonal pronouns "that" and "it": "If that be fair whereon my false eyes dote / What means the world to say it is not so?" Why not write "she"? One answer is that referring to someone as a "that" or an "it" expresses distance, even contempt, toward the person. The impersonal pronouns also suggest the absorption of the black mistress into the commonplaces of Renaissance misogyny, since these pronouns can refer not just to one person — the black mistress — but to the entire group she represents: "that" kind of thing whereon my eyes dote; "it"—the idea of woman's beauty—is not so. If we take Shakespeare to be writing about the black mistress as if she were a typical woman, then his question echoes Gasparo's: why do men love women and consider them "fair" when, really, the world knows that they are not?

The concluding lines of the sonnet underscore the generalization. Shakespeare quite viciously associates the debilitating blindness of his love for the black mistress with the dangers of love for women in general: "O cunning love, with tears thou keep'st me blind, / Lest eyes, well seeing, thy foul faults should find." Two phrases in these lines refer to the vagina. The sound of "cunning love" plays on "cunt love," while "foul faults" plays on "fault" as a slang term for the vagina.[50] The crudity of this slang especially suggests the abuse heaped on women. Since "fault" also means something imperfect or lacking—Aristotle's influential theory held women to be imperfect men—this way of referring to the vagina also recalls Shakespeare's question in sonnet 150 about how "insufficiency" is able to sway his heart.[51] If Stephen Booth is correct that "love's eye" in line 8 may also refer to the vagina, then the entire sonnet turns on the danger to men's eyes—their source of perception and judgement—presented by the only "eye"—the vagina—that women in this sonnet are said to have.[52]

Besides making men overly emotional, the dangers of loving women are specifically sexual. What happens to men when they have sex? We already know the answer. They are reduced to their penises.

> Love is too young to know what conscience is,
> Yet who knows not conscience is born of love?
> Then, gentle cheater, urge not my amiss,
> Lest guilty of my faults thy sweet self prove.
> For, thou betraying me, I do betray
> My nobler part to my gross body's treason.
> My soul doth tell my body that he may
> Triumph in love; flesh stays no farther reason,
> But rising at thy name doth point out thee
> As his triumphant prize. Proud of this pride,
> He is contented thy poor drudge to be,
> To stand in thy affairs, fall by thy side.
>   No want of conscience hold it that I call
>   Her 'love' for whose dear love I rise and fall.
>
>   [sonnet 151]

Shakespeare begins this sonnet with a statement about the "conscience," the sense of sin, that arises from his affair with the black mistress. Don't accuse me of sin—"urge not my amiss"—he tells the black mistress, since you might find yourself likewise guilty: "lest guilty of my faults thy sweet self prove."

The black mistress' sin is (at least) her infidelity. The "gentle cheater" betrays Shakespeare, presumably by sleeping with the young man.

We would expect a parallel statement of sin on Shakespeare's part. After all, by sleeping with the black mistress Shakespeare is cheating on his wife. Shakespeare, however, worries not about how he betrays another woman, but about how he betrays himself. Shakespeare has allowed his body rather than his "nobler part," his "soul," to command his actions.

In fact, as we have seen, Shakespeare writes about himself as if he were only his penis. He becomes "flesh ... rising at thy name," "contented ... to stand in thy affairs, fall by thy side." The sonnet's metaphor obviously refers to the penis before and after sex. Though in sonnet 135 Shakespeare may identify the black mistress' "will" with her vagina, sonnet 151 reminds us that in his affair with the black mistress Shakespeare too wishes to be called "will" (his first name but also slang for the male as well as female genitals). Sonnet 151, like sonnet 135, treats this reduction to "will" comically. In 151 Shakespeare is even tender. We can see, however, why other sonnets are more hostile. To become flesh is to become vulnerable to the diseases of the flesh. These include literal physical disease — sonnet 144 in particular associates sex with syphilis — but also spiritual sin.[53]

Once betrayed into flesh, moreover, the man becomes like the woman, losing the superior reason that justified his authority over her. Sonnet 151 presents this paradox of Renaissance manhood: sex is a male "triumph" and "pride," a sign of masculine mastery. In fact "pride," as we saw in chapter 15, is slang for the erect penis. But Shakespeare's pride equally submits him to the black mistress: his proud flesh "is contented thy poor drudge to be." In loving the black mistress, Shakespeare enslaves himself to what, as a man, he should triumph over: women, passion, flesh.

The sentiment echoes the antifeminist Swetnam, as well as this anonymous seventeenth-century verse:

> The woman's best part call it I dare
> Wherein no man comes but must stand bare
> And let him be never so stout
> T'will take him down before he goes out.[54]

This verse reminds us of sonnet 151 for its joke about male vulnerability during sex: the man/penis must "stand bare." The poem similarly implies that sex subordinates the man to the woman. Be the man/penis "never so stout," the woman/vagina will "take him down." A Renaissance common place: Rocky's coach ("women weaken legs") had seventeenth-century forebears.

21

More Perjured I?

The anonymous verse quoted in the previous chapter was copied into the commonplace books of a number of Oxford students. Commonplace books were storehouses of common knowledge. But could this knowledge be trusted? When Shakespeare calls the black mistress a "common place," does he suspect his own reliance on commonplaces?

The answer depends on whether Shakespeare thinks these familiar sayings and jokes are commonplace because their truth is everywhere evident or because they are clichés and stereotypes, popularly circulated but false. If commonplaces are true, then Shakespeare's black mistress is another example of the "common" Renaissance woman: low, sexually available, and typical. If commonplaces are abusive stereotypes, then the black mistress, like Shakespeare's Desdemona, is another of their victims. And Shakespeare, like his villain Iago, is an abuser of women. In fact, Shakespeare in his sonnets incorporates a good deal of the female (or sympathetic male) response to the stereotypes he echoes. The sonnets do not simply recirculate misogynist commonplaces. But neither do they simply reject them. Instead, Shakespeare often recognizes his insults as unfair slanders of the black mistress—and repeats them anyway.

Shakespeare even warns the black mistress to beware his "mad slanders" of her. But then he turns warning into threat. The black mistress had better grant him her love before she drives him to speak ill of her:

> Be wise as thou art cruel; do not press
> My tongue-tied patience with too much disdain,
> Lest sorrow lend me words, and words express
> The manner of my pity-wanting pain.

> If I might teach thee wit, better it were,
> Though not to love, yet, love, to tell me so —
> As testy sick men when their deaths be near
> No news but health from their physicians know.
> For if I should despair I should grow mad,
> And in my madness might speak ill of thee.
> Now this ill-wresting world is grown so bad
> Mad slanderers by mad ears believèd be.
>   That I may not be so, nor thou belied,
>   Bear thine eyes straight, though thy proud heart go wide.
>
> [sonnet 140]

Though the black mistress may grant her favor (including sexual favors) to others, Shakespeare complains that she is "cruel" to him. Renaissance sonneteers often use the word "cruel" to describe the customarily aloof courtly beloved. Shakespeare warns the black mistress that too much "disdain" on her part may lead him to express "the manner of my pity-wanting pain." Returning cruelty for cruelty, Shakespeare will "speak ill" of the black mistress, angrily describing how she lacks (is "wanting") pity for his love pains.

Surprisingly, Shakespeare does not advise the black mistress to love him in order to avert his anger. He advises her to *pretend* to love him, as physicians pretend to their dying patients that they are healthy: although she does not love him ("though not to love") she should tell Shakespeare that she does ("yet, love, to tell me so"). She should "bear thine eyes straight, though thy proud heart goes wide." She should seem to have eyes only for Shakespeare — not the roving eyes of misogynist complaint — even though these "straight" eyes disguise what's in her proud and undependable heart.

This sonnet is remarkable because Shakespeare acknowledges that the slanders he threatens will be unfair and unfairly believed: "Now this ill-wresting world is grown so bad / Mad slanderers by mad ears believèd be." The "ill-wresting world" interprets things — wrests meanings — in the most "ill" way possible.[55] In this bad world both the slanderer of a woman and those who believe him are mad. These lines remind us of the importance and vulnerability of women's sexual reputations in the Renaissance, as well as nearly mad attacks on women in Shakespeare's day, brought to a low art in Swetnam's 1615 *Arraignment*. Shakespeare's criticism in this sonnet of slanders against women also recalls the plot of *Othello*, just as the slanders themselves do. When Othello calls Desdemona a "whore," Emelia rightly says she "will be hanged if some eternal villain..., have not devised this slander."[56] In *Othello* Shakespeare sees both the deviser of the slander and the one who believes him — Iago and Othello — as "mad."

But the very advice this sonnet gives to avoid "mad" slander is the stuff of slander. If the mistress should bear her eyes "straight" even though her heart goes "wide" she will be sexually deceitful, only pretending to love Shakespeare. Shakespeare's knowing injunctions to be "wise" and his promise to "teach thee wit" insinuate this deceit. Both "wise" and "wit" in Shakespeare's day can have overtones of craftiness. Shakespeare does not expect of the black mistress that she can truly love him, only that she can be crafty enough to dissimulate love.

This expectation reaffirms just the kind of slanders the sonnet apparently dismisses. It also creates, in a subtly mocking manner, a double-bind for the black mistress. If she does not demonstrate her love for Shakespeare he will slander her. But if she does show her love for Shakespeare, she will not only be vulnerable to slander for her deceit, but also prove slanders of women to be true rather than "mad."

Shakespeare follows this pattern elsewhere in the black mistress sonnets. He sympathetically echoes criticism of male slanders against women, but then undercuts this sympathy with some cutting irony that repeats the slander. For example, in sonnet 131 Shakespeare defends his love of his mistress' black beauty, even though some say her "face hath not the power to make love groan." Against this opinion Shakespeare swears that in his judgment "thy black [beauty] is fairest." But the sonnet concludes: "In nothing art thou black save [except] in thy deeds, / And thence this slander, as I think, proceeds."

Shakespeare responds to a slander of the black mistress' looks with the more vicious slander that not her appearance but her deeds are black. These lines recall Renaissance attacks on women for having cosmetically fair outsides and black souls within. Shakespeare, however, delivers these lines not with Nashean sensationalism (of the sort we saw in chapter 18) but with quiet derision. He pretends he is defending her, when he is not. The bland tone of Shakespeare's expression, especially conveyed in the mock judicious phrase "as I think," implies Shakespeare's indifference to the black mistress, as well as his difference from other "mad" slanderers. At least in this sonnet, Shakespeare ends up writing about the black mistress with a cool contempt. The blandness also seems defensive, as if Shakespeare would like to insult the black mistress while pretending that he's not, or at least that he has no idea that he is. This pretended innocence again suggests that Shakespeare knows he is creating his portrait of the black mistress out of misogynist stereotypes — but uses them anyway.

There is another example of partial self-criticism in sonnet 152, which addresses the issue of male versus female responsibility for sexual infidelity:

> In loving thee thou know'st I am forsworn,
> But thou art twice forsworn to me love swearing:

> In act thy bed vow broke, and new faith torn
> In vowing new hate after new love bearing.
> But why of two oaths' breach do I accuse thee
> When I break twenty? I am perjured most,
> For all my vows are oaths but to misuse thee,
> And all my honest faith in thee is lost.
> For I have sworn deep oaths of thy deep kindness,
> Oaths of thy love, thy truth, thy constancy,
> And to enlighten thee gave eyes to blindness,
> Or made them swear against the thing they see.
>   For I have sworn thee fair — more perjured eye
>   To swear against the truth so foul a lie.

This sonnet echoes a point frequently made against misogynists such as Swetnam. Sexual affairs involve and make guilty two people, not one. While in misogynist complaint this one guilty person is invariably the women, prowomen writers like Sowerman and Anger, as we have seen, emphasize that if any single person is responsible it is likely to be the man.

Shakespeare similarly wonders about relative guilt. Both he and the black mistress in having an affair have broken vows to others. Shakespeare begins the sonnet acknowledging his own wrongdoing: "In loving thee thou know'st I am forsworn." Shakespeare is married; and he has vowed his unalterable faith to the young man, with whom he also enjoys a kind of "marriage" (sonnet 116). The black mistress knows ("thou know'st") that Shakespeare is being unfaithful to one or both of these two people, and this knowledge appears to give her the moral high ground. Hence Shakespeare reminds her of her own sins. She is "twice forsworn." The "bed-vow" broke, as we have seen, could refer either to her own marital infidelity, or to an informal vow to a former lover. Her "vowing new hate after new love bearing" could refer to this same broken vow (having found her new love for Shakespeare she has a new hate for her husband or former lover), to a new breaking of her vow of love to Shakespeare (after bearing new love for Shakespeare she now bears new hate for him) or even to a breaking of her vow to Shakespeare in favor of a new lover, perhaps the young man (she vows new hate for Shakespeare because she bears — perhaps in a sexual sense as well — a new love).[57] The very number of possible vows broken and people involved in these lines imply that the black mistress has plenty of reasons to be guilty.

In the following lines Shakespeare gives up on a literal accounting of guilt. Why accuse you of "two oaths" broken, he asks, "when I break twenty"? "Twenty" is no longer a real number but a figure of speech that intensifies Shakespeare's expression of his own guilt. He is "perjured most," since all his vows have been "oaths to misuse" the black mistress. At this point in the sonnet, Shakespeare writes in terms close to the pro-women responses to misogynist complaint. "What care if they [men] make a thousand oaths and commit ten thousand perjuries, so they may deceive a woman?" This is what Shakespeare has done. He has complimented the black mistress, perhaps to seduce her, swearing oaths of her kindness, love, truth, and constancy. Yet his phrasing of this deceit — "all my honest faith in thee is lost" — says more than that Shakespeare has dishonestly pursued the black mistress. The phrase strongly implies that the black mistress is somehow responsible for this fault, and perhaps also that trying to be honest or faithful to the black mistress is a losing proposition.

The end of this sonnet makes it even more clear that we cannot celebrate Shakespeare as a feminist, at least not from the evidence of the sonnets. True, Shakespeare admits his guilt for lying, but only in the sense explained by the acid joke of the final couplet: "For I have sworn thee fair — more perjured eye / To swear against the truth so foul a lie." Shakespeare's "eye," and punningly, "I," is "more perjured" than the black mistress'. This admission sounds like Sowerman, but it turns her emphasis on male guilt on its head. Shakespeare says he is most guilty for swearing the "foul lie" that the black mistress is "fair" — a word that refers to behavior as well as looks. In other words: I'm so bad because I said you were good. The sonnet in its conclusion returns to emphasizing in misogynist terms the "foul" woman and to blaming the woman for male sins. Shakespeare has been driven to lie because of the sexually tempting black mistress.

Why are Shakespeare's sonnets so ambivalent about whether to side with the misogynists or their opponents? Certainly Shakespeare the astute writer and observer could see the strong case to be made against crude misogynist accusation. Yet in seeing this side of the debate Shakespeare was not drawing solely on his own talents, nor was he taking a dissident position. Rather, the sonnets are contradictory because ideas in the Renaissance about women and men's relationships to them were contradictory. Male fears of losing self-control challenged their fantasies of sexual mastery. An ethos of courtly graciousness challenged ill-mannered antifeminism. The Galenic idea of women as perfect in their own sex challenged the Aristotelean idea of women as incomplete, imperfect men.[58] And the Protestant celebration of marriage challenged the detraction of the partner that God had ordained for man. The black mistress sonnets' guilt about adultery, once a staple of the literature of courtly love, especially suggests this influence of Protestant thought on marriage. Shakespeare was writing within a culture that treated male adultery with relative indulgence.[59] Protestant teaching, however, with its renewed celebration of the mutual love between husband and wife, was hostile to the sexual double standard.[60] This hostility may have influenced Shakespeare's admission that he shares the black mistress' guilt for adultery.

    Yet Shakespeare expresses this guilt as a joke, as he likewise jokes about unfair slanders of the black mistress. Jokes are a means of escaping contradiction. They allow us to say something, without saying that we mean it.

22

"The Expense of Spirit"

Do not "blame my verse of loose unchastity / For painting forth the things that hidden are, / Since all men act in speech what I declare." So unchaste was Thomas Nashe's poem "The Choice of Valentines" that, though written and circulated in manuscript around the time of the sonnets, the poem was not published until 1905. "The Choice of Valentines" tells the story of a young man who, failing to find his beloved at a rural celebration of Saint Valentine's day, discovers her instead at a London brothel, where he pays to have sex with her. When the young man is unable to satisfy his beloved (he comes too soon) she turns to a dildo — which it turns out has other advantages as well: "he'll refresh me well / And never make my tender belly swell." In Nashe's day the poem was also referred to as "Nashe his dildo" and the first evidence of the word occurring in English, according to the *Oxford English Dictionary*, is from Nashe's poem.[61]

We often associate Renaissance love poetry with the idealizing verse that Shakespeare writes for the young man, the kind of verse that, of course, is also written at this time for ladies "chaste and fair." In this courtly love poetry men and women love but don't have sex — and certainly not sex for pay, or with a dildo. Nashe's poem was not outside sixteenth-century literary tradition, however. The English Renaissance produced a strong countercurrent of bawdy poetry that combined frank and rebellious sexuality with a related satiric drive to "lay bare," literally and figuratively, all sorts of euphemizing ideals. Shakespeare's great dramatic forbear Christopher Marlowe draws on this more satiric style in his sexy and funny version of the Hero and Leander story, as does much of the early verse by the poet John Donne.

This alternative tradition became especially strong in the 1590s, when the hopefulness of the earlier part of Queen Elizabeth's reign gave way to a sense of decline and corruption at its end. At court too many men were chasing too few positions — straining the system of court patronage with disappointment and bribery. In London the scary energies of the market were pushing against the traditional feudal order and its values.[62] In this uneasy fin de siecle innocent rural celebration gives way to urban brothel, "natural" male potency to a woman's "artificial" desires.

Sometimes this more cynical love poetry mixes the disappointments of love with the trials of patronage and the dangers of court life. John Donne, long dependent on more powerful aristocratic patrons, likened the unsatisfied desire of the courtly lover to the frustration of serving "great men" who promise honors or riches but never deliver.[63] When, in his religious poetry, Donne reflected on the vanity of his earlier life at court he called his pursuit of "fame, wit, hopes" the love of "false mistresses."[64] Walter Ralegh wrote likewise of love that it "is a careless child / And forgets promise past; / He [love] is blind, he is deaf, when he list / And in faith never fast." These bitter words reflected a life at court of betrayal and danger, which ended with his execution on trumped-up charges of treason, promoted by a former friend.[65]

Another celebrated poet who turns in the 1590s to this counter-tradition in love poetry is Shakespeare. The black mistress sonnets include, after all, a beloved accused of wild sexual infidelity ("the bay where all men ride"), obscene punning on the word "Will," a joke about three-way sex, with Shakespeare sandwiched between black mistress and young man ("I, being pent in thee, / Perforce am thine, and all that is in me" [133]), and a general picture of sexual desire out of control. These sexually "dark" sonnets are often seen as an original transformation of idealizing courtly love convention. But the black mistress sonnets can clearly be placed in the literary and cultural history of the 1590s. Like Nashe's "Choice of Valentines," these sonnets are poems of "loose unchastity" that combine sexual rather than spiritualized love with the related satirical impulse to reveal "what all men act" — sexually and otherwise — but attempt to keep hidden.

This impulse takes its most mild form as anti–Petrarchanism. Love poetry in Renaissance England is called anti–Petrarchan when it rejects the much imitated and soon hackneyed idealizations of the Italian poet Petrarch, as Shakespeare does in sonnet 130:

> My mistress' eyes are nothing like the sun;
> Coral is far more red than her lips' red.
> If snow be white, why then her breasts are dun;
> If hairs be wires, black wires grow on her head.

I have seen roses damasked, red and white,
But no such roses see I in her cheeks;
And in some perfumes is there more delight
Than in the breath that from my mistress reeks.
I love to hear her speak, yet well I know
That music hath a far more pleasing sound.
I grant I never saw a goddess go:
My mistress when she walks treads on the ground.
 And yet, by heaven, I think my love as rare
 As any she belied by false compare.

This sonnet pokes fun at Renaissance rhetoric, particularly the conventional figures of speech that impossibly idealize the courtly beloved: eyes like the sun, lips like coral, breasts white as snow, and so on. All these similes are literally untrue, as sonnet 130, skeptical of Petrarchan idealism, declares. By rejecting them, Shakespeare takes his mistress down to earth: "she treads on the ground." Modern readers have admired this sonnet for portraying a love that seems real rather than sentimentally romantic.[66]

The realism of sonnet 130, though, may be less complimentary than it first appears. There is after all not much said about the black mistress in this sonnet that is actually complimentary. Shakespeare follows even the sonnet's nicest sentiment, "I love to hear her speak," with the enthusiastic admission that "music hath a far more pleasing sound." And Shakespeare does not mind telling us of "the breath that from my mistress reeks." "Reeks" during Shakespeare's day could mean "gives off" in a more neutral sense, but it also could mean smells.[67]

The final couplet of the sonnet is the key to its positive meaning. Shakespeare writes that the black mistress is "as rare" as sonnet ladies who have been praised with lying figures of speech ("false compare"). The couplet might mean that Shakespeare's down-to-earth love is better than the sonnet ladies men have sappily idealized, and readers often understand the couplet to say this. But the couplet's phrasing is evasive. Is the black mistress as good or as bad as all the rest? The indefinite point of reference in these lines creates the same veiled insult as this witticism of the humanist Sir Thomas More, concerning a rival writer's new book: "he composed quickly, but even so, with all the time in the world, he could not have written better."[68]

Sonnet 130's skepticism of idealizing love is playfully ambiguous. The previous sonnet in the sequence sheds idealism and ambiguity altogether. If in sonnet 130 Shakespeare brings his love from heaven to earth, in sonnet 129 love — or rather lust — brings Shakespeare from heaven to hell.

 Th'expense of spirit in a waste of shame
 Is lust in action; and till action, lust

> Is perjured, murd'rous, bloody, full of blame,
> Savage, extreme, rude, cruel, not to trust,
> Enjoyed no sooner but despisèd straight,
> Past reason hunted, and no sooner had
> Past reason hated as a swallowed bait
> On purpose laid to make the taker mad;
> Mad in pursuit and in possession so,
> Had, having, and in quest to have, extreme;
> A bliss in proof and proved, a very woe;
> Before, a joy proposed; behind, a dream.
>   All this the world well knows, yet none knows well
>   To shun the heaven that leads men to this hell.

As in sonnet 151, sex ("lust in action") is an "expense of spirit" that reduces the writer from a spiritual to a physical being. Even the poet's words share in this reduction. "Spirit" in Shakespeare's day referred not just to the soul but to semen. The "waste of shame" plays on the "waist" of shame, that part of the body where spirit/semen is expended. And if sex leads to disgust — it is "enjoyed no sooner but despised straight [i.e. immediately]" — sexual desire is equally contemptible. A string of feverishly compressed adjectives in lines 3 to 4 convey its dishonest, violent and ultimately mad energies.

The extremity of this madness suggests however that something more than guilt about sex drives the sonnet. Sonnet 129 might at first seem psychologically plausible. Lust is sometimes rude, cruel, or not to trust. But is it really bloody and murderous? And not just occasionally so, but typically, as this sonnet declares "the world well knows"! Shakespeare turns a reflection on sex into a shadowy story of lies, murder, blood, blame and loss, as if packing a tragedy into the space of a sonnet. Even the strong suspicion in the Renaissance of the body and its passions would not fully account for the corrupt world this sonnet evokes.

Rather, as with Nashe's "Choice of Valentines," the portrayal of sex in sonnet 129 conveys an entire, if unstated, worldview. Only Nashe is more cheerful. Writing in the nearly pornographic style of the black mistress sonnets rather than the polite euphemism of the courtly sonnets to the fair young man, Shakespeare expresses grief at an "expense of spirit" — both ejaculation and a lost idealism. Draw the curtain of love and find lust; lay bare the flattering pleas of devotion in patronage poetry and discover the violent energies of ambition and material self-interest.[69] To suggest that sonnet 129 implies these broader ideas does not mean ignoring its specific complaint about the desire for women. Instead, we can ask why Shakespeare transforms social complaint into sexual pessimism, centered around, like Donne's "false mistresses," a deceitful and dangerous female. If a fall is near, can a daughter of Eve be far away?

23

Fair Is Foul

By usually idealizing the young man and associating the loss of idealism with the black mistress, Shakespeare follows a familiar pattern. During Shakespeare's day maleness is often associated with a set of virtues, femininity with their opposing vices. The Renaissance inherited this association in part from classical authors such as Aristotle, who aligns men with unity, right, square, rest, straight, light and good, and women with plurality, left, oblong, moving, curved, darkness and evil.[70]

Men and women in the Renaissance were not inevitably seen in these crudely oppositional terms. But the organization of virtue and vice by gender remained available to relieve anxieties about a messier social reality. The Ralegh poem that calls love unreliable and untrustworthy ("a careless child ... in faith never fast") concludes that this love is merely for women:

> Of womankind such indeed is the love
> Or the word love abused,
> Under which many childish desires
> And conceits are excused:
> But true love is a durable fire
> In the mind ever burning.[71]

Ralegh's "true love" is probably love for God. The poem's false love, however, is not merely human love, but love "of womankind." The stressed position of these words at the beginning of the line especially contributes to the sense that women are responsible for the failures of men.[72] Swetnam in his *Arraignment* is more blunt: "if thou study a thousand years thou shalt find a woman nothing else but a contrary of man."[73] Woman is man's contrary in two related senses: she brings him down and she does so because,

143

as in the Aristotelean schema, she embodies vice while man embodies virtue.

Shakespeare appears to have similarly organized his sonnets by gendered contraries: virtuous young man and immoral black mistress. The gendering of virtue and vice is especially stark in sonnet 144, one of the sonnets that recounts the love triangle between Shakespeare, the young man and the black mistress.

> Two loves I have, of comfort and despair,
> Which like two spirits do suggest me still.
> The better angel is a man right fair,
> The worser spirit a woman coloured ill.

The young man is a love of comfort; he is a man, an angel, right and fair. The black mistress is a love of despair; she is a woman and a "worser spirit" who is "coloured ill." Sonnet 144 not only divides virtue and vice by gender, but also describes the principle of division of Shakespeare's sonnets as a whole. There is the idealistic world of the young man sonnets with its "marriage of true minds" and the earthly or, more usually, hellish world of the black mistress with its "expense of spirit."

Virtue and vice aren't really neatly divided by gender, however, and many of the sonnets suggest as much. Sonnet 93 may describe deceit as feminine but Shakespeare is writing about the young man, whose virtue may be no more than face deep: "heaven in thy creation did decree / That in thy face sweet love should ever dwell; / Whate'er thy thoughts or thy heart's workings be." The beginning of this sonnet, however, changes the young man's infidelity ("thy looks with me, thy heart in other place") into a wife's adultery: "So shall I live, supposing thou art true / Like a deceivèd husband." So does the sonnet's end. Its couplet relies on the untrustworthiness of women at its most commonplace: "How like Eve's apple doth thy beauty grow / If thy sweet virtue answer not thy show!"

On the other hand, sonnet 129 gestures toward a female "hell" ("hell" was also Renaissance slang for the vagina[74]) without blaming women outright for the evils of "lust in action." Even Shakespeare's sonnet 144 unexpectedly blurs what seem at first glance its absolute divisions: both loves are "spirits" that "suggest" Shakespeare, a word that connotes temptation to evil.[75] Still more damningly, as the sonnet continues Shakespeare worries that the black mistress will succeed in seducing the young man, making her hell his.[76] It takes two: if the young man sleeps with the black mistress, will he be guilty as well?

The very first sonnet to the black mistress hints at the young man's guilt while warning against black and white views of the world:

In the old age black was not counted fair,
Or if it were, it bore not beauty's name;
But now is black beauty's successive heir,
And beauty slandered with a bastard shame:
For since each hand hath put on nature's power,
Fairing the foul with art's false borrowed face,
Sweet beauty hath no name, no holy bower,
But is profaned, if not lives in disgrace.
Therefore my mistress' eyes are raven-black,
Her brow so suited, and they mourners seem
At such who, not born fair, no beauty lack,
Sland'ring creation with a false esteem.
   Yet so they mourn, becoming of their woe,
   That every tongue says beauty should look so.

[sonnet 127]

As in sonnet 129, Shakespeare tells in this sonnet a story as daring as the plots of his great tragedies. Black Othello is admirable and white Iago repellant. Sonnet 127 likewise challenges the "old age" preference of "fair" over "black." The reason for this challenge recalls *Othello* too: fair beauty is the dishonest product of cosmetic artifice, "art's false borrowed face," just as Iago turns out to be the play's great liar, whose evil deeds prove false the moral superiority of whiteness.

The sonnet's skepticism about telling good from evil also recalls the plot of *Macbeth*, whose witches chant "fair is foul, and foul is fair."[77] Though the witches are foul, they are fairly right about the difficulty of telling good from evil in that play. When Shakespeare introduces the black mistress he hits upon a phrase similar to this one from *Macbeth*. "Fairing the foul" is one of Shakespeare's names for the fraudulent appearance of "art's false borrowed face." Shakespeare's explanation of how the black mistress came to be considered beautiful also echoes his witches' logic. If fair is really foul, then perhaps foul is really fair. Because fair looks have proved fraudulent, black beauty, once denigrated, now earns the praise of every tongue.

This sonnet arouses suspicion that with the young man too, "fair is foul." Why else switch sonnet recipients from young man to black mistress with a complaint about the falsity of fairness? Is renouncing fairness in sonnet 127 Shakespeare's way of renouncing the young man? After all, some of the sonnets to the young man do imply that he is actually vain, arrogant, unfaithful and lascivious.[78] And if the young man is not really fair, then what about Shakespeare? When Shakespeare praises the young man despite his faults, he not only "fairs the foul" subject of his sonnets, but himself as well. Promises of honest praise rather than a poet's flattery turn out to be "foul" lies. Shakespeare may also tell these lies, moreover, in order to make more fair his own "foul" birth. Shakespeare announces his intimacy with a socially superior young man, in a literary form embraced by gentlemen poets like Wyatt and Sidney. But unlike these men Shakespeare was "not born fair," a phrasing that in Renaissance England evokes not just complexion or beauty but social status, especially when linked in sonnet 127 to beauty's "heir" and "bastard shame."[79]

Perhaps this sonnet, whose skepticism about fairness brings to mind both the young man and his poet, cut too close to the bone for Shakespeare fully to continue in the direction it points. The sonnets that follow 127 make a subtle but decisive change of course. Shakespeare stops treating the black mistress as the alternative to fair-is-foul beauty and starts describing her as its exemplar.[80] Many of the unconventional stances initiated by 127, such as that sonnet's anti–Petrarchan skepticism about ideal beauty, remain through the rest of the black mistress sonnets. But the subsequent embodiment of 127's skepticism *in* the black mistress and Shakespeare's love for her means that these unconventional stances are tamed by the conventional gender divide in the Renaissance between male virtue and female vice.

As we have seen, this divide was sometimes expressed in the language of white and black: even white women have black souls.[81] But, in addition to feminine "blackness," what about racial blackness? The echoes of *Othello* in sonnet 127 suggest this meaning of "black." So do other Shakespeare plays, in which, as we have seen, brunettes are already associated with racially black peoples.[82] Trying to prove the black mistress was really black is like trying to prove the young man was really William Herbert — a losing proposition. More promising is the proposition that the sonnets' first readers could have thought of race when they read the black mistress sonnets, and that the very indefiniteness of the references to blackness in the sonnets encourages such thoughts.

The idea that black in the sonnets had the same racial meaning in Renaissance England that it does for modern readers might at first seem anachronistic. A defining characteristic of "the Renaissance" is, however, the brave new worlds and encounters with new peoples that the period's global exploration and trade encouraged (and that plays like *Othello* and *The Tempest* record). Perhaps these brave new worlds are part of Shakespeare's contrast in sonnet 127 between the "old age" when black was not counted fair, and the contemporary moment, when it is.[83]

Nonetheless, the importance of race in the sonnets may lie, at least in part, in the very fact that "race" in Renaissance English more frequently refers to lineage than skin color. We often consider race and gender to be rooted in the body (of course these assumptions are problematic). In the

Renaissance, however, class is also physical, its primary language birth and blood rather than the economic "class" to which we are accustomed. "Race" most often means "lineage" in Shakespeare's plays. And this is how Sidney uses the word when he praises Stella for making "so fair my race."[84] "Race" means Sidney's ride on horseback, but it also glances at Sidney's pride in his family, his place as nephew to one of England's most powerful nobles, the Earl of Leicester. Even the word's primary reference to skillful horseman-ship points to Sidney's aristocratic "nature," since such skill belonged to nobles and gentlemen.

As we have seen, sonnet 127 complains of those who, though "not born fair," assume the marks of fair beauty — Sidney's fair race — and those peo-ple could include Shakespeare, mimic of aristocratic literary fashions, newly made gentleman, and usurper of the fair young man's affections, which should be directed toward the prudential reproduction of his race, that is lineage. But if, as Kim Hall argues, the sonnets in their striking contrast between "fair" and "black" beauty are beginning to nudge these terms toward modern racial ones, the story changes. For when race becomes, as we often think of it today, a matter of skin color rather than lineage, then Shakespeare and the young man are both born fair, and it is the black mistress — associ-ated with new days against the old — who becomes the inferior and threat-ening figure.[85]

I would argue, then, that the black mistress serves as a scapegoat for anxieties about duplicity or sin in the relationships between fair young men.[86] Worth noting in this respect is Colin Burrow's opinion (with which I agree) that the sonnets to the young man are more complex and compelling because they are really uncertain — we are frequently unsure where Shakespeare and the young man stand morally or in relation to one another — while the son-nets to the black mistress only play at uncertainty. Though the black mis-tress sonnets are full of paradox, the paradox is brittle, and in most of these sonnets there's never a real question about the black mistress' honesty or Shakespeare's cynical attitude toward her. Rather, as Burrow puts it, the son-nets in this group "focus sharply on distinctions between what the poet sees and what is, and as a result they seem far simpler than many of the poems before 126."[87]

Burrow attributes the more contrived cynicism of these sonnets to their early composition. Though last in the sequence, they were very likely writ-ten first.[88] But why were they placed last — whether by Shakespeare or some-one else? The answer may be simple: written to a woman rather than a man, these sonnets were seen as less serious, and hence tacked on to the end of the sequence. (In fact, as I have argued, I think Shakespeare sees them as less serious.) But there is another, related possibility that these sonnets made

a reassuring end to the increasing moral ambiguities of the young man sonnets.

Sonnet 127 speaks to these doubts about fair beauty — the young man's
or Shakespeare's — even as it nostalgically points to the old days when "black
was not counted fair." But many of the sonnets following 127 speak to these
doubts by more readily identifying them in a usual suspect.[89] Shakespeare
ultimately finds it easier to direct the energies of skepticism toward a black
woman who, as the obviously "dark" character in the sonnets, becomes the
embodiment of the wrongs that Shakespeare only more hazily admits that
he, or his fair young man, also commit.[90]

First, there's lying, which Shakespeare frequently associates with the
black mistress. In probably the wittiest of his sonnets, number 138, Shakespeare describes how she lies to him by vowing that she has been faithful.
Yet he lies to her as well when he pretends to believe these vows. Why does
he pretend belief? So that she will think him naïve — and hence a young man
rather than old. In other words, she lies to him about fidelity, and he lies to
her about his age (perhaps significantly, Shakespeare is more concerned about
his age than his own fidelity). The sonnet's final couplet makes sex and the
lovers' mutual deception the same lying together: "Therefore I lie with her,
and she with me, / And in our faults by lies we flattered be." When Shakespeare's self-accusation about lying turns from witty to angry, its resonance
to the young man sonnets — also obsessed with the problem of flattery —
becomes striking. "For I have sworn thee fair — more perjured eye / To swear
against the truth so foul a lie," Shakespeare concludes sonnet 152. These
lines are puzzling, if we think about how Shakespeare writes about the black
mistress. Shakespeare's praises for her black beauty are usually so faint, ironic
or outright sarcastic that they could hardly be the deceiving lies that Shakespeare in these lines admits to with such intensity.

Perhaps Shakespeare called the black mistress "fair," without irony, in
a sonnet we no longer have, or an unrecorded moment of lying seduction.
Still, the guilt and anger in "I have sworn thee fair" also strongly recalls the
sonnets to the young man. Shakespeare does frequently and solemnly praise
the young man for fairness in looks and behavior. It is the young man's sig-
nature quality — even while in several sonnets to the young man Shakespeare
worries that this fairness might be a lie. Whether or not the final accusation
of sonnet 152 is true about the black mistress as well, how satisfying must
it be for Shakespeare to write it, so much more directly, about her rather
than him — a satisfaction the reader could be imagined to share.

Then there's sex. The black mistress' promiscuity recalls various
sonnets in the series that allude to Shakespeare's or the young man's infidelities, including with the black mistress. It also recalls the same possibility

of sexual sin in the love between Shakespeare and the young man, especially in Renaissance England, where same-sex sodomy and heterosex adultery were considered more alike as sinful non-married sex than distinguished as either homosexual or heterosexual: John Rainolds refers to sodomy as "among the kinds of adulterous lewdness."[91] The potential social consequences of the black mistress' sex outside of marriage — the disrupted passing of inheritance from father to legitimate son — likewise shadows the disruption of class boundaries in Shakespeare's love for the young man. If the black mistress were really racially black then the social consequences of her sexual activity — race as well as class mixing — become even more apparent, especially to modern readers who may be more frequently confronted with taboos about cross-race than cross-class sex.[92]

Yet it is the sheer physical sexuality of the black mistress sonnets — their double entendres, their joking or angry complaints about the black mistress' sexual appetite, their compulsive expressions of Shakespeare's own — that most fundamentally express the anxieties that shadow the "fair" young man and Shakespeare's relationship to him. Physical desire, as we have seen, provides a metaphor for a fallen world that the idealism of courtly love or male friendship fails to capture — or intentionally conceals. And sex brings love into time as well as down to earth. The love in the sonnets to the young man lasts forever. The body lives and dies. Sexual desire ties us to that transient body and itself involves sudden physical change. Like other Renaissance poets, Shakespeare is fascinated by the vicissitudes of the penis, which becomes an equivalent of Fortune's Wheel.[93] At the climax, it falls. The grandiloquent expression of sonnet 55 ("Not marble nor the gilded monuments") may seem worlds apart from sonnet 151's bawdy chronicle of erection and detumescence. But their theme is really the same: what changes, what remains. Where sonnet 55 celebrates the love and poetry that endure past the fall of worldly princes, sonnet 151 contemplates the inevitability of change in the human world, signified by the human body in its "expense of spirit."

This change threatens what Shakespeare celebrates as permanent in the sonnets to the young man. At stake is the fate of poetry (or, we might say, of the pen rather than the penis as reproductive instrument), which elevates and eternally commemorates the love between Shakespeare and his beloved. Also at stake is Shakespeare's insistence that his love for the young man is not a time-serving one, that it does not depend on the rise and fall of courtly fortunes. "No, time, thou shalt not boast that I do change!," Shakespeare vows in sonnet 123, promising to be true to the young man. There is no room for sex, with its phallic rises and falls, its intense pleasure "enjoyed no sooner but despised straight," in Shakespeare's promise of fidelity to the young man. Still, inconstancy haunts these sonnets, as when in 56 Shakespeare nervously compares love and "appetite," worrying that that once "hungry eyes" have been satisfied with the sight of the beloved, the "spirit of love" will suffer "a perpetual dullness." So fragile is love in this sonnet that the satisfaction not of lust but only looks can kill it. Why so fragile? Even if Shakespeare did not change his loyalty to the young man, there is no way to guarantee that the socially superior and much admired young man will not change his loyalties to Shakespeare — as he does by sleeping with the black mistress or "marrying" the muse of some rival poet. The intensifying and slackening of sexual desire, registered in the sonnets to the black mistress, express Shakespeare's fear that love will not last.

24

Sonnet 20: A Reprise

Because sonnet 20 describes the young man as part woman, a "master-mistress," readers have focused on whether the sonnet proves or disproves Shakespeare's "homosexuality." Same-sex love in the Renaissance, however, did not depend on the idea that one of the partners in a male homosexual relationship plays the woman's role.[94] The joke about gender-bending in sonnet 20 is less evidence of Shakespeare's same-sex desire than of the way Shakespeare thinks about men and women. The sonnet, which praises the young man by dispraising "false women," exemplifies in a single poem Shakespeare's tendency in the sonnets to cast anxieties about the "fair" young man onto a "dark" woman.

Is Shakespeare being more risqué in sonnet 20 by writing about the young man's penis, or by calling him a woman? In Renaissance England male "effeminacy" was a frequent and damning charge, especially at court.[95] Turning the young man from social superior into gender subordinate, Shakespeare takes pleasure in bringing his "master" down to level of his "mistress." He also acknowledges that calling the young man a woman is not a compliment and insists that the young man is like a woman only in her positive qualities: "A woman's gentle heart, but not acquainted / With shifting change as is false women's fashion; / An eye more bright than theirs, less false in rolling." As in the sonnets to the black mistress, women in this sonnet represent the possibility of deceit and "shifting change" rather than truth and constancy.

Also as in the sonnets to the black mistress, Shakespeare associates men with love and women with sex: "But since she pricked thee out for women's pleasure / Mine be thy love, and thy love's use their treasure." Clearly men's love has the higher value than the "love's use" Shakespeare grants to women. "Use" and "pleasure" describe sex as something fleeting and merely self-gratifying. This is the sex of the black mistress sonnets. How much more ennobling is the generous and lasting "love" that Shakespeare would preserve for himself and the young man.

The word "love" does not exclude sex; it may, as we have seen, euphemize it. Still, sonnet 20 finally tells us less about whether Shakespeare had sex with the young man than about the way Shakespeare manipulates ideas of women in defining his relationship to him. First Shakespeare relieves his insecurity about his lower social status by calling the young man a woman. Then he takes an opposite tack, but one that also relieves this insecurity. Shakespeare emphasizes the young man's difference from women, and the difference between the exalted love of men (in Bush's words), which Shakespeare wishes to enjoy with him, and the fleeting and selfish sexual pleasure that is all Shakespeare expects the young man will enjoy with women. [96]

In writing this way, Shakespeare spiritually elevates his courtly client-patron relationship to the young man. He may be the young man's social inferior, but at least they share an ennobling, white masculinity.[97] Esther Sowerman's comment on the motives for male misogyny is apposite: "He who could devise anything more bitterly or spitefully against our sex hath never wanted [i.e. lacked] the liking, allowance and applause of our giddy-headed people."[98] Writing against women is a cheap way men win applause, presumably from other men whom they wish to impress.

If Shakespeare never had or wished to have sex with the young man, it is certainly not because he celebrates sex with women. At least not in his sonnets. Rather, Shakespeare burdens women with sex. Sometimes men are thought to be homosexual because they hate women. But it is not homosexual desire that prompts the misogyny of the sonnets. Just the opposite. It is the fear of sexual desire in the love between men that prompts Shakespeare to cast those fears onto men's love for women — what E.K. calls gynerasty.

Nor is this only a fear, we need to repeat, of homosexuality in the modern sense. Given the negative associations of sex in the sonnets, and in Renaissance culture more generally, Shakespeare hardly needed the moral imperative against male-male sex to wish to deny his sexual desire for the young man. Sex in the sonnets isn't bad because it's homosexual. It's just bad (unless it's for procreation).

It is ironic that in the centuries since the publication of Shakespeare's sonnets, this poetry has become an icon of heterosexual romance. For it is Shakespeare's sonnets to the young man that are romantic. And it is the sonnets to the woman that speak the fears that romance cannot. In the next section of the book I explore further how readers' understandings of the sonnets have changed over time. The sonnets are historical not only because they are shaped by the history of Shakespeare's own day, but also by the subsequent history of their publication, editing, and interpretation.

SECTION IV

"So Long Lives This"

25

The Sonnets Today

We often think of Shakespeare's sonnets as timeless and universal. But like all literature, they change with the times. The sonnets are as much a part of history in the varying way readers have received them as in the way they were written. Nor are these changing reactions to the sonnets just the product of readers' responses to them. The sonnets have been continually reimagined, from the moment they first saw print. Critics, editors, publishers, other writers and artists — all produce their own versions of the sonnets, often against the grain of text or history, and these reimaginings help to shape readers' responses to them. Their contemporary popularity as heterosexual love poetry is a twentieth-century creation. Their popularity as a whole is an invention of the nineteenth. This section of the book tells the story of how the sonnets only quite recently came to be seen as "the world's greatest love poetry."

In contemporary U.S. popular culture the sonnets are frequently imagined as heterosexual, romantic, and universal. In the 1998 film *Shakespeare in Love* a besotted Joseph Fiennes composes "Shall I compare thee to a summer's day?" (sonnet 18) for Gwyneth Paltrow. *Shakespeare in Love* is committed to a more historical Shakespeare, whom the movie sets to great effect in the down-and-dirty world of Renaissance London and the Elizabethan court. But the movie's historical imagination falters in its recreation of the writing of sonnet 18, one of the sonnets in the group to the young man. The movie glances at this homoerotic complication through Viola's initial cross-dressing. *Shakespeare in Love* avoids suggestions of homoerotic love, however, by quickly making Fiennes' "master-mistress" (sonnet 20) a woman. [1]

The plot of *Shakespeare in Love* also romanticizes the sonnets. It ignores the sonnets' misogyny, melancholy, jealousy, hostility, passive aggression, loneliness, frustration, suspicion of flattery, obscenity, and sometimes downright obscurity. Many of these attitudes appear in the movie and give it its depth and comic appeal. But Gwyneth Paltrow, the recipient of the sonnets, is no black mistress. (In the movie "Rosalind" plays that role.) And the scenes in which Fiennes writes sonnet 18 and Paltrow reads it make a pointed contrast to the otherwise troubled or sordid experience that the movie portrays. The sonnets symbolize the oasis of romantic love between Fiennes and Paltrow that will be troubled by their class difference or by the misogyny of the evil Earl of Wessex. The movie is not completely wrong in representing the sonnet in this fashion. The sonnets are romantic about the power of love — but only with regard to the young man. And even the sonnets to him are not always romantic.

Printed editions of the sonnets similarly frame them as the poetry of heterosexual romance. Men in doublets and hose and women in flowing gowns walk their pages, which come decorated with roses, cherubs and Venuses.[2] Illustrations of lovers embracing in gardens and walks are a long way off from the sonnets that give us Shakespeare writing to his "sweet boy" (sonnet 108), lying awake, alone and jealous in bed (sonnet 61) or attacking his mistress as "the bay where all men ride" (sonnet 137). One edition features sonnet 3 ("Look in thy glass, and tell the face thou viewest") illustrated by a man offering a mirror to a woman. The illustration fits the sonnet's injunction to "look in thy glass," that is, mirror. But it ignores the plain fact that the person so commanded in sonnet 3 must be a man.[3]

This dissonance between Shakespeare's poetry and modern reimaginings reaches a still stranger height in a book released to coincide with the movie *Shakespeare in Love*. Produced by the film's distributor Miramax, *Shakespeare in Love: The Love Poetry of William Shakespeare* features romantic sounding passages from Shakespeare's plays and sonnets, along with stills of Fiennes and Paltrow looking lovingly at one another. What is the reader to make of the picture of Paltrow smiling and about to kiss Fiennes, juxtaposed with sonnet 138, the sonnet that begins "when my love swears that she is made of truth / I do believe her, though I know she lies"?[4] The frame is all, since the sonnet's illustration only succeeds if the sonnet remains unread — at least past the first line and a half.

The lovers that decorate these editions of the sonnets often look Elizabethan or pre–Raphaelite. But this historical distance is costume drama, in which the past provides a quaint romantic atmosphere for a version of the sonnets that strips them from their origins. For the transformation of the sonnets into a story of heterosexual romance goes hand in hand with assertions of their universality, another aspect of the contemporary repackaging of the sonnets. As the "world's greatest love poetry" the sonnets are said to transcend time or place. As one sonnet book puts it on its dust-jacket blurb, "Shakespeare's poetic lines have inspired, and will continue to inspire, hosts of writers, musicians and, of course, lovers."[5] A note "About Shakespeare" in the Miramax *Shakespeare in Love* selection of the sonnets tells us only when the sonnets were published, their number, and that "they retain a remarkable universality of themes expressed in metaphorically rich language."[6]

Certainly the sonnets have wide appeal. The idea of the sonnets' universality becomes troubling, however, when it results in a culturally particular version of the sonnets that claims to be true for all times. Writers, editors and filmmakers not only impose a modern fantasy of heterosexual romance onto the sonnets, but also suggest that this heterosexual romance has always been what everyone feels — including the famous author of the sonnets, even in the face of evidence otherwise. A consultant for the movie *Shakespeare in Love*, the literary critic and Shakespeare biographer Stephen Greenblatt, suggested a homoerotic love plot. Worried about alienating a large part of their commercial audience, the movie's producers demurred.[7]

Though less romanticizing, classroom editions of the sonnets have likewise downplayed or denied their homoeroticism. W.H. Auden, in his introduction to the Signet Classics edition, finds the sonnets to the young man erotic, but subordinates this eroticism to a mystical love. He criticizes the "homosexual reader" who is "uncritically enthusiastic about the first one hundred and twenty-six of the sonnets" while preferring to "ignore those to the Dark Lady in which the relationship is unequivocally sexual." As a reminder about *these* sonnets a man and woman hold hands on the front cover of the edition, even though the young man sonnets outnumber the black mistress sonnets more than four to one.[8] The introduction to the Bantam edition of the Shakespeare' sonnets likewise stresses that only the sonnets to the black mistress refer to "sexual consummation." And it similarly distinguishes between Shakespeare's emotional or spiritual love for the young man (their bond is "extraordinarily strong") and his sexual desire for the woman. This distinction is confirmed by interpretive glosses that provide sexual meanings only in words about the black mistress but not about the young man. The Bantam cover art similarly shifts focus to the smaller number of sonnets to a woman, or pretends that they all are, by taking the rose associated with the young man and giving it to a woman to hold.[9] An edition of Shakespeare's sonnets sponsored by the renowned Folger Shakespeare library — in use from 1967 to 2004 — advises that Shakespeare's love for the young man was "not abnormal," that is, homosexual. Its cover features a beautiful Renaissance lady, adapted from Titian's *Venus of Urbino* (figure 2).[10]

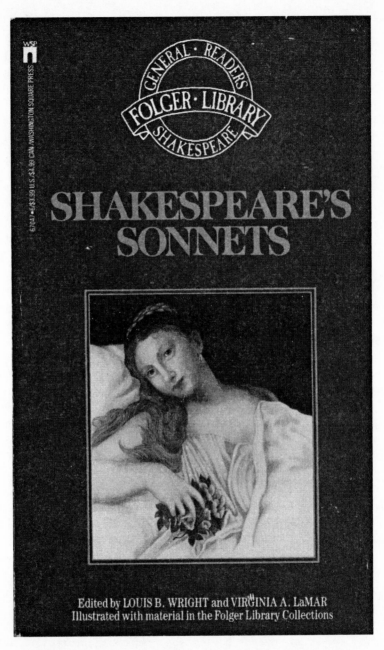

Figure 2: The front cover of this Folger General Readers edition of the sonnets pictures a woman rather than a man. The woman has also been made more ladylike than the sonnets describe her. In fact, she's literally been dressed up, since this picture is adapted from Titian's *Venus of Urbino*, where the woman was originally a nude. This "dressing up" is typical of romanticizations of the sonnets.

Since all three of these editions, the Signet, Bantam and Folger, are meant for students, they introduce Shakespeare's sonnets to many readers for the first time. Their skewed portrayals of the sonnets are just beginning to change. As part of a gradual updating of its editions of Shakespeare's work, the Folger Library in 2004 replaced its previous *Shakespeare's Sonnets*. This New Folger Library edition no longer find it necessary to give Shakespeare a clean bill of sexual health. Still, even this new edition provides mixed messages about the centrality of homoeroticism to the sonnets. Its introduction cautions against assuming that the sex of the beloved is identifiable in most of the sonnets, while an essay following the sonnets argues against that position.[11] The cover art of the New Folger edition, which features the words "Shakespeare's Sonnets" written out in flowing cursive, is consistent with the style of the New Folger Shakespeare series as a whole. Nonetheless, this cover also obscures the sex of the sonnets' chief recipient.

Of all the editions of Shakespeare's sonnets that I know of, only the 2000 Cambridge School edition puts a man on the cover. This edition features a miniature portrait by Nicholas Hilliard, who also painted "Young man among the roses." Called "Unknown man against the flame," the portrait is of a fashionable young man, white shirt loosely covering his chest and open almost to his navel, a dangling earring, locket in hand, and a suggestive glance. Flames of love shoot out in the portrait's background. Is he the lover or the beloved? This cover reminds us that our ideas of the sonnets are changing. They always have.

26

From "Sweet Boy" to "Sweet Love"

How much have readers' ideas about the sonnets changed? The sonnets today are now among Shakespeare's most popular works, so much so that it is often imagined that they have always been admired. In their own day, however, and for nearly two hundred years after, the sonnets were among Shakespeare's least popular works. The first edition of Shakespeare's sonnets was printed once in 1609 and then, as one critic has put it, "sank without a trace."[12] There was no new edition of the sonnets for over thirty years. During this same period Shakespeare's other poetry — now relatively obscure — was wildly popular. His *Venus and Adonis*, first published in 1593, was republished 16 times by 1638, including 3 editions after 1609. Another narrative poem, *The Rape of Lucrece*, first published a year later, went through 7 editions during this time, including, like *Venus and Adonis*, 3 editions following 1609.[13]

The sonnets similarly failed to inspire other writers of the time. Scholars have found few verbal borrowings from them in the seventeenth century. A study of direct references to Shakespeare's work from 1591 to 1700 records that of his writings the sonnets came in nearly last. (They do beat *Love's Labour's Won*, a play "by" Shakespeare that may never have been written.) *Venus and Adonis*, on the other hand, comes in fourth, and *Rape of Lucrece* comes in sixth.[14] The record of manuscript circulation of Shakespeare's sonnets tells a similar story. There are no surviving manuscript copies of Shakespeare's sonnets from the sixteenth century and relatively few from the seventeenth. Their scarcity contrasts with the poetry of Shakespeare's contemporaries, such as John Donne, Ben Jonson and Walter Ralegh.[15]

Literary historians have speculated that the scandalous content of the sonnets is responsible for these absences. Once the 1609 quarto was published, the argument goes, Shakespeare or the nobleman to whom the sonnets were addressed persuaded the authorities to call the sonnets in and forbid their further sale.[16] Or perhaps the sonnets were not actually censored, but readers shunned them because they found their sexualizing of the language of friendship disturbing — especially in describing Shakespeare's relationship to someone who was not his social equal. Or perhaps the problem was not homoeroticism at all but the lewd and angry poems to the black mistress.[17]

More likely, neither sexual scandal was responsible for the initial lack of response to Shakespeare's sonnets. 1609 may just have been a bad year to publish them. Lyric poetry — the poetry of personal expression — became less popular in the early seventeenth century, at least in print form, its rate of publication clearly falling from its sixteenth-century heights.[18] The tide turned particularly against sonnets, which in the 1590s had become so fashionable that by the end of the decade they provoked the fatigue and ridicule that often end fads.[19]

Shakespeare himself expressed this ridicule, early on. In *Love's Labour's Lost*, often thought to have been written around 1595, the writers of sonnets are witless narcissists who do not get their girls at play's end. We might have expected Shakespeare's own sonnets to be more successful than those of his inept lovers. They did have advantages. There was Shakespeare's contemporary fame as a playwright. And the edginess of many of these sonnets would have had greater appeal to an early seventeenth-century audience.[20] But neither Shakespeare's name nor his sonnets' more fashionable style seem to have ensured their fame.

Shakespeare, or the publisher of his sonnets, would probably not have been surprised that the sonnets did not achieve immediate fame. Despite what the pages of the book grandly declared, the 1609 *Shakespeare's Sonnets* appears to have been designed for an ordinary rather than an eternal summer. As was often the case with lyric poetry, *Shakespeare's Sonnets* was published in quarto format, the flimsiest of book types. It was just papers held together with string. Poetry published in this manner literally did not last — nor was it expected to.[21] And when in 1623 John Heminges and Henry Condell edited the first Works edition of Shakespeare, the more prestigious, and durable, folio-sized volume contained only his plays.[22]

The sonnets finally saw print again in 1640 when the publisher John Benson sought to give Shakespeare's poetry the grand presentation that Heminges and Condell had given to the plays. The entrepreneurial Benson, who around the same time was also bringing out unpublished work by Ben Jonson, collected the sonnets and other poetry by Shakespeare no longer in print, just as Heminges and Condell had gathered together all of Shakespeare's plays. His more elaborate presentation of Shakespeare's poetry — front matter included a portrait of Shakespeare and commendatory verses — also echoed the Works editions of Shakespeare's plays. Even the octavo format in which Benson published the sonnets was sturdier and more prestigious. Benson glanced at the wish to give Shakespeare's poetry a presentation equal to his plays when he observed, in the preface to his edition, that Shakespeare's poems had failed to achieve "proportionable glory, with the rest of his everliving Works."[23] If not ever-living, Benson's *Poems* did have staying power. For almost 150 years it remained the most influential edition of the sonnets.[24]

But nothing, the sonnets warn us, achieves permanence: Time's fell hand defaces all. The agent of Time in this case was Benson, who radically altered what he preserved. Notoriously, Benson rearranged the 1609 quarto's order of sonnets, as well as added poems from *The Passionate Pilgrim* (1599), a pirated edition of poetry by Shakespeare (including versions of sonnets 138 and 144) and others. Benson often ran sonnets together in groups of up to five — violating what now seems their all but sacred sonnet form. Readers of Benson's edition would not first encounter sonnets urging the young man to marry. Benson leads off with sonnets 67 to 69 run together under the title "The Glory of Beauty." Then follows a second group, comprised of sonnets 60 and 63 to 66, under the new title "Injurious Time." In the process of rearranging the sonnets Benson left out eight of them altogether, for reasons that remain unclear. [25] These include sonnet 18 ("Shall I compare thee?"). Even if Benson omitted 18 accidentally it's worth noting that this sonnet, so favored today, did not seem compelling enough to Benson to keep him from missing it.

More notoriously, Benson changed some of the male nouns and pronouns in the sonnets to female or gender neutral ones. The last line of sonnet 101, "To make him seem long hence as he shows now," becomes "To make her seem long hence as she shows now." Sonnet 108's "sweet boy" becomes "sweet love." Similarly, some of the titles Benson gave to the sonnets written to the young man suggested that they had been written to a woman. For example, sonnets 113 to 115 are grouped together under the title "Self Flattery of Her Beauty," and sonnet 125 is "An Intreaty for Her Acceptance."[26]

Why Benson sometimes changed the gender of the sonnets' recipient is controversial. These changes have been interpreted as marking the end of the Renaissance acceptance of male love, or to suggest that even by Renaissance standards the friendship of the sonnets was too obsessive, too eroticized, and too fraught with differences of age and class for Benson's comfort. More recently, some critics have contested the view that Benson begins the sonnets long (and, as we'll see, not always steady) march to heterosexual romance. They point to the fact that Benson let stand more nouns or pronouns pointing to a male beloved than he changed. And his new arrangement of the sonnet order began the sequence with sonnets clearly addressed to a man as, it might be added, did the 1609 edition. This fact has led one critic to reverse received wisdom and argue that Benson preferred the sonnets' homoeroticism over their sordid and socially transgressive portrayal of the black mistress.[27]

I believe the case for Benson's incipient heterosexualization of the sonnets is stronger. Some of the opening sonnets in Benson's edition obviously have a male recipient but they are not pointedly erotic — at least not to the Renaissance reader accustomed to affectionate language between men. Benson might have associated these sonnets with the tradition of elegy, an important form during the Renaissance. Elegies contained moralizing complaints about the times, lavished sonnet-like praise on their (often male) subjects and were sometimes written in sonnet form.[28] The two sonnets that open the edition describe the young man in elegiac terms as the last vestige of better days. The title under which they are grouped, "The Glory of Beauty," while stressing physical appearance, is philosophical rather than personal.

A third sonnet clearly written to a man follows in the next grouping of sonnets in Benson's edition. Sonnet 63 concerns the deaths of the beloved and the speaker. Its vow to preserve the memory of its subject ("His beauty shall in these black lines be seen, / And they shall live, and he in them still green") echoes the promises of sonnet lovers writing to women, and there is an erotic aspect to Shakespeare's invocation of his "sweet love's beauty." Yet the title given to the group including this sonnet, "Injurious Time," is even more abstract than the title given to the first. With its shadow of death hanging over all, sonnet 63 is not especially sexy. Including the sonnet in a group that emphasizes the destructive effects of time, Benson calls attention to this aspect of sonnet 63. Again he seems to have understood this group in elegiac rather than erotic terms. A seventeenth-century annotator of a copy of Benson's edition at the Folger Shakespeare library saw these sonnets similarly, retitling them "Eternity of verse, spight of Injurious Time that destroys all things else."[29]

The sonnets in which Benson altered pronouns come later in his edition and follow groupings of sonnets with titles that more frequently imply a lover's pursuit (for example: "A request to his scornfull Love."[30]) Benson may have taken for granted the sonnets' affectionate address of the young man, in a way typical for the Renaissance, but altered sonnets in which the literary styles of courtly love and male friendship appeared to him too mingled.[31] That such changes are relatively few — they number five — may be because Benson assumed the gender neutral sonnets were written to a woman.[32] Moreover, although Benson's alterations of gender are small in number so too are the number of times he altered entire words, rather than changes he could have viewed as correcting the quarto's many spelling errors. That almost half these instances involve words relating to the gender of the beloved suggests Benson found the issue significant.[33]

But not central: Benson's handling of references to the young man in the *Poems* may reflect Renaissance standards of publication no more preoccupied with editorial care than the Renaissance understanding of sexuality was preoccupied with gender choice. Benson did correct obvious typographical errors in the 1609 edition of the sonnets. But whole sonnets in Benson's edition appear in groups to which they clearly do not belong and many group titles are inaccurate.[34] So when Benson let stand Shakespeare's description of his beloved in sonnet 110 as a "god in love" did that mean he accepted this masculine deity, didn't notice it, or misunderstood the phrase? The difference between "he" and "she" (or god and goddess) — so important to the sexual and editorial expectations of modern readers — might have been to Benson one more detail to which he paid only partial attention.[35]

Whatever Benson intended, we know that other readers in the seventeenth and eighteenth centuries did turn the male beloved into a female. One reader who copied Shakespeare's sonnet 68 ("Thus is his cheek the map of days outworn") from the *Poems* altered the male pronouns that Benson did not to either neuter ones ("thee," "thy") or to a female "she." Two instances of sonnet 106 ("When in the chronicle of wasted time") copied into seventeenth-century verse miscellanies were headed "On his Mistress's Beauty." The most frequently copied sonnet in the seventeenth century was often given titles suggesting a female beloved. Of the thirteen manuscript copies of Sonnet 2 ("When forty winters shall besiege thy brow"), one has the title "A Lover to his Mistress" and four more are headed "To One that Would Die a Maid."[36]

Even more decisive about the sex of the sonnets' beloved was an edition published in 1711. It was titled *One Hundred and Fifty-Four Sonnets, All of Them in Praise of His Mistress*. Hyder Rollins, the sonnets' most indefatigable editor, has suggested that the "Mistress" in the title of this edition reflects the influence of Benson's *Poems*. If it doesn't, we have an even stronger example of the reluctance during this time to read any of the sonnets as being written to a man, since this 1711 edition followed the 1609 quarto. It had none of the misleading alterations of sex introduced by Benson.

Benson has long been blamed for the changes he made to the sonnets. How could this now anonymous publisher have dared to alter Shakespeare's words? The question isn't fair. Benson was acting in accord with the assumptions of his time. After all, until the end of the eighteenth century Benson's edition formed the basis for most subsequent publication of Shakespeare's sonnets, even after editions that more closely followed the 1609 quarto became available again. Benson's edition satisfied his readers' expectations.[37] These readers would not have expected to see the sonnets treated as hallowed texts in which no word must be other than that we suppose Shakespeare wrote. Benson could readily alter the sonnets because Shakespeare, though an admired playwright and author, had not achieved cult status. His works were not yet "sacred objects" to be venerated but not profaned.[38]

The sonnets were not only not sacred, they were being ignored. Benson may have changed the sonnets, but his edition at least made available in some form the poetry just left out of the early "Complete" Works of Shakespeare. In fact, this edition marks Shakespeare's rising star. Its publication suggests that it has become important to put into print, in a format more lasting than the flimsy 1609 quarto, anything that Shakespeare wrote. The assumption that Shakespeare is so great an author that his texts must be published with complete accuracy will come later.[39]

No matter how popular the sonnets, moreover, neither Benson nor his readers would have seen his changes to them as tampering with an author's unique vision. This is how we often understand literature today, but it was not yet generally prized in these terms. The title of Benson's edition — *Poems: Written by William Shakespeare, Gent*— marks the difference between a Renaissance sense of authorship and our own. Not genius, but gent. Imagine a modern edition of Shakespeare announcing in its title that the writer is a gentleman. What would being a gentleman — an elite, social, inherited, and traditional identity — have to do with what we now regard as the creative, self-expressive, custom-busting power of the poet?

For Benson and his contemporaries, however, being a good writer and being a gentleman went together, because they believed that good writing came from and expressed good social standing. Benson praises Shakespeare's sonnets for being "elegantly plain" and "perfect eloquence," as if Shakespeare were giving dinner-table speeches rather than allowing readers to overhear his most difficult private experience. Plain and eloquent speech are the gentleman's accomplishments, not lyric utterance or idiosyncratic self-expression.

Changes Benson made to the sonnets similarly reflect this view of the poet as decorous rather than self-expressive. His reordering and titling of them made their already fuzzy personal story even more difficult to discern. Rather than self-revelation, Benson's editorial changes emphasized a set of mannered literary poses, with sonnets regrouped under titles such as "A Bashful Lover," "A Lover's Affection Though His Love Prove Unconstant," "A Lover's Excuse for His Long Absence." The speaker of the sonnets becomes not Shakespeare but a generic lover, performing actions that any suitor in the courtly style might.[40] For the same reason, Benson felt free to join to the end of the *Poems* the verse of other men contemporary and near contemporary with Shakespeare who were especially associated with courtly elegance and gentility. In doing so the *Poems* do not stress Shakespeare's individual genius, as we usually do today, but the opposite: Shakespeare becomes a member of a circle of genteel, court-centered poets.[41]

Since the sonnets exemplified a genteel style, it was more acceptable for others, who shared that style, to change Shakespeare's poetry — which belonged to the literary circle as well as to any one member of it. Art was a communal activity. Renaissance readers copied and passed on work they admired, building personal collections and arranging the work of many authors as they saw fit — their iPod was the commonplace book. They often altered this work as they copied it, either inadvertently or as part of their own participation in a circle of writers and readers.[42]

Publishers participated in this circulation of writers' work by making manuscript collections available in print to a wider audience. They also made changes to that work, a practice that followed the precedent of manuscript circulation. Authors lacked control over such alterations, since at the time there was no strong copyright protection for them. Publishers like Benson had to be careful about the rights not of authors, but of other publishers, who were the focus of laws regarding the protection of copyright. Authors did not have the privileged place in the production of their work that they now enjoy.[43]

It's worth considering, however, that the situation of Shakespeare's sonnets has changed less from 1640 to the present than might first appear. To be sure, editors are now much more concerned to stay true to Shakespeare's words. Their changes most frequently involve modernizing Renaissance spelling and punctuation, or fixing obvious mistakes made in the setting of the sonnets' first edition for printing. No modern editor fails to fix, usually silently, the printer's error that rendered in 1609 "Lou's not times fool" what we always read as sonnet 116's "Love's not time's fool" (a boon for lovers over the world, but a blow for Lous). More substantive changes to the 1609 sonnets are usually identified by the editor.[44] But accurate reproduction of Shakespeare's words — or rather, those words as the 1609 quarto reproduced them — is only one aspect of an edition of the sonnets. Even with texts that remain closer than Benson to the words and sonnet arrangement of 1609, editions like the Signet, Bantam or Folger Sonnets, with their cover art and editorial comment, transform the poetry in ways just as substantial as Benson's *Poems*.

27

"Piteous Constraint to Read Such Stuff"

Wrong-headed or not, Benson's changes to the sonnets, and his praise of them as "serene, clear, and elegantly plain" did not save their reputation.[45] For nearly 200 years the story about the sonnets was the same: readers didn't like them. In the seventeenth and eighteenth centuries readers frequently ignored or condemned them. Most editors of Shakespeare during this period left all his poetry, including the sonnets, out of their editions of Shakespeare's works. Shakespeare was esteemed as a dramatist. The poetry, when it appeared, was equivocally published as supplemental volumes, sometimes unauthorized, to existing editions of Shakespeare's plays. The poetry was half in, half out, of the Shakespeare canon.[46]

Editors who included the poetry in their editions from the start sometimes found it necessary to justify their decision.[47] Francis Gentleman, who edited a 1774 Works of Shakespeare, explains to his readers that he has included the poetry not because it is good, but for the sake of completion.

> If Shakespeare's merit, as a poet, a philosopher, or a man, was to be estimated from his Poems, though they possess many instances of powerful genius, he would, in every point of view, sink beneath himself, in these characters. Many of his subjects are trifling, his versification mostly laboured and quibbling, with too great a degree of licentiousness.[48]

But because he has promised to provide an "entire edition" of Shakespeare's works, and because he wants to avoid "prudery," Gentleman has allowed "some passages to remain, which we are ourselves as far from approving, as the most scrupulous of our readers."[49]

Six years later an edition of the sonnets edited by Edmond Malone, a prominent Irish lawyer turned man-of-letters, brought to a head the question of their place in the Shakespeare canon. Like other editions of the sonnets during the seventeenth and eighteenth centuries, Malone's 1780 sonnets first appeared as part of a collection of Shakespeare's poetry intended to supplement an already published set of Shakespeare's plays, this one edited by George Steevens and Samuel Johnson. But Malone's work was pioneering in his commitment to using the earliest printed editions of Shakespeare's writings, and in his detailed historical investigations of Shakespeare's life as a context for understanding them. Unlike previous editors who produced supplemental volumes of Shakespeare's poetry, Malone used for his text of the sonnets the 1609 quarto rather than Benson's 1640 *Poems*, as he did again when he included the sonnets in his own 1790 Complete Works of Shakespeare. Malone also gave to the sonnets the serious editorial attention that previously only Shakespeare's plays had received. Two other editions from the eighteenth century that broke ranks with Benson to follow the 1609 quarto lacked either annotation or influence.[50]

The publication of the sonnets with detailed notes by a major editor might have indicated a new, higher valuation of them. But the tone of these notes was not laudatory. Readers of Malone's edition of the sonnets would find not veneration, but a debate between Malone and Steevens over the merits of the sonnets, carried out in notes beneath them. Each note carried the name of Steevens or Malone as its contributor. The first in the edition was by Steevens, who calls the final two lines of sonnet 1 ("From fairest creatures we desire increase") nonsensical and laments his "piteous constraint, to read such stuff." The edition that reintroduced the sonnets to the world is filled with these complaints. "Such laboured perplexities of language, and such studied deformities of style, prevail throughout these sonnets," Steevens writes about a line in sonnet 30 ("When to the sessions of sweet silent thought").[51] And so on.

Malone defends the sonnets, but without the same energy with which Steevens attacks them. He more frequently justifies their shortcomings than praises their merits. In response to Steevens' complaint about the obscurity of sonnet 1 Malone grants that the couplet is "quaintly expressed" and merely suggests that the couplet's "obscurity rises chiefly ... from the awkward collocation of words for the sake of the rhyme." Elsewhere Malone grants that the sonnets sometimes contain "far-fetched conceits," but so, he observes, do the plays, the meaning of which the sonnets help illuminate. He acknowledges that some of the sonnets are not as "simple and clear" as they should be but points out that others are written with "perspicuity and energy." None of this is the high praise lavished on the sonnets today. As Malone himself writes, "I do not feel any great propensity to stand forth as the champion of these compositions." He is just able to muster the reply that the sonnets have been "somewhat under-rated."[52]

The debate played out in the notes to Malone's edition of the sonnets reflects in part a different relationship among critic, reader and author in the eighteenth century. A modern reader comes to an edition of the sonnets, as with other now canonized literary texts, assured of their value (usually in an introduction) by a professional critic. The reader, on the other hand, is usually not an expert. The attitude encouraged by the edition is one of reverence for the author, and deference to the critic. In the eighteenth century, critics were not yet professionally trained as such, and ordinary readers were encouraged to develop opinions about the works they read, to become, in effect, critics themselves. Of course, it helped that the number of readers in the eighteenth century was relatively small, so that confidence in their ability to make judgments was also a product of the exclusion of many who did not judge at all.[53] Malone's edition of Shakespeare reflected these different sensibilities. The conversation in the notes, rather than instructing the reader and paying tribute to the author, exemplified and encouraged active participation in the evaluation of a literary text. Sometimes in eighteenth-century editions of Shakespeare these conversations take up more space on the page than Shakespeare's own writing.[54]

The conversations were not always polite. Editors freely quoted and attacked one another in the prefaces to their editions. Alexander Pope, who produced a 1725 edition of Shakespeare, took revenge on another Shakespeare editor, Lewis Theobald, by naming him King of Dullness in his mock-epic poem *The Dunciad* ("Old puns restore, lost blunders nicely seek / And crucify poor Shakespear once a week").[55] The friendship between Steevens and Malone, strained by their competition as editors of Shakespeare, broke down completely when Malone, about to publish his own, new edition of Shakespeare (the 1790 *Plays and Poems of William Shakespeare*) fought with Steevens over how their notes would appear in it. Malone had offered Steevens the final word in the notes to his new edition. But he reserved the right to change notes he had previously written, if Steevens had convinced him the notes were incorrect. Steevens, however, wished these notes to appear unchanged, "with all their imperfections on their head" (as Claudius kills his brother, King Hamlet). When Malone refused to reprint these notes without revision, Steevens "declared that all communication on the subject of Shakespeare was at an end between them."[56]

The sonnets provided fit ground for these sort of acrimonious debates over literary value. Since Shakespeare's reputation was more closely connected to his work as a dramatist, it was easier to doubt the value of his poetry. While Malone included that poetry in his 1790 *Plays and Poems of William Shakespeare*, Steevens, now Malone's rival, pointedly refused to reproduce Shakespeare's sonnets or other poetry in his 1793 *Plays* of Shakespeare. "We have not reprinted the *Sonnets* &c. of Shakespeare," Steevens wrote, "because the strongest act of Parliament that could be framed would fail to compel readers into their service."[57]

Nathan Drake, author of a set of essays on reading called *Literary Hours*, agreed. He criticized Malone for including the sonnets in his edition of Shakespeare and praised Steevens for *excluding* them from his. Steevens has acted, Drake writes, "with greater judgment in forbearing to obtrude such crude efforts upon the public eye; for where is the utility of propagating compositions which no one can endure to read."[58] As late as 1810 Alexander Chalmers in his *Works of the English Poets* could write that Shakespeare's poems "have never been favourites with the public, and have seldom been reprinted with his plays." He observed that Steevens' criticisms of Shakespeare's poetry, though "severe," represented the general opinion of the reading public.[59]

When Malone's protégé and literary executor James Boswell (son of Johnson's Boswell) published his important edition of 1821, which collected the fruits of the previous' century's scholarship and ran to twenty-one volumes, he restored Shakespeare's poetry to it. His defense of doing so, however, first took up the argument for completion. "The editor who undertakes to publish Shakespeare, is bound to present the reader with all his works." Moreover, Boswell continued, these poems were "youthful performances," and though they could not compare to great plays like *Othello* and *Macbeth*— written by the mature Shakespeare — they were "entitled to a high rank among the lighter productions of our poetry" and would not "suffer much" in comparison to the earlier dramas such as *The Two Gentleman of Verona* or *The Comedy of Errors*.[60]

Shakespeare's sonnets of all his poetry were at a particular disadvantage because the sonnet as a poetic form had fallen out of favor during the eighteenth century. The preferred poetry of the time reflected Enlightenment values of reason and order. It was, moreover, public poetry: the epic, the verse essay, poetic satire. And it was modern. The sonnet frustrated all these expectations. Its small size seemed to impose arbitrary limits on expression, as well as instance what the age would have called "false wit": elaborate rhetorical ornament substituting for reasonable discourse. The customary subject of the sonnet, passionate, frustrated love, was hardly an exercise in reason. Nor was it a matter of public interest. And the sonnet's popularity during the great age of absolute monarchs rendered it suspect to an age (as it saw itself) of commerce and rational thought.[61]

The sonnet, a writer declared in a 1789 issue of the *New London Magazine*, "appears in a state of almost rusticated barbarism, or refined absurdity." The sonnet's "studious turn of phrase and abstract conceits," are "totally repugnant to true poetry, and its genuine principles of harmony." Another commentator, in 1803, declares of a collection of sonnets that "a few of them are good, good at least for sonnets," since most poems of this kind "are little better than ravings ... aped by hysterical affectation, or drivelling incoherencies, lisped by sentiment in her dotage, than which nothing can be conceived more hostile to genuine poetry."[62]

Steevens' debate with Malone reflected this eighteenth-century appraisal of the sonnet. In a note to sonnet 54 Steevens objects that the "canker," or dog rose, does not in fact, as the sonnet states, "have full as deep a dye / As the perfumèd tincture of the roses." Unmoved by the verse's imagery, Steevens soberly complains that Shakespeare had "not yet begun to observe the productions of nature with accuracy.... But what," Steevens asks, "has truth or nature to do with Sonnets?" Elsewhere Steevens remarks that the approval of a sonnet is assured as soon as its "admirers ... have counted their expected and statutable proportion of rhymes" and, echoing a nationalism that also frequently accompanies eighteenth-century criticism of the sonnet, he wishes that the form had "expired in the country [Italy] where it was born."[63]

And Shakespeare's sonnets had a third strike against them. Most appeared to be written to a man. Benson's influential *Poems* somewhat obscured this recognition. Malone's edition, which removed Benson's titles and restored the sonnets to their original order and text, did not. Nor did Malone simply ignore the young man of the sonnets, as did Lintott's 1711 edition, even though it was based on the 1609 quarto. Malone was the first editor to suggest a break between sonnets about a man and sonnets about a woman at 126/127 — a break that took 150 years to identify but that has generally prevailed to this day.[64]

Three strikes and you're out. Thomas Warton, author of the influential *History of English Poetry* (1774–1781), suggested the sonnets would lose "their impropriety and give pleasure without disgust" only if the reader were to imagine the first 126 sonnets "of our divine dramatist as written by a lady": for they are "addressed with more of fondness than friendship, to a beautiful youth." Steevens likewise records his special revulsion that Shakespeare has written his sonnets to a man. In a note to sonnet 20 ("A woman's face with nature's own hand painted") he writes that "it is impossible to read this fulsome panegyric, addressed to a male object, without an equal mixture of disgust and indignation."[65] The hysterical affectation and lisped sentiment of the sonnet are bad enough — worse if that affectation and sentiment are directed to a man.

Malone defended Shakespeare on this point, though again not whole-heartedly. "Such addresses to men, however indelicate, were customary in our author's time, and neither imported criminality, nor were esteemed indecorous."[66] The crime raised and denied, of course, is sodomy. By the late eighteenth century, as the modern nuclear family becomes increasingly central, Malone finds even the casual homoeroticism of Shakespeare's day disturbing.[67] Benson saw Shakespeare's sonnets in terms of friendship or courtly love: marriage was unimportant. The longest commentary in Malone's edition, by contrast, was a debate between him and Steevens over whether Shakespeare was jealous of his wife.

Malone's reply to Steevens regarding sonnet 20 initiates what has long since been one of the ways editors of the sonnets have dodged their homoeroticism: it was customary for men to write that way back then.[68] The same impulse toward historical accuracy that drove Malone to reedit the sonnets according to the original 1609 quarto would also, Malone believed, save the sonnets from accusations of indecorum or crime.[69] But Malone does not appear completely reassured. In a separate note to this sonnet he floats the idea that the sonnet's "master-mistress" might mean a "sovereign mistress," an unusually bad gloss for Malone, given that the sonnet turns on (as Shakespeare is turned on by) the young man's female attributes. Moreover, elsewhere Malone grants that one of the sonnets' defects is their failure to be directed to a female, to whom "alone such ardent expressions of esteem could with propriety be addressed."[70]

Similarly troubled by the sonnets' male beloved, Malone's protégé Boswell would add a second dodge of homoeroticism, one that also has a long editorial tradition.[71] In the preface to his 1821 edition of the sonnets Boswell argues that Shakespeare does not speak "in his own person." Rather, the sonnets are fictions, works of poetry and imagination, "written upon various topics for the amusement of a private circle."[72] Why Shakespeare's "private circle" took pleasure in the imitated declarations of one man's love for another, Boswell does not say. In any case, this suggestion that the sonnets were merely fictions would have to compete with the contrary tendency in the nineteenth century to emphasize that in the sonnets Shakespeare does indeed "speak in his own person." In fact, Boswell was probably responding to the growing opinion that the sonnets were autobiographical.[73] These autobiographical readings helped renew interest in the sonnets, which during the nineteenth century finally became popular.

28

A Lover and a Man

What is a poet? We often imagine someone who writes from the heart, whose poetry is as much a product of a deep need for self-expression as it is a formal art. This poet is quirky or tortured, a rebel, an inhabitant of society's margins rather than its respectable center. But what is marginal is also exceptional. The poet is a visionary, a genius, a prophet who utters truths that challenge convention.

The poet so imagined is largely a product of the Romantic movement in early nineteenth-century Europe. During the Romantic period poetry left salons and satire for the woods and lyricism. Espousing rules gave way to encounters with madness. Feeling came first. The great Romantic poet William Wordsworth wrote an epic poem not about the fall of Troy (Homer), the founding of Rome (Virgil) or the fall of man (Milton)—but about himself. And the sonnets became Shakespeare's great poetry of self. "With this key / Shakespeare unlocked his heart," Wordsworth declared of the sonnets.[74]

The ground for this new, autobiographical reading of the sonnets had been encouraged by Malone, who in the notes to his edition of the sonnets repeatedly identified the speaker of them with Shakespeare. The notes similarly treat the other figures in the sonnets as real people and speculate on their identities. Was Mr. "W.H." William Hart, Shakespeare's nephew? Or was he W. Hughes, an identification made by working from proper nouns presumed to be hidden in the sonnets? Did the beginning of sonnet 93, "So shall I live supposing thou art true / Like a deceivèd husband," reveal that Shakespeare was jealous of his wife? Malone's edition was the first to raise these sorts of questions about the sonnets, now so familiar—and fundamental, fascinating or infuriating, depending on your point of view. The sonnets' "I" had ceased to be Benson's generic "lover." They were now pointedly framed as a record — however enigmatic — of Shakespeare's feelings and experience.[75]

Prominent men and women of letters declared the same. The German Romantic critic August Wilhelm Schlegel observed in 1811: "These sonnets paint most unequivocally the actual situations and sentiments of the poet; they make us acquainted with the passions of the man; they even contain remarkable confessions of his youthful errors."[76] Wordsworth similarly wrote in 1815 that "there is extant a small Volume of miscellaneous Poems in which Shakespeare expresses his own feelings in his own Person." He goes on to criticize Steevens' shallow response to the "beauties" of the sonnets, in which Shakespeare (like a good Romantic poet) was able to encompass as nowhere else in his works "a greater number of exquisite feelings felicitously expressed."[77] The essayist Anna Jameson praised the autobiographical sonnets for making a God-like Shakespeare flesh: "It is not Shakespeare as a great power bearing a great name, — but Shakespeare in his less divine and less known character, — as a lover and a man, who finds a place here. The only writings he has left through which we can trace any thing of his personal feelings and affections, are his Sonnets."[78]

While this celebration of selfhood and individual genius was an elite, intellectual phenomenon it was also a popular one. Something like the culture of celebrity in the modern U.S., early nineteenth-century England developed cults of celebrity around authors such as Shelley and Byron, whose private lives were made public not only in their poetry, but through gossip, autograph hounding, voyeurism (complete with telescopes), and pilgrimages to authors' homes. One publisher defended his newspaper's promotion of interest in poets' private lives by remarking that "personalities, among fashionable people, are the very best ingredient in a morning newspaper." Advances in printing and commerce helped fuel this fascination with authorial private lives. More books to buy meant more fame, and more interesting personalities sold more books, magazines and newspapers — not to mention what we might now call "spin-off" products — while the growing distance between readers and writers in that very marketplace intensified curiosity about the hidden lives of famous writers.[79] But there was no living Shakespeare for his fans to pursue. If admirers wanted to discover "Shakespeare's less known character" they could, as Jameson advises, "trace ... his personal feelings and affections" through the sonnets.

Trace they did. While Malone's notes to the sonnets had prompted brief guesses about the identity of figures in the sonnets, during the early nineteenth century the speculation began in earnest. Both of the nobles still considered the most likely candidates were proposed during this period. Nathan Drake, now converted to an admiration of the sonnets, published in 1817 *Shakespeare and His Times*, which provided a detailed argument for identifying the young man with Henry Wriothesley, Earl of Southampton. Anna Jameson in her *Memoirs of the Loves of the Poets* (first published 1829) also identified Wriothesley as the young man. Though frustrated in similarly identifying the black mistress, she declared her conviction that the sonnets to her are "inspired by the real object of a real passion." James Boaden countered the Southampton theory with the publication of his *On the Sonnets of Shakespeare* (1837), which proposed the first full-scale argument for identifying the young man with William Herbert, Earl of Pembroke. Arguments in favor of either of these two major candidates, and many minor ones, would dominate and then dog nineteenth-century criticism of the sonnets.[80]

The new appeal of the sonnets in the Romantic period was aesthetic too. The cultural shifts that prompted a new and more positive reading of the sonnets as autobiography also encouraged a newly positive evaluation of the sonnet form. Wordsworth's much quoted pronouncement that "with this key / Shakespeare unlocked his heart" came from a sonnet written in that form's defense. Most of the Romantic poets wrote sonnets (except for Byron, who still considered sonnets "puling, petrifying, stupidly platonic compositions"). In fact, the form became so popular in the first decade of the nineteenth century that, as in the seventeenth, it began to generate its own backlash.[81]

The extravagant emotion that disgusted the Enlightenment critics of the sonnet captivated the inward-looking poets of the Romantic era. The shortness of the sonnet form, rather than an arbitrary limit, was now seen to facilitate the intensity of the emotional experience. It also suited the Romantic interest in discovering the large in the small, the whole in the part. The sonnet was a small key that nevertheless unlocked a great heart. Wordsworth wrote of Shakespeare's "exquisite" sonnets that they were "treasures contained in ... little pieces." His friend and collaborator the poet Samuel Taylor Coleridge similarly praised the sonnets for being "so rich in metre, so full of thought and *exquisitest* diction." The sonnets are teeming with riches and fullness on the jeweler's fine scale.[82]

Though Coleridge admired the sonnets as works of art, and assumed they expressed Shakespeare's personal voice, he worried over their content. The biographical approach to the sonnets generated controversy not only about the identity of their addressees, but also about the feelings they seemed to reveal. When Drake identified the young man with the Earl of Southampton, he followed Malone in assuring his readers that in the Renaissance "the language of love and friendship was mutually convertible." That Shakespeare was expressing friendship for a great lord and patron explained for Drake the intensity of the sonnets' affection and admiration for the young man.[83]

Coleridge was more troubled. In a note written in the margins of a poetry anthology containing some of Shakespeare's sonnets, Coleridge promises his six-year-old son Hartley that one day these sonnets "will help to explain the mind of Shakespeare," who felt a "pure love" for the young man, a love that he appears "to have been in no way ashamed of ... or even to have suspected that others could have suspected it." Observing that Shakespeare's plays contain "not even an allusion to that very worst of all possible vices," he implores his son not to join, when he grows up, the ranks of those who doubt: "O my son! I pray fervently that thou may'st know inwardly how impossible it was for a Shakespeare not to have been in his heart's heart chaste."[84]

For historically-minded readers like Malone and Drake the possibility of Shakespeare's sexual desire for another man was refuted by the idea that in the Renaissance the language of love and friendship was "mutually convertible." Coleridge, on the other hand, finds reassurance in personal feeling, not history. At the deepest level, in Shakespeare's "heart's heart," we find that Shakespeare's love for the young man was chaste. The grounds for this belief are partly Shakespeare's plays, more writings that reveal what Shakespeare really felt. But they are also what readers must feel in their own hearts as they read the sonnets. Coleridge feels certain he can discern in the sonnets the "mind of Shakespeare" and prays that the sonnets will help his son do the same, "know inwardly" that Shakespeare's love was pure.

The place these observations were written also suggests the inward turn of the Romantics. The Steevens-Malone notes were published and formed a public conversation about the sonnets. The anthology in which Coleridge inscribed his handwritten note belonged to his friend Wordsworth, who had written in the anthology his own note about the sonnets. This marginalia made for a private rather than public conversation. Coleridge recorded his feelings as he read the sonnets — expressed in a fervent prayer for his son — just as he viewed the sonnets themselves as the record of Shakespeare's own inward heart. Rather than an occasion of genteel and sociable debate, the sonnets had become a more intimate medium for all — writer and readers.

Another report of Coleridge's understanding of the sonnets comes from a conversation repeated many years later by his son-in-law. In that conversation the poet mused that "a man may, under certain states of the moral feeling, entertain something that deserves the name of Love towards a male object — an affection beyond friendship and wholly aloof from Appetite." He concluded however that "the sonnets could only have come from a man deeply in love, and in love with a woman." Coleridge went on to suggest that Shakespeare disguised his female beloved as a man, but does not explain why.[85]

This interpretation of the sonnets — romantic in the literary and popular senses of the word — remains the most influential. The sonnets are assumed to be profoundly personal, the product of a man "deeply in love." The sonnets also seem to be getting more universal — no fastidious historical observation about patronage or the language of male friendship here. And who has not been deeply in love? Yet at the same time the sonnets seem to broaden, they have also narrowed: the deep love of a man must be for a woman — even in the face of evidence to the contrary.

29

The Science of Sonnets

By the early 1800s Shakespeare's sonnets had finally become popular, but not without controversy. As readers newly valued the sonnets for the intensity of their emotional expression and self-revelation, they also subjected them to a newly intense scrutiny and argument over the feelings that the sonnets revealed.[86] Not all readers liked what they found.

When the eminent Victorian historian Henry Hallam turned his attention to literature, he gave Shakespeare's sonnets short shrift. In his *Introduction to the Literature of Europe in the Fifteenth, Sixteenth, and Seventeenth Centuries* (1839), Hallam wrote that "notwithstanding the frequent beauties of the sonnets ... it is impossible not to wish Shakespeare had never written them." The likelihood that the sonnets were written to a nobleman (Hallam supposes Pembroke) insufficientiy justified the way Shakespeare humiliates himself by addressing this man "as a being before whose feet he crouched."[87] The Victorian poet Robert Browning likewise wished that Shakespeare had kept his heart shut. Browning quotes Wordsworth, "With this same key Shakespeare unlocked his heart," and offers the reply: "Did Shakespeare? If so, the less Shakespeare he!"[88]

Yet just as John Benson's praise of the sonnets failed to turn the tide of pre–Romantic opinion against them, so these protests against the sonnets little quieted the post–Romantic rage for them. Like the Romantics, Victorian readers often connected life and art. They liked their Shakespeare in the world. Since the Victorians — pushing the bounds of science, industry and empire — labored in that world as never before, must not their greatest poet have similarly toiled? The Romantic poet of feeling and imagination became a heroic god-man who struggles and triumphs in tempestuous life.[89] This was a new story that the sonnets could readily tell. The essayist Thomas Carlyle, in an 1840 lecture titled "The Hero as Poet," sounded early notes on the theme:

> Yet I call Shakespeare greater than Dante, in that he fought truly, and did conquer. Doubt it not, he had his own sorrows: those *Sonnets* of his will even testify expressly in what deep waters he had waded, and swum struggling for his life.[90]

But Shakespeare conquers rather than drowns. In the words of *King Lear's* Edgar: the worst returns to laughter.[91]

This idea of the sonnets received detailed exposition in the Victorian period by William Dowden, a professor in the new field of English literature and chair of the English department at Trinity College, Dublin. His influential *Shakspere* (1877) plotted Shakespeare's psychic development along the presumed chronology of the plays. According to Dowden, Shakespeare progresses from youth to experience to despair to redemption, each step necessary to the progressive maturation of Shakespeare's vision.[92] In the plays, however, one had to get at Shakespeare's mind through the art of his drama. For Dowden readers are attracted to the sonnets particularly because they give us more immediate access to the poet's mind. We are attracted by the sonnets "in a peculiar degree by the possibility that here, if nowhere else, the greatest of English poets may — as Wordsworth puts it — have 'unlocked his heart.'"[93]

Dowden structured his 1881 edition of the *Sonnets* to fit these ideas. He composed for it a prose narrative of the sonnets to the young man, making continuous autobiography out of the sonnets' more fragmentary lyric utterance. His notes similarly encouraged the reader to interpret the sonnets as a single, coherent story by emphasizing links among them. For Dowden, moreover, the sonnet's story is coherent psychically as well as formally. He found the same pattern to Shakespeare's life in the sonnets as he had in his plays: Shakespeare falls to rise again, like a great ship returning from sea. Expressing injured faith in the young man and youthful indiscretions with the black mistress, the sonnets are Shakespeare's songs of experience. "Driving his shafts deeper towards the centre of things," Shakespeare transmutes "worldly wisdom into spiritual insight."[94]

Other Victorian editors similarly frame the sonnets as autobiographical revelations of Shakespeare's depths, but not his degradation. Francis Palgrave, editor of the frequently republished "Gem" edition of Shakespeare's poetry (1865), writes in his introduction to this general reader's edition that he cannot agree with Hallam's wish that the sonnets had never been written. Without the sonnets, not only would we be denied the passion characteristic of great genius and great Poetry, but also the pleasure we receive in the idea that the sonnets' "phase of feeling" was "transient." From "ecstasy" Shakespeare regained his "sanity," which was "not less ... an especial attribute of the great poet."[95] William Sharp likewise writes in the introduction to his edition of the sonnets (1885) that in them we discover the young Shakespeare had to "pass through the dark valley of humiliation." "Unreasoning devotion to a boyish friend" and adultery are the humiliations Sharp has in mind. But the result of our troubling discovery is finally healthy and moral, for we gain from the sonnets "strength and refreshment in the great nature they reveal, — self-abnegating, loyal, reaching down from the heights of Supremacy with a humility that has in it something of pathos as well as of spiritual nobility."[96]

So much for Hallam and Browning. In the introduction to his popular *Leopold Shakespeare* (1877) Frederick Furnivall — a pioneering editor who founded a number of societies dedicated to English literature and publishing, including the New Shakespeare Society — presented the debate over the moral status of the sonnets as a marital dispute between the poets Robert and Elizabeth Barrett Browning. Furnivall rebuts the husband's censure of the sonnets by quoting his wife, who Romantically hailed the sonnets as "short sighs" from Shakespeare's "large poetic heart." Furnivall likewise praises the sonnets as a record of Shakespeare's "spiritual struggles."[97]

The Victorian emphasis on Shakespeare's progress — his struggles and triumphs in the world — was reflected in the method of Victorian sonnet criticism, which combined industrious historical research into the "facts" of the sonnets' origin with a belief in the scientific nature of this research.[98] Dowden compares discovering Shakespeare's personal life in the sonnets to penetrating "the secrets of Nature." Gerald Massey, author of the confidently titled *Shakespeare's Sonnets, Never Before Interpreted: His Private Friends Identified* (1866) complains that no one has done for the sonnets what Richard Owens (the Victorian paleontologist credited with naming the dinosaur) did for the earth's fossil record:

> Sought out the scattered and embedded bones of fact, and put them together again and again, until they should fit with such nicety that the departed spirit which they once breathed and had its being in these remains, should stir with the breath of life, and clothe itself in flesh once more, and take its original shape.[99]

Similarly, John A. Heraud emphasizes that his new work on Shakespeare will bear the imprint of Victorian progress. Just as scientists have now "by artificial aid" identified individual stars in nebulae, so contemporary readers have become more aware of, and able to understand, the greatness of Shakespeare: "The contemplative mind grows from century to century; and observation

... acquires an instrumentality and a habit, by aid of which what was once secret or neglected is brought into light."[100]

This scientific approach changed the critical evaluation of the sonnets. For Thomas Tyler, another prominent Victorian editor of the sonnets, the interest of these poems depends mainly on the factual knowledge they provide about Shakespeare's life. The poetry itself is less important. We are drawn to the sonnets, Tyler observes, not for their "beauty and sweetness, nor majestic strength," but from the wish to gain more knowledge about Shakespeare. Like a good scientist, Tyler is committed to the objective pursuit of this knowledge, even if what we learn from the sonnets might prove embarrassing for Shakespeare. The sonnets bear the "impress of reality"—a truth that must be maintained "whatever the consequences."[101] We are a long way from Benson's fanciful lovers.

Tyler's edition of the sonnets promoted his supposed discovery of what was thought to be an insoluble problem, the identity of the black mistress. Tyler believed her to be Mary Fitton, one of Queen Elizabeth's ladies-in-waiting, a theory based on Fitton's affair with the Earl of Pembroke, whom Tyler considered the sonnets' young man. Thus the requisite love triangle. To confirm his theory Tyler visited Fitton's tomb and observed that traces of dark paint could still be discerned on her effigy. No metaphor for Tyler. Not only was the black mistress literally black, but, like a natural scientist, the Shakespeare scholar could solve her riddle by careful observation of the physical world.[102]

Facts can be as elusive as the desire to know is strong. There was no evidence that Shakespeare had ever met Mary Fitton. Moreover, while the sonnets point to a married black mistress (if that is how we understand her broken "bed vow" in sonnet 152), Fitton is only recorded as having wed in 1607, a date too late for usual chronologies of the composition of the sonnets and of the story they tell. Undaunted, Tyler hypothesized, again with no evidence, that Fitton must have had a marriage earlier than the 1607 one, which was then annulled.[103]

Could that dark paint Tyler discovered have been the product of long-hardened dirt and a hopeful eye? It was not long before portraits of Mary Fitton were identified that showed her to be fair rather than dark. Tyler had better luck with a portrait of William Herbert, Earl of Pembroke, which he found to display the girlish face described by the sonnets. Others argued against Pembroke because his portrait showed him not to be handsome, or because he was known to smoke tobacco, and hence could not have the sweet breath alluded to in sonnet 54![104]

Though Carlyle warned against a "mechanical" approach to history that simplified its complexity and missed its higher meaning, Tyler's literal minded — and desperate — hypothesizing was not atypical for the time.[105] The second half of the nineteenth century is the great age of loopy theories about the sonnets (though loopiness about the sonnets is always with us). This theorizing was the other side of Victorian pride in science and progress. Where the Romantic Wordsworth saw the sonnets as the key that unlocked Shakespeare's heart, the Victorians saw the sonnets as ciphers requiring a key. The reader, by means of keen observation, had to provide it.[106] Victorian scholars sometimes acted like literary Sherlock Holmeses, ingeniously able to solve the mystery of the sonnets by tracing the slightest clues in their language or in the ever-increasing store of literary and historical research on Renaissance England. But their discoveries were often every bit as fantastic, and imagined, as Holmes's.

Take Massey's byzantine theories about the sonnets. He argues that some of the sonnets to the young man do express Shakespeare's love and admiration for Henry Wriothesley, Earl of Southampton. Some of these sonnets, however, make the speaker sound too lover-like and their recipient too much like a woman. These, Massey deduces, must have been written by Shakespeare *for* Southampton, dramatizing his courtship of the lady Elizabeth Vernon, whom the earl married. Such a theory had been suggested earlier by Anna Jameson in her *Loves of the Poets*.[107] But Massey's book, which runs to over six hundred pages, was the heroic Victorian version written by the man who was also author of *Ancient Egypt, The Light of the World: A Work of Reclamation and Restitution in Twelve Books*.

As befitting the reclaimer of Egyptian mysteries, Massey offers new and still more astonishing discoveries. Some of the sonnets are written by Shakespeare in the voice of Elizabeth Vernon to Southampton. Some of these dramatize Elizabeth Vernon's jealousy over a possible affair between Southampton and the lady Penelope Rich. The black mistress sonnets also turn out to be about Penelope Rich, but this time dramatizing her affair with the *other* proposed young man of the sonnets, William Herbert, Earl of Pembroke. Massey also proposes that Herbert had a hand in writing some of these sonnets himself, especially if he does not like the sonnet (included among this "apprentice work" is 130, "My mistress' eyes are nothing like the sun"!).[108]

Massey wished his work to emulate the paleontological science that reconstructed the dinosaur; but the lumbering tome has met rather with the dinosaur's extinction. For though it is full of Elizabethan history, none of it truly supports his claims. There is, for example, no record of a Pembroke-Rich affair.[109] It is enough for Massey that Rich — whom he calls the "Cleopatra of the Elizabethan court" — was described by the poet Philip Sidney as having dark eyes and that she did have an affair and illegitimate children with another courtier, Charles Lord Mountjoy.[110] If Rich had an affair with

Mountjoy, why not Pembroke? As Katherine Duncan-Jones points out, speculations on the identity of the black mistress even today often rely on the sexist assumption that a woman who has had sex outside of marriage with one man is likely to have had sex with many.[111]

Massey's connections between the sonnets and their supposed historical referents hang by equally invisible threads. Here is how Massey interprets sonnet 122 (which we might now call the "regifting" sonnet) in which Shakespeare apologizes to the young man for giving away a commonplace book the young man had previously given to him. According to Massey this sonnet is written by Shakespeare to dramatize Southampton's apology to Elizabeth Vernon for giving to Pembroke the commonplace book she had given Southampton, in which Shakespeare had narrated in sonnets the record of their courtship. This story neatly accounts for the genesis of the sonnets about Pembroke and Rich too. Once Pembroke got this commonplace book, Massey reflects, "it followed, as a matter of course, that Herbert should be ambitious of having sonnets by Shakespeare devoted to himself."[112] Of course.

Other Victorian critics pursued philosophical rather than historical speculation by turning the sonnets' characters into allegorical representations of abstract concepts. These interpretations were idealist rather than based on the discovery of "facts." But they bore a similar confidence in discovery, based in this case on a new "science" of man.[113] For the German critic Barnstorff, whose 1862 *A Key to Shakespeare's Sonnets* promises more unlocking of Shakespeare's heart, the sonnets to the young man "form an appeal addressed by his [Shakespeare's] mortal man to his immortal man," or "genius." The mistress is a symbol for what that genius will make fertile, his Drama or Art. Barnstorff interprets the imperative to have a child in the procreation sonnets as Shakespeare imploring himself not to die without leaving his art to the world. The ambiguously gendered addressee of sonnet 20 ("A woman's face with nature's own hand painted") represents Shakespeare's "duplex mind," which possessed the affections of a woman and the reason of a man all under his artistic control. Barnstorff speculates that the mysterious dedicatee of the sonnets, Mr. W.H., is none other than William Himself.[114]

An American writing at about the same time as Barnstorff similarly proposes that the young man is "the better part of the poet himself, meaning undoubtedly the spirit of life."[115] Undoubtedly. For Heraud, also an allegorist, progress is Protestant. The young man begins as the Ideal of "universal humanity," but — as the increasing scriptural allusions in the later young man sonnets suggest — he eventually symbolizes "a Messiah" and the black mistress "the Church." More particularly, the self-deifying lady of the sonnets represents the Catholic Church, and Shakespeare's dark view of her makes him "a thorough-going Protestant." In the sonnets Shakespeare "par-abolically opposed the Mariolatry of his time to the purer devotion of the Word of God, which it was the mission of his age to inaugurate." Naturally, the sonnets are anti-celibacy.[116]

In these novel interpretations Victorian discovery protects Victorian morality. Shakespeare becomes not an adulterer, not a lover of young men, but an artist, a seeker of the ideal, a forward-looking Protestant. Shakespeare maintains his place as hero and guide — especially for those readers less ready to accept that Shakespeare first suffered. Thus for Barnstorff, an allegorical interpretation of the sonnets is required if they are not to appear "the feeble effusions of an unhealthy mind." For Massey, the sonnets that Shakespeare wrote to Southampton in proper persona show his relationship with the earl to have been "of the purest, loftiest, most manly kind." There is not one sonnet in which Shakespeare is certainly the speaker, Massey declares, that "can possibly be pressed into showing that the friendship had the vile aspect into which it has been distorted."[117] If some of Shakespeare's own sonnets to Southampton seem too warm it is because Shakespeare, promoting Southampton's courtship and marriage, expects Elizabeth Vernon will read them![118]

30

Wilde Sonnets

However dubious Massey's reconstruction of the sonnets, his complaint about those who suspected a "vile aspect" to the relationship between Shakespeare and Southampton might have been confirmed at the 1895 trial of Oscar Wilde. Wilde was charged with "acts of gross indecency."[119] The charges involved Wilde's alleged sexual involvement with men who were substantially younger than he and of a lower social class. Just as important to the charges, however, was another younger man not included in them, the aristocrat Lord Alfred Douglas. This relationship was suspected as well, including by Douglas's father, the Marques of Queensbury, whose animus against Wilde led to the prosecution. Wilde first took Queensbury to court, for libel, after Queensbury publicly accused Wilde for "posing as a sodomite." When Wilde's libel case failed, the government turned around, probably at Queensbury's urging, and charged Wilde with "gross indecency." After the jury in a first trial could not reach a decision, the case was re-tried and Wilde convicted.[120]

The love between the celebrated Victorian writer Wilde and the younger aristocrat Douglas looked a lot like the relationship between the celebrated Renaissance writer Shakespeare and the younger aristocratic man of the sonnets. And Shakespeare's sonnets figured repeatedly in Wilde's trial. At the libel trial, Queensbury submitted as evidence of the truth (and therefore legality) of his charges a letter Wilde had written to Douglas, in praise of one of Douglas's sonnets. In the letter Wilde marvels that "those red rose-leaf lips of yours should have been made no less for the music of song [Douglas's poetry] than for madness of kisses." When questioned about the letter in court, Wilde maintained that it was merely a prose sonnet, which he compared to *King Lear* or "the sonnets of Shakespeare."[121] In his first trial on "gross indecency" charges, Wilde passionately defended the nobility of male love, calling it perfect and pure, and invoking the names of Plato, Michelangelo — and Shakespeare. Another piece of evidence leveled against Wilde: his novella "The Portrait of W.H.," which, as we shall see, located the origin of the sonnets in Shakespeare's love for — and perhaps sin with — a beautiful boy.

Notably, Shakespeare's sonnets figured in Wilde's defense as well as in the prosecution. We might expect that in the Victorian courtroom Wilde's invocation of Shakespeare's sonnets could only fail, could only sully the name of Shakespeare rather than clear Wilde's own. And yet when Wilde defended male love by calling on, among other great names, that of Shakespeare, the courtroom audience erupted into applause. What Wilde said about male love and Shakespeare resonated with his Victorian audience, which was not merely composed of Wilde supporters. Indeed, Wilde's reading of the sonnets as a testament to noble male love is a typically Victorian one — as was Wilde's relationship to Douglas.[122] The final verdict on Wilde was indeed conviction, to two years hard labor. But this verdict was not that of an oppressive Victorian morality squelching the first modern reader of the sonnets as openly homosexual. It was a product rather of warring aspects of Victorian culture, a warring evident as well in Victorian opinion about the sonnets.

For the scandal of the sonnets has not always concerned Shakespeare's possibly homoerotic desires. Biographical readings of the sonnets have been more mixed, varying their alarm between at least two possible scandals: an ambiguously sexual relationship with the young man, and a more clearly adulterous relationship with the black mistress. While Coleridge fretted over Shakespeare's love for the young man, his friend and fellow poet Wordsworth believed it was the sonnets to the black mistress that were "abominably harsh, obscure and worthless." Their contemporary Drake was of the same opinion, deeming her identity impossible to discern and "not worth the enquiry; for a more worthless character ... no poet ever drew." Boswell, editor of the 1821 variorum edition of Shakespeare, was dismayed both by Shakespeare's fawning on the young man and the "criminal connection" implied by Shakespeare's adulterous relationship with the black mistress. In his 1904 edition of the sonnets H.C. Beeching labels the sonnets to the black mistress merely an "appendix" to the young man sequence, and tells readers that they describe a woman "without great beauty and without virtue." Beeching comments as well that it is with regard to these sonnets, rather than those to the young man, that we may agree with Henry Hallam's wish that they had never been written.[123]

Hallam was a Victorian, but he does not represent the whole of Victorian opinion. In fact, during the Victorian period biographical readings of the sonnets shift appreciably toward favoring the young man and those sonnets written to him. Thus for Dowden the friendship portrayed in the young man sonnets "climbs to a high sunlit resting-place," while the series to a "dark temptress" is, by contrast, a "whirl of moral chaos."[124] Furnivall similarly assumes that the scandal of the sonnets is not homosexual desire but adultery. Like Dowden, he sees the relationship between Shakespeare and the young man as the noble and manly love that *redeems* the sonnets from sin. Furnivall finds words for this love between Shakespeare and the young man in no less exalted a source than the Bible, in David's lament for his dead friend Jonathan: "I am distressed for thee, my brother Jonathan: very pleasant hast thou been unto me: thy love to me was wonderful, passing the love of women."[125] Even Massey's objection to any "vile aspect" in the relationship between Shakespeare and Southampton comes in the course of praising it as "of the purest, loftiest, most manly kind."

It is no coincidence that Furnivall also compares the sonnets to a famous Victorian testament to the love between men, the poem *In Memoriam, A. H. H.*, in which Alfred, Lord Tennyson expressed his grief over the death of his beloved friend Arthur Henry Hallam, the son of Henry Hallam. In fact, Tennyson declared in the poem that his love for Hallam, whom Tennyson had met when both were students at Cambridge, was equal to Shakespeare's love for his young man: "I loved thee, Spirit, and love, nor can / The soul of Shakespeare love thee more."[126] While Henry Hallam found something untoward in Shakespeare's expressions of love for the young man, Tennyson could equally draw on that love, with the approval of his Victorian readers, to express the depths of his devotion to Hallam's son Arthur Henry.[127]

Victorian celebrations of the love between men were driven by responses to Victorian progress. On the one hand, Victorians admired masculine power, and the bonds between men, which ran the new worlds of business and industry. While women were increasingly confined to domestic spheres and ideals, it was men who built, invented, and reformed. Men, together, were reshaping the world. For such work men were to be admired, including by other men. And when this progress — with its factory smoke, urban poverty, ruthless competition, mass conformity and religious doubt — appeared in more gloomy Dickensian lights, Victorians likewise sought in the love of man for man a remedy for the ills of their modernity. Notable Victorian educational reformers such as Matthew Arnold and Benjamin Jowett promoted the close relationships of elite young men with one another and their male teachers. These reformers believed that if students and teachers shared strong emotional bonds, they would turn to their studies with greater seriousness and energy, and the spiritually regenerating effects of education would be intensified. When bands of elite boys became elite men, they would help to regenerate the nation as well.[128]

For Jowett, the Oxford classicist, the study of Plato provided both model and occasion for the bonds between men. And so did Shakespeare. A student at Arnold's Rugby School, writing an article about Shakespeare's sonnets for the school magazine, had no trouble understanding the male beloved of Shakespeare's sonnets. Writing under the pseudonymous initials M.V.B., the student first observes that passionate addresses among men were common in the Elizabethan age. So far this sounds like Malone or his nineteenth-century followers. But not only does M.V.B. approve of this older custom (unlike Malone), he also suggests that one need not look to the past to understand Shakespeare's passionate feelings for another man. There is, instead, the experience of life at school. Do we not recognize, M.V.B. asks his student and alumni audience,

> Looking inwards, and avowing from the histories of the feelings written there, that our school-attachments,— the yearning towards, and confiding in, our school-boy friends,— the previous desire of obtaining their affection,— the exceeding comfort of it when obtained,— the fear of losing it,— the jealous measuring of its depth by our own,— at one time, maybe, the torturing doubt of its existence or its sincerity, then the overwhelming happiness, when any trifling circumstance has assured us that it is strong and warm as ever,— the desolateness of heart on any estrangement,— the deep joy of a reconciliation,— still more, the dependence and uplooking of a younger boy on a friend older and more powerful than himself; and in his turn, the fond attention and submission of the elder to the childish pleasures or the runaway wishes of his companion — that such records as these, taken from that Bible within us, our clean and yet unfettered Conscience, may well justify the truth and fitness of our mighty poet's language.

The Bible of our conscience; the scriptural Bible that praises the love "passing the love of women"; the culture of the Greeks, which celebrated the love between a younger male and an older, more experienced male who would mentor him; the elite Victorian schools and universities that promoted this Greek idea for their own educational purposes; great philosophers, artists and poets such Plato, Michelangelo, and Shakespeare — in a way that reminds us of the moment of the sonnets' origin in the Renaissance, central cultural authorities and institutions lined up in the Victorian period to exalt the love between men.

But M.V.B. adds the complaint that "in this day" the passionate language Shakespeare addresses to the young man is "dropt from our locked lips into the ear of woman only." The Victorian idea of male-male love as distinctively "manly" clashed with a second definition of manliness, that of the breadwinner husband, who looked for spiritual uplift from his wife and home, rather than from another man. Fear of homosexuality also clashed with the Victorian promotion of male-male love.[129] Some critics of Victorian schools, especially as the century progressed, worried about just what the "childish pleasures" and "runaway wishes" of this passionate schoolboy love involved.[130] Tennyson's love for Hallam, whom he met at Cambridge in the 1830s, was celebrated. Wilde's love for Douglas, a fellow Oxfordian, was, in effect, put on trial in the 1890s.

Wilde's own important contribution to the history of the sonnets' reception, "The Portrait of W.H.," brilliantly captures the Victorian response to Shakespeare's sonnets. The "Portrait" begins with the narrator having dinner with his older friend Erskine. The two begin a discussion of literary forgeries. Erskine tells the story of his friend Cyril Graham, who once proposed to him that the young man of the sonnets was a boy actor, Willie Hewes, who played the heroines in Shakespeare's dramas. Erskine is taken with Cyril's theory but suggests they need more proof. Unable to find any written documents testifying to the existence of a Willie Hewes, proof finally comes in a picture Cyril claims to have found of him. This "portrait of W.H." displays a young man of about seventeen years, "of quite extraordinary personal beauty, though evidently somewhat effeminate," resting his hand on a book of Shakespeare's sonnets, which are dedicated to him.[131]

Erskine soon learns that the picture is a forgery. He confronts Cyril, who kills himself the next day. Cyril tells Erskine in a suicide note that he still believes in the Willie Hewes theory, and that he is "going to offer his life as a sacrifice to the secret of the Sonnets" (311). Erskine's faith in Willie Hewes is shattered, but the story of Cyril Graham has the opposite effect on the narrator, who upon hearing it begins an obsessive two-month search to prove Cyril's theory true. No sooner, however, does the narrator commit his proofs of the theory to writing and send them off to Erskine than the narrator too loses faith in the theory.[129]

When he and Erskine meet the following day it is Erskine who is convinced, and the narrator who remains skeptical of Willie Hewes. Erskine goes to Germany. Two years later he writes the narrator that he still believes in, but has not been able to prove, the Willie Hewes theory. But to demonstrate his faith in it, and to honor Cyril Graham, Erskine intends to kill himself. Erskine begs the narrator not to reject the theory "for it comes to you now, stained with the blood of two lives" (348). ("To die for a literary theory! It seemed impossible," the narrator muses.) There is, however, one more forgery. It turns out that Erskine knew he would die of consumption, and merely claims to kill himself in order to win back the narrator's belief that Willie Hewes was the young man of the sonnets. The story ends with the narrator still a doubter of the Willie Hewes theory. But the narrator tells us that at times when he gazes at the forged portrait, which he has inherited from Erskine, he nonetheless feels there is "really a great deal to be said" (350) for the idea that the boy actor Willie Hewes was the young man of the sonnets.

In "The Portrait of W.H." Wilde mischievously undermines Victorian interpretation of the sonnets. On the one hand, "The Portrait" echoes Victorian ideas of the spiritualizing love between men, especially at school. The theory of Shakespeare's love for the boy actor is first proposed by one schoolboy friend to another. Erskine explains that he was "absurdly devoted" (304) to Cyril Graham when they both attended Eton. The narrator similarly attributes his sympathy for the Willie Hewes theory to the Hellenic spirit he imbibed at Oxford (344), and he includes in his explication of the sonnets a long disquisition on the Renaissance neo–Platonic theories of male friendship, in which "there was a kind of mystic transference of the expressions of the physical world to a sphere that was spiritual, that was removed from gross bodily appetite" (325).

Wilde leaves it doubtful, however, that his characters' interest in the sonnets, or Shakespeare's interest in the boy actor, really do exclude "bodily appetite." The narrator lingers on the beauty of Willie Hewes: "From those finely curved lips ... had come the passionate cry of Juliet, and the bright laughter of Beatrice" (328). And he imagines that Shakespeare's relationship with Willie Hughes is shadowed by something secret. "I did not care to pry into the mystery of [Willie Hewes's] sin or of the sin, if such it was, of the great poet who so dearly loved him" (320). The narrator recognizes too that he is attracted to Shakespeare's sonnets because, like all great art, they bring to consciousness a secret in his own heart: "Suddenly we become aware that we have passions of which we have never dreamed, thoughts that make us afraid, pleasures whose secret has been denied to us, sorrows that have been hidden from our tears" (343).

It has been easy for readers of "The Portrait" to understand this pleasure — secret, forbidden and perhaps tragic — as homosexual desire. Wilde's narrator sounds as if the sonnets have awakened him to his previously unrecognized homosexual identity, just as the narrator himself seems to be "outing" Shakespeare. But the force of Wilde's "Portrait" does lie not in its revelation of particular persons — the story's narrator or Shakespeare — as homosexuals. Its effect was larger. Readers heard homosexual desire within the same culturally celebrated male bonds that shaped Wilde's own life and that characterized orthodox Victorian readings of the sonnets.[132]

Wilde's "Portrait" is also striking, though less well known, for undermining another aspect of the Victorian reception of the sonnets: the belief that a historical account of them, modeled on scientific inquiry, could ferret out their secrets.[133] Cyril Graham is conversant in the minutiae of the latest biographical theorizing. He is able to rehearse and refute the Southampton theory, the Pembroke theory, and the allegorical theories of Heraud and Barnstorff, before proposing his own Willie Hewes as the candidate for the young man (305–308). When the narrator determines to prove Cyril's theory, he likewise immerses himself in Victorian sonnet criticism, beginning with "Mr. Tyler's facsimile edition of the Quarto" (313). The narrator has also read, among others, Dowden and Massey. His own theorizing about Willie Hughes is thick with hypotheses about the relationship between historical fact and the blurry story of the sonnets that characterizes Victorian sonnet criticism.

But "The Portrait" parodies Victorian scientific biography, rather than exemplifies it. The narrator excitedly discovers in the historical record a "Will Hewes" who was musician to the first Earl of Essex. This musician, the narrator decides, must be Shakespeare's young man, whom Shakespeare describes in a sonnet as "music to hear." But there's a problem. The earl died in 1576, a date that makes his musician too old for the young man of the 1590s. Then the narrator recalls that there was a Margaret Hews who became in the 1660s one of the first professional actresses. "What more probable," the narrator asks, "than that between her and Lord Essex' musician had come the boy-actor of Shakespeare's plays" (327). But then why is there no record of a Willie Hewes in the available lists of actors during Shakespeare's day? The absence of the name, Erskine offers, "is rather a proof in favour of the existence of Willie Hewes than against it, if we remember his treacherous desertion of Shakespeare for a rival dramatist." If this hypothesis fails to convince, Erskine has another ready to hand: "There is no reason at all why Willie Hewes should not have gone upon the stage under an assumed name. In fact it is extremely probable that he did so," given the English Renaissance prejudices against the acting profession (347).

Wilde loads "The Portrait" with such extremely probable fact. His sonnet clue-seekers with their elaborate theories and rationalizations to fit an already-framed hypothesis sound just like a Tyler or a Massey, but Wilde the writer — unlike the characters he writes about in the "Portrait" — recognizes the flimsiness of this sort of "highly probable" fact. It's no wonder that "The Portrait" is a fictional story about the sonnets that reads as if it were a critical essay on them, or that the story turns on the forged evidence of the Willie Hewes portrait. All biographical speculation in the story comes to be a kind of forgery. It is a testament to the allure of this speculation that Wilde's "Portrait" has been and still is occasionally taken as offering a serious biographical theory about the sonnets, rather than a send-up of such theorizing.[134]

Wilde's parody of Victorian criticism ingeniously exposes its contradictions. He pits readings of the sonnets that celebrate male friendship against increasing Victorian concern about homosexuality. And he pits the optimistic Victorian belief in science against the reaction of Victorian aestheticism, which warned of a crudely mechanistic society sacrificing the visionary power of art to dull and "discreditable" fact.[135] Wilde's "Portrait" prophesies the end of Victorian criticism by providing its best example.

But the work equally prophesies the mode of reading Shakespeare's sonnets that would succeed Victorian criticism and dominate much of the twentieth century. For Wilde's narrator also insists that the great attraction of the young man is that he is both the medium for Shakespeare's drama and himself a work of art: in the actor Willie Hughes "Shakespeare found not merely a most delicate instrument for the presentation of his art, but the visible incarnation of his idea of beauty" (327). This understanding of the young man's attraction removes Willie Hughes and the sonnets from history and homosexuality, and puts them in the realm of art. Many twentieth-century critics wary of fact, and worried about sexual sin, have been happy to keep the sonnets and their young man there.

31

Love Poetry at Last

We come at last to the beginnings of our own most popular story about Shakespeare's sonnets. Charles Knox Pooler's 1918 scholarly edition of the sonnets exemplifies the trend. Pooler begins with more than 30 pages of a densely and intelligently argued survey of the historical background of the sonnets and the succeeding debates over that background. The survey reads like a culmination of nineteenth-century research, until Pooler declares (on page 32) that "the interest of such speculations, great as it seems, has nothing in common with a feeling for poetry." And then in a new paragraph Pooler announces even more decisively: "Hitherto, no theory or discovery has increased our enjoyment of any line in the Sonnets or cleared up any difficulty."[136]

Like Wilde's forgeries, speculations on the sonnets' historical background have merely seemed great. With the zeal of the converted Pooler denies "theory or discovery," including his own, any achievement at all. What matters for the sonnets instead is feeling, enjoyment and poetry. The sonnets count as art to be experienced, not records to be analyzed for information about the poet's life and times.

Other editions of the sonnets from around the turn of the century similarly mark this shift. Most striking is George Wyndham's edition of 1898. Wyndham contentiously eschews beginning his introduction to the sonnets with the heretofore usual discussion of historical background. His edition starts by identifying the sonnets' genre. The sonnets are framed as belonging to the history of the writer's art, not to a particular writer's life or the times in which he lived. Wyndham classifies the sonnets as lyric and elegy and — not uncoincidentally — emphasizes that these genres take art as their

193

chief concern. Lyric and elegiac poetry, Wyndham maintains, express the "quintessence of man's desire for Beauty." Nor is it a coincidence that this Beauty (with a capital B) is greatest when "abstracted from concrete and transitory embodiments." Wyndham scorns those who try to locate the sonnets, with their "portentous mass of theory" (think Massey), in the transitory world that Beauty transcends. For, Wyndham argues, we are not concerned about Shakespeare the man, but Shakespeare the artist. Indeed, according to Wyndham, Shakespeare's gift as an artist was to turn whatever was squalid in his career and world into a compensatory lyric beauty. [137]

In its repudiation of history, Wyndham's edition marks what will be another distinguishing quality of twentieth-century sonnet editions: the concern with "theme." Readers educated in twentieth-century literature courses may be under the impression that "themes" are a natural product of literary works, or at least of literary critical readings of them. But "themes" have not always been so emphasized. They are really the product of a twentieth-century compromise between two critical schools, formalism and historicism: the former, especially as art's for art's sake, maintains that the literary work is "about" nothing more — or less — than the craft or beauty of its composition. The latter is concerned with the literary work as biographical and historical document, and neglects its aesthetic qualities or distinctive status as an artwork. "Themes" represent a compromise between these two positions: the work of literature is about something (so not merely beautiful), but what it is about is universal, rather than located in a writer's life or times (and so not merely documentary). Wyndham lists the themes of the sonnets as "love," "absence," "beauty," "decay," "immortality" and "identity with friend."[138] Many of these sonnets themes would be reiterated through the twentieth century.

Similarly, Israel Gollancz's 1899 edition of the sonnets tells their story in the manner of nineteenth-century biographical accounts, but uses generic rather than proper names. The sonnets are not about Shakespeare but "the poet." This usage will be repeated in the familiar warning in twentieth-century editions of the sonnets — and twentieth-century criticism more generally — not to confuse the "I" of a poem with the author's biographical "I." The other players in what Gollancz calls the "drama" of the sonnets — emphasizing their fictive quality — are also generic figures and feelings: "the friend," "friendship" and "love."[139]

These themes of love and friendship, death and immortality would seem to bring us all the way back to Benson's generic lovers. But there is an important difference. Benson's lovers were displaying the courtly manners of the elite, just as poetry was a game for gentleman. In the twentieth century as opposed to the seventeenth, the generic lover is assumed to be universal, as are the feelings that the poet describes. For John Dover Wilson, writing in his 1968 edition, the sonnets are nothing less than "the greatest love-poetry in the world."[140] The category "love poetry" itself wafts the sonnets into a realm of the universal. Wilson chooses this term over more scholarly generic designations such as "lyric" or "sonnet," which he likely finds too particular and too literary, too removed from the universal feelings of love that Shakespeare is seen to express.

As capacious as Dover's claim for the sonnets would seem, it excludes the way the sonnets were understood for hundreds of years: as gentlemen's verse, as execrable, as revelations of Shakespeare's heart, as a mine for facts about Shakespeare's life, as poetry of a beautiful male friendship, as intimations of a secret homosexual sin. None of this history is captured by calling the sonnets the world's "greatest love-poetry," a phrase that leaves out hundreds of years of readers' hesitations about the sonnets' literary merits or morality. And Wilson himself admits that though the view of the sonnets as great love poetry, rather than as "biographical puzzle," seems "so obvious and so natural," this view has "in point of fact only recently been realized."[141]

As Wilson's recognition suggests, the apparently obvious idea of the sonnets' universal appeal itself has a history. It was not always thus. This idea partly comes, as we have seen, from a backlash against the Victorian idea that sufficient critical ingenuity could reveal the highly probable facts of the sonnets' composition. So profound has been the reaction against this kind of fact-finding, that even in a climate much more friendly to historical criticism, interpretations that purport to solve the sonnets' biographical mysteries are now generally viewed as embarrassments. The call for papers for a panel on the sonnets at the 2002 annual conference of the Shakespeare Association of America warned that no essays that "speculate about hidden biographical identities in the sonnets" will be accepted.[142] While calls for papers often implicitly communicate the kinds of critical work most desired, this is the only time I have ever seen one explicitly exclude a particular kind of criticism.

The rise of universalizing readings of the sonnets depends on more, however, than a despair about achieving localized ones. It reflects a despair about history itself. Victorians like Dowden read the sonnets, and understood their own criticism, as manifestations of historical progress. But a very different view of English literature was beginning to develop in the Victorian period, one that would view literature as an antidote to the fears generated by change. In this view, advanced most famously by the great Victorian literary critic Matthew Arnold, literature and science no longer marched in tandem on the road to progress. Rather, literature by virtue of its unworldliness would redress the dangerous loss of faith created by scientific skepticism. Belief in the transcendent poem would replace belief in a transcendent God.[143]

Critics such as Arnold also hoped that the transcendence of literature would redress the class conflict generated by modern industrialism, a wish intensified by fears of lower-class rebellion in England, and, after Arnold's death, by an actual communist revolution in Russia. In this view, the universally appealing wisdom and joy of literature provided a meeting ground for all classes that transcended petty local interests — such as the lower-class demand for better wages and working conditions.[144]

Dover Wilson's 1968 pronouncement on the universal appeal of Shakespeare's sonnets (the world's greatest love poetry) is rooted in these particular historical concerns. They led him, all the way back in 1921, to describe literature in Arnoldian terms as "an embodiment of the best thought of the best minds." So Wilson wrote in an influential report on the teaching of English literature in England, in which he warned that the lower classes, and particularly "organised labour movements," were dangerously hostile to literature. These groups had to be persuaded that literature created "a fellowship which 'binds together by passion and knowledge the vast empire of human society, as it is spread over the whole earth, and over all time.'" A nation that "rejects this means of grace, and despises this great spiritual influence," Wilson predicts, "must assuredly be heading to disaster."[145] Literature in this view is defined exactly by its capacity to transcend — like the religious spirit Wilson's language draws on — local times and places. Love poetry that is simply the world's greatest can speak to all.

Wilson draws not only on the language of religion when he refers to the bonds that literature creates and that transcend time and place. He also speaks the language of colonialism in his description of the "vast empire of human society, as it is spread over the whole earth." The vast empire that had spread over human society at the time of Wilson's report was really the British empire. And the bonds by which it drew peoples together were not just those of good fellowship. But as with class conflict within England, the relationship between colonizer and colonized could be imagined as reconciled on the higher plane of literature, which transcended time and place. This transcendence was a shadow of empire, both literally and ideologically. Literally, the British empire spread British writing over the globe, making it appear to be universal. Ideologically, the idea of the universality of English writers like Shakespeare suggested the cultural superiority of Great Britain, and hence its entitlement to rule the inferior and merely particular culture of the colonized.[146]

In the United States the movement now referred to as the New Criticism was also instrumental in advancing an ahistorical approach to literary analysis. The movement, which originated in the American South of the 1920s and 30s, had its roots in a protest against what its founders saw as the materialism and mass culture of Northern industrial capitalism. But the New Criticism's antipathy to exploring the historical contexts of literature also well accommodated the environment of post–World War II America, where the cold war, McCarthyism, Viet Nam and the Civil Rights movement made political discussion threatening. In this environment literature could be seen as a safe zone, above and beyond worldly historical phenomena like politics.[147] The world's greatest love poetry does not know left and right.

There were practical reasons for the popularity of this view as well. Following World War II in the United States new groups were gaining access to post-secondary education for the first time, and they were coming without the historical knowledge that would have allowed them to read literature in historical context. Rather than attempt to supply that knowledge, it was easier to have students read literature in historical isolation.[148] You could hand students a copy of the sonnets and have them identify patterns of light and dark imagery or trace the theme of death. No knowledge of Elizabethan patronage was required.

Nor of early modern friendship. What Wyndham called "identity with his friend" disappears over the course of the twentieth century from lists of sonnet "themes." As late at 1904 H.C. Beeching in the introduction to his edition of the sonnets emphasizes their portrayal of an older man's attraction to a younger. He calls this attraction a natural theme for poets, who are sensitive to beauty and fearful of its decay. W.H. Hadow's 1907 edition of the sonnets similarly emphasizes the bond of friendship in the sonnets. The story the sonnets tell of this bond being stressed by passion for a woman is, Hadow observes, as "old as romance itself." As the century progresses, however, the sonnets' friendship increasingly becomes a problem to be solved or avoided, rather than a great theme of art and literature.[149] Katherine Duncan-Jones has suggested that the Wilde scandal made it increasingly difficult to talk about male friendship in the sonnets without generating anxiety that this friendship was sexual. Additionally, by the beginning of the twentieth century the science of psychology had defined the "homosexual." The more science defined the identity of the homosexual, the more pressure there was to assert that Shakespeare was not one, that the great poet could not, as asserted in the 1967 Folger edition of the sonnets, be "abnormal."[150]

Since Malone, critics responded to anxieties about male same-sex desire in the sonnets by turning to the sonnets' historical origins. Male friendship, readers were assured, was different back then: more intense and lovingly expressed, but not sexual. In the twentieth century these claims continue to be made, but interpreters increasingly take the opposite tack, by simply removing the sonnets from history, including biography, so that even the male address of most of the sonnets is obscured. If the sonnets are about a set of themes — "love," "longing," "death," "art" — then no particular persons, especially male persons, need be attached to them. This ahistoricism has likely seemed the safer defense of the sonnets' sexual content in a post–Freudian world, in which the notion of unconscious desire may have rendered more doubtful the claim that men's intense friendships in the Renaissance had no sexual content. But this ahistorical approach has also been enabled by the general shift in the twentieth-century toward universalizing readings.

Wilson's description of the sonnets as "the world's greatest love poetry" might imply it doesn't matter if you're hetero or homo: this love poetry appeals to everyone. Such a universal appeal is all very well, except that the universal often excludes the homoerotic. As T.H.W. Crosland put it in 1917:

> We require the *Sonnets* because of the poetry they contain, and for no other reason. The best thing that could happen to them would be a rearrangement destructive of their alleged sequentiality and 'story': and as regards 1 to 126, destructive of their reference to a man. In effect, the reading-mind has already accomplished these destructions for itself. Only the scholars know or read the *Sonnets* for a sequence or for a history. Ordinary people content themselves with the most beautiful and human of them, and skip the rest. And somehow they manage to forget that 1 to 126 were not addressed to a lady.[151]

Given this desire to forget that the first 126 sonnets "were not addressed to a lady," it's not surprising that during the twentieth century the reputation of the "black mistress" skyrockets. Before then the black mistress poems were frequently treated as embarrassments, since they are less elegantly written than the poems to the young man, and they describe an avowedly adulterous and lurid love triangle. Nineteenth and early twentieth-century editors tend to ignore these sonnets altogether, or treat them as merely an appendage or after-thought to the "main" sonnet sequence to the young man.[152] This treatment seems reasonable, given that the 126 young man sonnets far outnumber the 28 black mistress sonnets. By the mid–twentieth century, however, the black mistress sonnets, despite adulteries or aesthetics, achieve parity with those to the young man (see figure 3). A single sonnet, 130 ("My mistress' eyes are nothing like the sun") is largely responsible for this change. In contrast to other now popular sonnets, it is only anthologized once before 1900, and the vast majority of its anthologizations come after 1950 (see figure 4).[153]

Why these changes? Sonnets 98 ("From you I have been absent in the spring") was probably valued for its extended nature imagery, a hallmark of the earlier nineteenth-century sonnet.[154] Sonnet 54 ("O how much more doth beauty beauteous seem") also contains a good deal of nature imagery, and its moral tone might have attracted Victorian readers (while its refer-

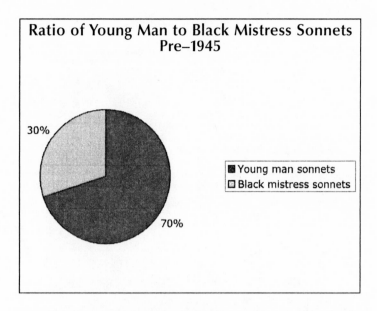

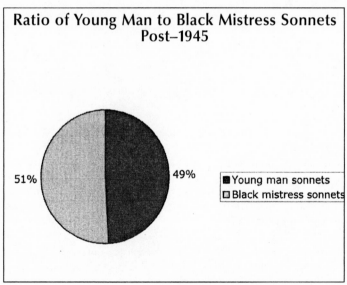

Figure 3: These pie charts show the ratio of the average anthologizations for the young man versus the black mistress group. The increase in popularity of the latter in the second half of the twentieth century is striking.

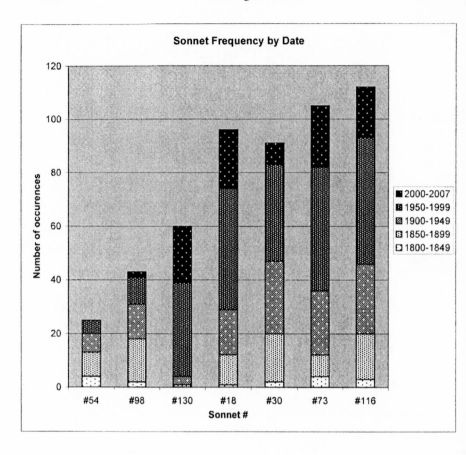

Figure 4: This graph shows the rate of anthologization by date of some currently and once popular Shakespeare sonnets. While sonnets 18, 30, 73, and 116 have been fairly consistent in their popularity, sonnet 130 is striking because almost all its growth in popularity has been post–1950. Also striking is the decline in the anthologizations of 54 and 98, which were once as or more popular than current favorite sonnets.

ence to a "youth" may have put off later twentieth-century ones). Sonnet 18, which begins with a flattering compliment, makes a good love sonnet. Sonnet 130 is also romantic. Its literary self-consciousness and ironic stance toward courtly love convention has something to do with its steep rise in popularity. But at least as important is the fact that this sonnet, from its second word, is about a "mistress." If you want to find romantic heterosexual love in Shakespeare's sonnets, sonnet 130, which is neither angry nor lascivious, offers one of the very few possibilities.

The frequent anthologization of sonnet 130 helps create the illusion of emotional parity between young man and black mistress sonnets. The "two loves" of the sonnets become not contrasting loves of "comfort" and "despair" (sonnet 144) but similar objects of affection, even though only one "black mistress" sonnet really conveys this parity. (Anthologizing 130 along with other popular sonnets to the young man, such as 18 and 116, additionally allows readers, not informed otherwise, to assume that these sonnets are also to a "mistress," since none of the popular young man sonnets refers directly to the recipient's gender.) Such parity also fends off worries about the sexual identity of the sonnets' author. For once there is an essential homosexuality so is there an essential heterosexuality. The literary critic and historian A. L. Rowse is certain Shakespeare was "a red-blooded heterosexual" stirred by "the frou-frou of skirts."[155] Heterosexual love, as we have seen, will also get first billing on sonnet book covers.

Of course, covers sell books. And the twentieth-century universalizing of the sonnets as great love poetry also relates to the expanding market in the twentieth century for Shakespeare. A Shakespeare stripped of historical baggage circulates more freely as a product in the marketplace. You can sell more editions of the sonnets if they're about the love everyone has felt, rather than a particular love that Shakespeare experienced, or that Shakespeare had for another man, or that Shakespeare invoked in the pursuit of patronage. There is a historical irony here, since many of the twentieth-century critics who developed a notion of the literary work as transcendent of its history did so because they were apprehensive about the historical moment they were living in of modern market capitalism. A transcendent literature was supposed to provide an alternative to capitalist materialism and mass conformity.[156] But instead capitalism has captured this idea of transcendence for the market.

History has a way of coming back. In the preface to his edition of the sonnets, Dover Wilson invokes the idea of literature as a better place. "I begin this edition of the finest love poetry in the world in what I think must be the loveliest garden on earth."[157] Garden and poem are enjoyed as parallel experiences. The garden, with its suggestions of nature, of Edenic paradise and of pastoral retreat from the modern (and corrupt) city, provides a more lovely and perfect place outside the tumult of history. A place shared by literature in general and Shakespeare's fine love poetry in particular. Except it turns out that this "loveliest garden on earth" is located in 1963 apartheid South Africa. The history of colonialism, racism and violence that secured South Africa's lovely gardens fails to register on Dover Wilson.

When I studied English in college about twenty years later, the student South Africa divestment movement was in full gear. And in the classroom, professors were now talking and writing about Shakespeare in terms of the cultural, social and political history of Renaissance England. They were employing the identity categories like class, gender and race that shaped how people lived in that world — and live in our own. History had come back.

Coda: Universal Shakespeare?

> Nothing of him that doth fade
> But doth suffer a sea-change
> Into something rich and strange.
> — Shakespeare, *The Tempest*

A student once asked a colleague of mine at George Mason University how she could still like the sonnets, now that she knew they were written by one man for another. After all, she wasn't a gay man. My colleague replied that she thought this knowledge broadened their appeal. I agree: anyone can appreciate the literary qualities of the sonnets or identify with the experiences of love registered in them. We always bridge gaps in time, place and situation when we read. Readers of the sonnets who identify as gay do, and have done, the same, while finding particular value in the sonnets' story of homoerotic desire. That story may also appeal to readers who do not, or do not yet, identify as gay. Moreover, framed historically the sonnets offer all their readers the recognition of historical difference, and therefore human freedom, rather than false assertions of tradition or human nature. If we know the past was different, we know that the future can be as well. I wouldn't call these wide appeals of the sonnets universal. I would call them diverse.

My colleague's student might also have wondered whether she could continue to appreciate the sonnets as a woman, given their misogyny. While the young man sonnets' appeal continues in several respects (though not in their own vision of a woman as "some vial"), less can be said for the sonnets to the black mistress. They have been defended as feminist, but much of this defense relies on a single sonnet, "My mistress' eyes are nothing like the sun" (130). And while they are more sexually frank than the ones to the young man, this frankness is so often tinged with anger or fear it's hard to celebrate them as sexually liberatory. Modern feminism is not responsible for the lack of appeal of these sonnets. Most of them have never been admired by the sonnets' readers.

Should it matter if we can reckon the diverse particular ways one might or might not like the sonnets, while abandoning belief in their universal appeal? I don't think so. In fact, I think it's time to lay this idea to rest. Besides its vagueness, the disturbing thing about praise of Shakespeare's universality is that it can really mean the opposite: the universal excludes rather than includes, by implying that what interests someone else in Shakespeare is too particular (or wrong, or inconsequential, or inhuman) to count.[1] A 2000 report by the conservative National Association of Scholars complains, "Shakespeare may have been a white male, but — with the appropriate postmodern mutations — he can be enlisted in any number of gender-bending crusades. How much of his liberating vision and stunning beauty survive the faculty press-gangs is anyone's guess." The writers of this report stand up for liberty and against coercive "faculty press-gangs."[2] Yet how coercive is the report's own language. Couldn't gender-bending be a form of liberty? Isn't there bullying in calling different approaches to Shakespeare "mutant"? Perhaps instead we are experiencing a "sea-change."

The sonnets have survived for four hundred years, but not because their vision and beauty were properly cultivated until the press-gangs of postmodernism. As we have seen, the sonnets have never been read in a single way. For almost half their history there was not even wide agreement that the sonnets should be included among the "stunning beauty" of Shakespeare's work. To read the sonnets (or Shakespeare) in new ways today is not to corrupt his work, but to participate in a long conversation about it. There are worse things one could do with literature.

Notes

Preface

1. Lisa Jardine and Alan Stewart, *Hostage to Fortune: The Troubled Life of Francis Bacon* (New York: Hill and Wang, 1998), 220–221, 138; Paul E.J. Hammer, *The Polarisation of Elizabethan Politics: The Political Career of Robert Devereux, 2nd Earl of Essex* (Cambridge, 1999), 323; Daphne du Maurier, *Golden Lads: Sir Francis Bacon, Anthony Bacon and Their Friends* (Garden City, NY: Doubleday, 1975), 192–93.

2. Jardine and Stewart, 240–52.

3. Jardine and Stewart, 17, 163; Alan Bray, "Homosexuality and the Signs of Male Friendship in Elizabethan England," *Queering the Renaissance*, ed. Jonathan Goldberg (Durham: Duke, 1994), 44, 60n15.

Introduction

1. John Dover Wilson, ed. *The Sonnets* (Cambridge, 1966), xvii. For discussion of Wilson's view, see chapter 31.

2. As Stephen Booth observes, *Shakespeare's Sonnets* (New Haven: Yale, 1977), 545–46.

3. Here I also follow up Jonathan Crewe's call to no longer "genteely" refer to the "dark lady" sonnets (*Trials of Authorship: Anterior Forms and Poetic Reconstruction from Wyatt to Shakespeare* [Berkeley: University of California, 1990], 120).

4. See *Shakespeare's Sonnets*, ed. Katherine

Duncan-Jones (London: Thompson Learning, 1997), 422.

5. Readers have however tried to find punning clues to these names in the sonnets. See for example Hyder Rollins, ed. *A New Variorum Edition of Shakespeare: The Sonnets (Vols. 24–25)*, 2 parts (Philadelphia: J.B. Lippincott, 1944), 2:194, which describes how one reader found in the sonnets' repeated references to roses the name "Wriothesley" and see note 7 below for one problem with this identification — no one knows if the name did sound like "rose-ly."

6. Katherine Duncan-Jones, introduction to *Shakespeare's Sonnets*, 57–58. See Joseph Pequigney, *Such Is My Love: A Study of Shakespeare's Sonnets* (University of Chicago, 1985), for a counterargument that the young man is not of high social status (12).

7. On the pronunciation of "Wriothesley" see Rollins, 2:194.

8. G.P.V. Akrigg, *Shakespeare and the Earl of Southampton* (Cambridge: Harvard, 1968), 31–34, 201–202.

9. Rollins, 2:195–96. See Duncan-Jones, *Shakespeare's Sonnets*, for indirect evidence that Pembroke could have been an intimate of Shakespeare's (66–67).

10. Rollins, 2:210.

11. On the problem of the "Mr." see Rollins, 2:200; and see Duncan-Jones, *Shakespeare's Sonnets*, for one attempt to solve it (59). The introduction to *Shakespeare: The Poems*, ed. David Bevington (New York: Ban-

tam, 1988) points to the "unconvincing possibility" of reversing "W.H." (184). For "W.H." as William Shakespeare see Donald Foster, "Mr. W.H. R.I.P.," *PMLA* 102 (1987): 42–54. "W.H." as William Himself was first suggested in 1860 (Rollins, 2:214).

12. See chapter 29 on Thomas Tyler's desperate theorizing for Fitton.

13. Samuel Schoenbaum, "Shakespeare's Dark Lady: A Question of Identity," in *Shakespeare's Styles: Essays in Honour of Kenneth Muir*, ed. Philip Edwards et al., (Cambridge, 1980), 233–35; Marvin Hunt, "Be Dark But Not Too Dark," in *Shakespeare's Sonnets*, ed. James Schiffer (New York: Garland, 2000), 372.

14. G.B. Harrison in *Shakespeare at Work* (1933; reprint with a new preface, Ann Arbor: University of Michigan, 1958) first identified the black mistress with a joking reference to a black prostitute nicknamed "Lucy Negro" (64, 310–11). Leslie Hotson, in *Mr. W.H.* (New York: Knopf, 1964) countered that this Lucy Negro was a brothel-keeper nicknamed Black Lucy, whose real name was Lucy Morgan and who was a white gentlewoman who once waited on Queen Elizabeth before falling into prostitution (238–55). More recently, Duncan Salkeld, examining court records, has argued that the Lucy Morgan Hotson identified as Black Lucy, though also a prostitute, was a different person from a brothel-keeper nicknamed Black Lucy who could have been black. Salkeld concludes that this Black Lucy could not have been Shakespeare's black mistress, presumably because records of her date to the late 1570s (when Shakespeare would have been about 12 and living in Stratford). Yet since the court records Salkeld draws on are missing from the period between 1579 and 1597, it's not absolutely clear that she was not still active later, when Shakespeare would have been older. See Duncan Salkeld, "'Black Luce' and the 'Curtizans' of London," *Signatures* 2 (2000): 5–15 (electronic journal available at http://www.chiuni.ac.uk/info/Signatures.cfm).

15. See Kim Hall's collection of Renaissance love poems written by white Englishmen about women who were racially black in *Things of Darkness: Economies of Race and Gender in Early Modern England* (Ithaca: Cornell, 1995), 269–90. Hunt, 379, observes Shakespeare's substantial interest in interracial relationships in his plays. Robert Fleissner, "Hebert's Aethiopea and the Dark Lady," *College Language Association Journal* 19 (1976): 458–60, argues for Shakespeare's influence on George Herbert's "A Black Woman Courts

Cestus, a Man of a Different Skin Color." Petrarch, *The Canzoniere*, trans. Mark Musa (Bloomington: Indiana, 1996), poem 187.

16. *A Midsummer Night's Dream*, 3.2.258. See also Hall, *Things of Darkness*, 1, 22–44; Ania Loomba, *Shakespeare, Race, and Colonialism*, Oxford Shakespeare Topics (Oxford, 2002), 59.

17. *Oxford English Dictionary*, "negro," 1.a; Loomba, 59–63. Hall, *Things of Darkness*, observes the critical reluctance to understand black in racial terms (69–70).

18. See the survey in Rollins, 2:277–94. Some of the rival poet sonnets, such as 82, speak of writers more generally, a fact that should warn us again too literally searching for *the* rival poet, but which has also had the opposite effect of suggesting to readers that there might have been a group of specific rival poets (see Rollins, 2:277).

19. See Rollins' survey, 2:133–56. A recent version of this position, emphasizing the sonnets as primarily works of literary art, can be found in Helen Vendler, *The Art of Shakespeare's Sonnets* (Cambridge: Harvard, 1997).

20. See the chapters in section 1.

21. Giles Fletcher, *Licia, or, Poems of Love in honour of the admirable and singular virtues of his Lady. To the imitation of the best Latin poets, and others* (1593) in *Elizabethan Sonnets*, ed. Sidney Lee, 2 vols. (*An English Garner*, 1877–1890, reprint, New York: Cooper Square, 1964), 2:28.

22. Alexander Judson, *The Life of Edmund Spenser*, vol. 11 of *The Works of Edmund Spenser: A Variorum Edition*, ed. Edwin Greenlaw, et al. (Baltimore: Johns Hopkins, 1954), 166–71.

23. Colin Burrow, introduction to *The Complete Sonnets and Poems*, The Oxford Shakespeare, ed. Burrow (Oxford, 2002), 118; Heather Dubrow, "'Incertainties now crown themselves assur'd': The Politics of Plotting Shakespeare's Sonnets," *Shakespeare Quarterly* 47 (1996): 293–95; Paul Edmondson and Stanley Wells, *Shakespeare's Sonnets*, Oxford Shakespeare Topics (Oxford, 2004), 39–40, 46. Stephen Greenblatt, *Will in the World* (New York: Norton, 2004), 232. Greenblatt raises the question, but — wisely — avoids offering an answer.

24. As Pequigney observes, regarding the idea that the sonnets have more than one male subject (218–19).

25. Burrow, 123; Edmondson and Wells, 46; Dubrow, 300–303. I find unpersuasive Dubrow's claim that the duplicity or "infinite variety" (300) of the black mistress means that

a version of her — good or bad — might appear anywhere in the sequence (300–301). Rather, the black mistress is monotonously changeable, palpable in her duplicity, and predictably in accord with Renaissance stereotypes of deceitful women.

26. Burrow, 123, invokes sonnet 53 ("What is your substance, whereof are you made / That millions of strange shadows on you tend") to suggest the sonnets' engagement with variety. But what interests Shakespeare in this sonnet is not variety in itself, but that a single "you" contains it.

27. See chapter 14.

28. See chapters 1–4.

29. Edwin Haviland Miller, *The Professional Writer in Elizabethan England* (Cambridge: Harvard, 1959), 141–49; W. W. Greg, *Some Aspects and Problems of London Publishing Between 1550 and 1650* (Oxford: Clarendon, 1956), 63–65. Often authors claimed their work was pirated as a means of protecting themselves from looking too eager to share their writing in print.

30. W.H. Auden, introduction to *Shakespeare: The Sonnets and Narrative Poems: The Complete Non-Dramatic Poetry* ed. Sylvan Barnet (Harmondsworth, England: Penguin, 1964, 1989), xxxv; Rollins, 2:3, 6; Burrow, 96, 98–99.

31. As Arthur Marotti observes though, it's not clear that in 1609 Shakespeare would be as desperate for money as in 1593–1594, when he was just beginning his career ("Shakespeare's Sonnets," in *Soliciting Interpretation: Literary Theory and Seventeenth-Century English Poetry*, ed. Elizabeth D. Harvey and Katherine Eisaman Maus [University of Chicago, 1990], 171 n.34.) While Duncan-Jones suggests that the closing of the theaters in 1609 would have even greater economic consequences for Shakespeare because by then he was highly invested as a sharer in them (*Shakespeare's Sonnets*, 8–9), he also had more assets by that time including an investment that yielded a sizable £40 annuity (see Park Honan, *Shakespeare: A Life* [Oxford, 1998], 290–94; Honan nonetheless agrees with Duncan-Jones that Shakespeare might have sold the sonnets to raise money [360]).

32. Duncan-Jones, *Shakespeare's Sonnets*, 8–13; 34–37. See also her "Were the 1609 Shake-Speares Sonnets Really Unauthorized?" *The Review of English Studies*, n.s., 34 (1983): 151–71; and Rollins, 2:6–18.

33. Duncan-Jones, *Shakespeare's Sonnets*, 32.

34. Rollins, 2:17–18; 84.

35. *King Lear* (conflated text), 3.4.22.

36. On this point see Booth, 545–46.

37. Duncan-Jones, "Unauthorized," 168. For example, Leighton Brewer (*Shakespeare and the Dark Lady* [Boston: Christopher, 1966]) rejects sonnet 106 as having been written to a man because "one can hardly imagine a man extolling the beauty of another man's foot" and assumes that Shakespeare was writing about a woman in sonnet 116 ("Let me not to the marriage of true minds") unless he was "a homosexual," which the author doubts (14). Sidney Lee assumes that when there is no "clear indication of the addressee's sex" they are to a woman (*A Life of William Shakespeare*, new ed. [New York: Macmillan, 1916], 166). See also Rollins' summary of defensive attempts to redistribute the "black mistress" over many sonnets before 126 (2: 242–49). As I detail further in chapter 31, however, this defensiveness has not always been about homosexual desire — as Rollins' summaries of attempts to make the sonnets' mistress into Shakespeare's wife attest (2:256–60).

38. As Dubrow points out, 302–303.

39. Edmondson and Wells, 28–32. Also see Dubrow, "Incertainties."

40. Dubrow admits that "even if one relies only on poems that gender their addressee, the sequence paints a picture more critical of women than of men" (305).

41. See chapter 17.

42. Dubrow suggests that when sonnet readers identify the negative but ungendered sonnets with a woman they make women the source of sin, a "frailty whose name is woman" (305). But it is not readers who do this; it's Hamlet ("frailty thy name is woman," he says) and perhaps *Hamlet*'s author, just as Shakespeare does, as Dubrow notes, in sonnet 129 (305). Why blame this scapegoating on readers or make the more improbable assumption that only the clearly gendered sonnets participate in this scapegoating?

43. Quoted in Rollins, 2:53.

44. Though, as Duncan-Jones observes, we can't be absolutely certain that the sonnets to which Meres refers are the ones that would eventually be published (*Shakespeare's Sonnets*, 13).

45. Rollins, 2:25–55, 73.

46. MacDonald P. Jackson dates the writing of the sonnets as beginning in 1590 and ending by 1604 ("Vocabulary and Chronology: The Case of Shakespeare's Sonnets," *The Review of English Studies*, n.s., 52 [2001]: 59–

75). Donald W. Foster dates composition to between 1598 and 1609 ("Reconstructing Shakespeare Part 2: The Sonnets," *The Shakespeare Newsletter*, Fall 1991, 26–27). A. Kent Hieatt, Charles W. Hieatt, and Anne Lake Prescott believe composition covered that entire period, from 1591 to 1609 ("When Did Shakespeare Write Sonnets 1609?" *Studies in Philology* 88 [1991]: 69–109).

47. These problems with stylometry are well detailed in Katherine Duncan-Jones's introduction to her edition of the sonnets, 13–17. Burrow observes additionally that individual sonnets within particular groups could be earlier or later than the majority of sonnets in that group (105).

48. Hieatt et al. date the black mistress sequence (127–154), as well as 1–103, all within the range of 1591 to 1595. Foster dates 127–154 in 1598 and 1599, overlapping with 18–36 and 37–55, which he dates to 1599. Jackson assumes the least overlap, with only 1–17 overlapping with the black mistress sonnets. Of the remaining young man sonnets, Jackson thinks they follow the black mistress sonnets.

49. As Rollins observes, 2:56.

50. Rollins, 1:263–67. See also 2:59–62. The other, even less helpful (or even clearly) "dated" sonnets are 35 and 104.

51. Duncan-Jones, *Shakespeare's Sonnets*, 29–31, 15–16; Burrow, 106.

Section I

1. Quoted in Norbert Elias, *The Civilizing Process*, trans. Edmund Jephcott, ed. Eric Dunning et al., rev. ed., (Oxford: Blackwell, 2000), 110, 122, 73 and 129 respectively.

2. Elias, 52–57.

3. *De civilitate morum puerilium* [of civilized manners for boys], quoted in Elias, 122.

4. See Elias, 67, 126; M. Braun-Ronsdorf, *The History of the Handkerchief* (Leigh-On-Sea, England: F. Lewis, 1967), 19.

5. English medieval kings did seek to assert their power, however. The Tudors' more centralized rule was already being established by their Yorkist predecessors, Edward IV and Richard III (Norman F. Cantor, *The English: A History of Politics and Society to 1760* [New York: Simon and Schuster, 1967], 325–26, 332–35).

6. Lawrence Stone, *The Crisis of the Aristocracy, 1558–1641* (London: Oxford, 1965), 200–201, 239–40; 265–66; Penry Williams,

The Tudor Regime (Oxford, 1979), 110–111, 237–238, 240–241, 436–439.

7. "Teares of the Muses," lines 95–96, in *Spenser: Poetical Works*, ed. J.C. Smith and E. De Selincourt (Oxford, 1912), 481.

8. Derek Wilson, *Sweet Robin: A Biography of Robert Dudley, Earl of Leicester* (London: Hamish Hamilton, 1981), 269–95, esp. 271, 276, 294–95. Sir Robert Naunton, *Fragmentia Regalia, or Observations on Queen Elizabeth, Her Times and Favorites*, ed. John S. Cervoski (Cranbury, NJ: Associated, 1985), 52. Williams, 134, 439.

9. Stone, 672–73.

10. Naunton, 52.

11. Ten editions of *The Courtier* were published in England between 1561 and 1611, four in Hoby's English translation and six in Bartholomew Clerke's Latin translation of 1571 (Peter Burke, *The Fortunes of the Courtier* [University Park: Pennsylvania, 1996], 65–66).

12. Baldesar Castiglione, *The Book of the Courtier*, trans. Charles S. Singleton (Garden City, NY: Anchor, 1959), 29.

13. See Raleigh Trevelyan, *Sir Walter Raleigh* (New York: Henry Holt, 2002), 46–54.

14. *Hamlet*, 3.1.150.

15. *King Lear*, 2.2.16.

16. Elias, 128, 134, 216–217, 396–98. Frank Whigham, *Ambition and Privilege: The Social Tropes of Elizabethan Courtesy Theory* (Berkeley: University of California, 1984), 13.

17. *As You Like It*, 5.4.81–82. On the (somewhat) pacifying effects of the code of the duel see Stone, *Crisis*, 242–47.

18. Skiles Howard, *The Politics of Courtly Dancing in Early Modern England* (Amherst: University of Massachusetts, 1998), 1–25.

19. *Astrophil and Stella* 41 in *Sir Philip Sidney: A Critical Edition of the Major Works*, ed. Katherine Duncan-Jones (Oxford, 1989).

20. See *Sir Philip Sidney: A Critical Edition* for possible identification and description of the specific tournament recalled in the sonnet (363; 299–311).

21. On the sonnet as an expression of literary mastery see Arthur Marotti, "'Love Is Not Love': Elizabethan Sonnet Sequences and the Social Order," *ELH* 49 (1982): 396–428.

22. Walter Bourchier Devereux, *Lives and Letters of the Devereux, Earls of Essex* (London: John Murray, 1853), 1:328. Quoted in Stone, 675. Francis Bacon, Renaissance courtier, essayist and philosopher, may also have had a hand in the letter that contains this comment, and the letter as whole has sometimes been as-

cribed to him. That Bacon may have been the earl's ghostwriter suggests both the new importance of the learned noble and its uncertain achievement. Paul E. J. Hammer suggests that the earl was consciously trying to create a reputation for himself as a man of learning by employing Bacon and others to help him with his writing ("The Earl of Essex, Fulke Greville, and the Employment of Scholars," *Studies in Philology* 91 [1994]: 170–172).

23. The gentleman accused was Sir Ralph Eure. See Stone, *Crisis*, 675. On the literacy of the medieval nobility and the degree of change in the Renaissance see Nicholas Orme, *From Childhood to Chivalry: The Education of the English Kings and Aristocracy, 1066–1530* (London: Methuen, 1984), 142–56. See also chapter 2 of my *Defending Literature in Early Modern England: Renaissance Literary Theory in Social Context* (Cambridge, 2000) for Sir Thomas Elyot as a transitional figure.

24. Catherine Bates, "Literature and the Court," in *The Cambridge History of Early Modern English Literature*, ed. David Loewenstein and Janel Muller (Cambridge, 2002), 345–46; Stone, *Crisis*, 672–74; Whigham, 13. On multiple styles of gentility see also my *Defending Literature*, 17–19, 36–39, 56–60.

25. Graham Perry, "Literary Patronage," in *The Cambridge History of Early Modern English Literature*, 125.

26. Bates, 343–44, 346. On the disappointment of hopes, see Perry, 126–27; and Edwin Haviland Miller, *The Professional Writer in Elizabethan England: A Study of Non-dramatic Verse* (Cambridge: Harvard, 1959), chapter 4.

27. T. W. Baldwin, *Shakspere's Small Latine and Lesse Greeke*, 2 vols. (Urbana: University of Illinois, 1944), 1:134–63. See also Helen M. Jewell, *Education in Early Modern England* (New York: St. Martins, 1998), 93, 102.

28. For example Thomas Wilson's *Arte of Rhetoric*, Richard Sherry's *A Treatise of Schemes and Tropes*, Angel Day's *The English Secretary* or George Puttenham's *Arte of English Poesie*. For an introduction to these English works see Baldwin, 2:29–68.

29. George Puttenham, *The Arte of English Poesie*, ed. and intro. Gladys Doidge Willcock and Alice Walker (Cambridge, 1936). I've drawn on the superb website *Silva Rhetoricae* (*http://rhetoric.byu.edu/*) for definitions of these figures rendered into modern English. What Puttenham calls traductio is more commonly defined as the related figure "polypto-

ton" and what he calls antitheton is more commonly defined as the related "antithesis."

30. Gladys Doidge Willcock and Alice Walker, introduction and appendices to *The Arte of English Poesie*, lix, 328–33.

31. Desiderius Erasmus, *De duplici copia verborum and rerum*, in *Collected Works Of Erasmus*, vol. 24, trans. Betty I. Knott (University of Toronto, 1978), 349–54. Stephen Greenblatt, General Introduction, *The Norton Shakespeare*, ed. Greenblatt et al. (New York: W.W. Norton, 1997) similarly refers to this example of variation as an instance of Renaissance rhetorical culture (61).

32. R.R. Bolger, *The Classical Heritage and Its Beneficiaries* (Cambridge, 1954), 314, 448. Baldwin, 2:32, 37, 41, 62, 179. Baldwin discusses evidence in Shakespeare's plays of his familiarity with and attitude toward the art of varying, 2:182–96.

33. Erasmus, 302.

34. Janet M. Green, "Queen Elizabeth I's Latin Reply to the Polish Ambassador," *Sixteenth Century Journal* 31 (2000): 2002–03. See also Neville Williams, *Elizabeth: Queen of England* (London: Weidenfeld and Nicholson, 1967), 8–9.

35. Whigham, 8.

36. Stephen Booth, *Shakespeare's Sonnets* (New Haven: Yale, 1977) notes the influence of Ovid's *Metamorphoses* on this sonnet (239). On the influence of Ovid in the English Renaissance see Elizabeth Story Donno, *Elizabethan Minor Epics* (New York: Columbia, 1963), 1–20. Baldwin, 2:417–18.

37. Park Honan, *Shakespeare: A Life* (Oxford, 1998), 43, 58.

38. Honan, 60–61.

39. Erasmus, 359.11–12; 361.14–15; 364.7.

40. Dates are of initial publication and from *Elizabethan Sonnets*, ed. Maurice Evans, rev. Roy J. Booth (Vermont: Everyman, 1994). While Shakespeare may have begun writing his sonnets in the 1590s, they were published at a late date for the form. See chapter 26 of this book on their belatedness, and see the preface on possible dates of composition.

41. Greville quoted in Lisle C. John, *The Elizabethan Sonnet Sequences* (New York: Russell and Russell, 1964, 1938), 24. This dedication is also emphasized by Marotti, "Love is not love," 419.

42. Marotti, "Love is not love," 405–10; John, 18–24.

43. *Amoretti* 1, *Spenser: Poetical Works*, 562.

44. Miller, 95–97; Lauro Martines, *Society*

and History in English Renaissance Verse (Oxford: Basil Blackwell, 1985), 27, 94.

45. Barnabe Barnes, *Parthenophil and Parthenophe: A Critical Edition*, ed. and intro. Victor A. Donyo (Carbondale: Southern Illinois University, 1971), 132.

46. See G.P.V. Akrigg, *Shakespeare and the Earl of Southampton* (Cambridge: Harvard, 1968), 35–38, 183–88; Honan, 163–64, 175–177.

47. Honan, 172. Katherine Duncan-Jones, *Ungentle Shakespeare: Scenes From His Life* (London: Arden Shakespeare, 2001), 56, 72. Introduction: "Venus and Adonis," in *Shakespeare: The Complete Sonnets and Poems*, ed. Colin Burrow (Oxford, 2002), 8–9. "Textual Note" to "Venus and Adonis" in *The Norton Shakespeare*, 606.

48. Dedication to *Venus and Adonis*, 607.

49. Dedication to *The Rape of Lucrece*, 641.

50. On this point, see also chapter 7.

51. Helen Vendler, *The Art of Shakespeare's Sonnets* (Cambridge: Harvard, 1997), 2. James Boswell makes a similar argument in his 1821 *The Plays and Poems of William Shakespeare*, 20 vols. (London: C Baldwin, 1821), 2:219.

52. Ralegh seems to have intended for the queen to see, or at least hear about his bitter "Ocean, to Cynthia" (*The Poems of Sir Walter Ralegh: A Historical Edition*, Medieval and Renaissance Texts and Studies 209, ed. Michael Ruddick [Tempe: Arizona State, 1999]), li. Ralegh's client the poet Edmund Spenser, moreover, seems to have known this poem and to have referred to its bitterness in print (Katherine Koller, "Spenser and Ralegh," *ELH* 1 [1934]: 53–60). Since these references to the poem were part of Spenser's "propaganda" for his patron (Koller, 53), Spenser must have thought that the bitterness of "Ocean, to Cynthia" was not an embarrassment. Louise Simons suggests that Nashe's dedication to Southampton, which seems "designed to give offense" did not appear in the second edition of the *Unfortunate Traveller* because it "misfired" ("Rerouting the *Unfortunate Traveller*: Strategies for Coherence and Direction," *Studies in English Literature, 1500–1900* 28 [1988]: 19–20). The offensive dedication may have misfired, but unruly Nashe was first willing to risk offense. On stances toward patronage, see also below, chapter 7.

53. Marotti outlines a similar reading in "Love is not love."

54. See Booth's gloss on this phrase, 180.

55. *Oxford English Dictionary* "friend," sb.

5c. Shakespeare uses the proverb in *2 Henry IV*, 5.1.26–27.

56. Felicity Heal, *Hospitality in Early Modern England* (Oxford: Clarendon, 1990), 33–34.

57. As Marotti, "Love is not love," argues about Sidney's sonnets, 399–402, 405.

58. As Booth points out, the syntactically ambiguous phrase could also mean that the young man (the "fair subject" of line 4) indiscriminately blesses (and gives patronage to) any book (280). This alternative reading does not, however, change the general sense of the poem's accusation.

59. Puttenham, *Arte of English Poesie*, 154.

60. Louis Montrose, "Of Gentlemen and Shepherds: The Politics of Elizabethan Pastoral Form," *ELH* 50 (1983): 440, 450–52.

61. In a review of over 2,000 anthologizations of Shakespeare's sonnets from 1803 to the present, I found only one instance of sonnet 125 being anthologized, in an anthology of Elizabethan poetry from 1992.

62. If the rumor and the identity of the informer are obscure, even more so is the question of who "suborned" — encouraged or paid for — it.

63. My reading of this sonnet here and in what follows has been shaped by Thomas Greene's wonderful essay, "'Pitiful Thrivers': Failed Husbandry in the Sonnets" in *Shakespeare and the Question of Theory*, ed. Patricia Parker and Geoffrey Hartman (New York: Routledge, 1985), 240–42.

64. *Oxford English Dictionary*, "obsequious," a., 1b; "oblation" n., 1a, 2a, 2b. See Booth's comments on "obsequious," "oblation," and the thread of religious metaphor in this entire sonnet (427–30).

65. See Booth's commentary on the word, 427. *The Oxford English Dictionary* first witnesses the word's pejorative meaning in 1602 ("obsequious," a., 2a).

66. William Fulwood, *The Enimie of Idlenesse: Teaching a Perfect Platform How to Endite Epistles and Letters* (London, 1586), 67–68. Examples of Shakespeare's sonnets that most closely echo Fulwood's advice — Point 1: 26, 38, 103. Point 2: 17, 106. Point 3: 21, 82, 125.

67. Honan, 228–229. See also Duncan-Jones, *Ungentle Shakespeare*, 96, 100–103.

68. See Felicity Heal and Clive Holmes, *The Gentry in England and Wales, 1500–1700* (Stanford, 1994) for this idea and its rivals (27–33).

69. Barbara Correll's quip from "Malleable

Material, Models of Power: Woman in Erasmus's 'Marriage Group' and *Civility in Boys*,"
ELH 57 (1990): 253.

70. "An Exhortation Concerning Good
Order and Obedience to Rulers and Magis-
trates," in *Certain Sermons or Homilies (1547)
and A Homily Against Disobedience and Willful Rebellion (1570): A Critical Edition*, ed.
Ronald B. Bond (University of Toronto, 1987),
161.

71. I've drawn on Whigham's discussion of
these laws, 156–69, and the charts of the 1580
law that he includes, 164–67.

72. Ian Archer, "Material Londoners?" in
Material London ca. 1600, ed. Lena Cowen
Orlin (Philadelphia: University of Pennsylva-
nia, 2000), 176–77. Steve Rappaport, *Worlds
Within Worlds: Structures of Life in Sixteenth-
Century London* (Cambridge, 1989), 84–86,
367–72. Not all London lives were as success-
ful as Shakespeare's however. The 1590s in
London especially were a "decade of excep-
tional hardships" (Rappaport, 378).

73. Jean-Christophe Agnew, *Worlds Apart:
The Market and the Theater in Anglo-American Thought, 1550–1750* (Cambridge, 1986),
8–9, 43–46, 111–12, 120–125; Archer, 178–84.
Life in sixteenth-century London put pressure
on traditional notions of status and social reciprocity. Archer notes however, that even in
London a premodern ethos of "collective values" moderated the pressures of consumerist
individualism (187).

74. Thomas Nashe, *Christ's Tears Over
Jerusalem, The Works of Thomas Nashe*, ed.
Ronald B. McKerrow, 5 vols. (Oxford: Basil
Blackwell, 1958), 2:104–105. The quotations
are from 105 and also quoted in Agnew,
46.

75. Heal and Holmes, 29.

76. Stone, *Crisis*, 76–77.

77. See e.g. *The London Daily Telegraph* 16
June 2001:4 and 20 June 2001:23 for a favor-
able quoting of this line from Polonius and a
corrective response.

78. Booth, 190.

79. For how the address to the young man
provides Shakespeare with a broader range of
emotion and ideas, see Gordon Braden,
"Shakespeare's Petrarchism," in *Shakespeare's
Sonnets: Critical Essays*, ed. James Schiffer
(New York: Garland, 2000), 170–71; and F.J.
Lever, *The Elizabethan Love Sonnet* (London:
Methuen, 1966), 166–68.

80. Marotti, "Love is not love," 411–413,
422 n52.

81. Heal and Holmes, 31.

82. *King Lear* (conflated text), 1.2.9–10.

83. *Oxford English Dictionary*, "outbrave,"
v., 2b. Booth observes this secondary sense of
the line (308).

84. John Fuller, *The Sonnet* (London:
Methuen, 1972), 15.

85. On "sweetness" and "salty" wit in the
sonnets see Rosalie Colie, *The Resources of
Kind: Genre-Theory in the Renaissance*, ed.
Barbara K. Lewalski (Berkeley: University of
California, 1973), 68–75; Fuller, 2–3; 14–20;
and Marotti, 413.

86. For the praise, see for example sonnets
104–106, 115. For the hiatus see sonnets 97–103.

87. See sonnets 110 and 111.

88. Marotti, "Love is not love," 412. Other
poems on this theme earlier in the sequence
could be interpreted similarly. Alan Sinfield,
*Shakespeare, Authority, Sexuality: Unfinished
Business in Cultural Materialism* (London:
Routledge, 2006), nicely picks up on the sonnet's calling the boy Nature's "minion" in revenge for being put in a subordinate position
as the young man's "minion" (178).

89. Joel Fineman, *Shakespeare's Perjured
Eye: The Invention of Poetic Subjectivity in the
Sonnets* (Berkeley: University of California,
1986), notes how frequently the sonnets observe the act of observation (158–159).

90. Some hints, however, have been discerned. Readers have heard an echo in the Earl
of Southampton's last name, Wriothesley (perhaps pronounced Rose-ly, though, alas, perhaps Wrisley), in the rose with which the
young man is often associated. "Hewes" in
sonnet 20 has been heard as referring to a last
name of Hughes, the H. of the mysterious
dedicatee W.H. See Hyder Rollins, ed., *A New
Variorum Edition of Shakespeare: The Sonnets
(Vols. 24–25)*, 2 parts (Philadelphia, J.B. Lippincott, 1944), 2:180–85, 194. Neither of these
suppositions are persuasive, especially the
latter. But one can't say there aren't jokes in
the sonnets that have been lost to time. The
point of a hint, after all, is that some won't get
it.

91. Hence some readers argue that there is
no evidence the young man is noble. See for
example, Joseph Pequigney, *Such Is My Love:
A Study of Shakespeare's Sonnets* (University of
Chicago, 1985), 12, 88 233–34n13. For the
opposite view, with which I would agree, see
Lever, 164.

92. On this point I have benefited from
Fineman's reading of sonnet 44 (222–25).

93. Barnes, sonnet 63 in *Parthenophil and
Parthenophe*, 39.

94. E.g. Sidney's *Astrophil and Stella*, 1.

95. See *Silva Rhetoricae*, "epanalepsis."

96. *As You Like It*, 4.1.91–92.

97. In making this point I follow Stephen Greenblatt's brilliant conclusion to his discussion of Thomas Wyatt's poetry, which is worth quoting in full: "Courtly self-fashioning seizes upon inwardness to heighten its histrionic power, inwardness turns upon self-fashioning and exposes its underlying motives, its origins in aggression, bad faith, self-interest and frustrated longing" (*Renaissance Self-Fashioning: From More to Shakespeare* [University of Chicago, 1980], 156).

Section II

1. On contemporary representations of the sonnets see section 4 and Michael Keevak, *Sexual Shakespeare: Forgery, Authorship, Portraiture* (Detroit: Wayne State, 2001), 122–23.

2. For example, *Love Speaks Its Name: Gay and Lesbian Love Poems*, ed. J.D. McClatchy (New York: Knopf, 2001).

3. Katha Pollitt, "Adam and Steve — Together At Last," *The Nation*, 15 December 2003, p. 9.

4. Jess Winfield in *What Would Shakespeare Do?: Personal Advice from The Bard* (Berkeley: Seastone, 2000) makes this connection between gay marriage and sonnet 116.

5. Michel Foucault, *The History of Sexuality, Vol. I: An Introduction*, trans. Robert Hurley (New York: Vintage, 1980), 43.

6. Certainly, however, not everyone who has same-sex sex sees him- or herself as "being" homosexual. And the legal case against homosexual persons has long been made in the U.S. on the basis of a supposed tradition of laws against homosexual acts. On these issues see Jeffrey Weeks, *Coming Out: Homosexual Politics in Britain from the Nineteenth Century to the Present*, rev. ed. (London: Quartet, 1990), 32–35; Eve Kosofsky Sedgwick, *Epistemology of the Closet* (Berkeley: University of California, 1990), 47–48; Jonathan Goldberg, *Sodometries: Renaissance Texts, Modern Sexualities* (Stanford, 1992), 6–16.

7. Jonathan Ned Katz, *The Invention of Heterosexuality* (New York: Penguin, 1995), esp. 99.

8. Alan Bray, *Homosexuality in Renaissance England* (N.p: Gay Men's Press, 1982), 14–16.

9. Bray, *Homosexuality*, 14–16; and Bruce Smith, *Homosexual Desire in Shakespeare's England* (University of Chicago, 1994), 19. See also Goldberg, *Sodometries*.

10. Bray, *Homosexuality*, 15–16.

11. *The Works of John Wilmot, Earl of Rochester*, ed. Harold Love (Oxford, 1999), lines 36–40. Also cited in Bray, *Homosexuality*, 50.

12. Bray, *Homosexuality*, 16–17, 54–55; John Rainolds, *The Overthrow of Stage-plays* (1599; reprint, New York: Johnson, 1972), 10; Edward Coke, *The Third Part of the Institutes of the Laws of England* (London, 1797; reprint, Buffalo, New York: William S. Hein, 1986), 59. Rainolds quoted in Bray, *Homosexuality*, 17, and Coke at 16. Smith, 166, also cites Coke's remark. *The Third Part of the Institutes* was first published in 1644, though written earlier.

13. See Bray, *Homosexuality*, 62, 71, and Smith, 48–53.

14. Katz, 38–40. Katz observes that the modern revaluation of heterosexual desire as positive leads to the particular stigmatization of homosexuality (82, 92–93, 111–12). Bray, *Homosexuality*, 47.

15. Bray, *Homosexuality*, 19–26, 68, 71–76.

16. Stephanie A. Sanders and June Machover Reinisch, "Would You Say You 'Had Sex' If...?" *JAMA: Journal of the American Medical Association* 281 (1999): 275–77. The study was conducted by the Kinsey Institute in 1991 but reported on in JAMA in 1999, when, because of the Clinton-Lewinsky affair, this question took on new political consequence. The editor of the journal was fired because he was said to have politicized the journal by allowing the article to be published at this moment ("AMA Journal Editor Fired Over Article," *Wall Street Journal*, 18 Jan. 1999, p. B7) .

17. To be prosecutable, homosexual sodomy under Elizabethan law usually had to involve the rape of a minor (Smith, 53).

18. *Lawrence v. Texas*, 539 U.S. (2003), Opinion of the Court, 7–10, Concurring Opinion, Justice O'Connor, 3–8.

19. Quoted in Paul Hammond, *Figuring Sex Between Men: From Shakespeare to Rochester* (Oxford, 2002), 28–29, who provides Bodley's Latin and translates it.

20. *Beowulf: A New Prose Translation*, trans. E. Talbot Donaldson (New York: Norton, 1966), 33; *Battle of Maldon*, in *Norton Anthology of English Literature, Volume I*, 6th ed. Abrams et al. (New York: Norton, 1993), 75; Sir Thomas Malory, *Le Morte D'Arthur*, intro. John Lawlor, ed. Janet Cowen, 2 vols. (New

York: Penguin, 1969), 2:458. Medieval lord-vassal relationships need not be seen as genitally sexual — in contradiction to a classical tradition — but they do suggest male intimacy, physical affection and love. On this point see Allen J. Frantzen, *Before The Closet: Same-Sex Desire from "Beowulf" to Angels in America* (University of Chicago, 1998), 69, 91–98, 107.

21. See chapter 1.

22. See Eve Cantarella, *Bisexuality in the Ancient World*, trans. Cormac Ó Cuilleanáin (New Haven: Yale, 1992).

23. On the influence of the classical world on Renaissance same-sex eroticism see Smith, esp. 35–41, 191–97, 81–91.

24. Desiderius Erasmus, *De ratione studii*, in *Collected Works Of Erasmus*, vol. 24, trans. Brian McGregor (University of Toronto, 1978). This commentary is also cited in Smith, 90, and Alan Stewart, *Close Readers: Humanism and Sodomy in Early Modern England* (Princeton, 1997), 123. Stewart notes that a fourth-century commentary on the eclogues, often included in Renaissance editions of them, identified Virgil as Corydon and Alexis as either a beautiful slave given to Virgil by his patron or as the great patron Caesar himself (122). Even if Shakespeare did not know the Erasmian commentary on the poem he likely knew this one (see T.W. Baldwin, *William Shakspere's Small Latine and Lesse Greeke*, 2 vols. [Urbana: University of Illinois, 1944], 2:478–79), which links love, patronage and authorial frustration.

25. Smith, 81–115. Goldberg, *Sodometries*, 64–76.

26. Smith, 84–88. Kenneth Charlton, *Education in Renaissance England* (London: Routledge and Kegan Paul, 1965), 149–50. See also Bray, *Homosexuality*, 51–53.

27. Bray, *Homosexuality*, 45–51.

28. Alan Bray, "Homosexuality and the Signs of Male Friendship in Elizabethan England," *Queering the Renaissance*, ed. Jonathan Goldberg (Durham: Duke, 1994), 42–45.

29. Alan Bray, *The Friend* (University of Chicago, 2003), 88. See also 82–83, 94–95, 110–15, 124, 128.

30. *Oxford English Dictionary*, "friend" sb. a4 ("A lover or paramour, of either sex"); "lover" (1) 1a ("One who is possessed by sentiments of affection or regard towards another; a friend or well-wisher"). Hammond provides an excellent discussion, keyed to Shakespeare's sonnets, of the overlaps and multiple meanings of "friend" and "lover" in the Renaissance (18–21).

31. See chapter 2.

32. *The Correspondence of Philip Sidney and Hubert Languet*, ed. William Aspenwall Bradley (Boston: Merrymount, 1912), 3, 6.

33. Alan Stewart, *Philip Sidney: A Double Life* (New York: St. Martins, 2000), 103–114.

34. Bray, "Friendship," 44–45; Stewart, *Close Readers*, 144–47.

35. Bray, "Friendship," 42–43.

36. Bray, "Friendship," 48–51; Goldberg, *Sodometries*, 117. *Edward II* in *Christopher Marlowe: Doctor Faustus and Other Plays*, ed. David Bevington and Eric Rasmussen (Oxford, 1995), 1.4.391.

37. Baldesar Castiglione, *The Book of the Courtier*, trans. Charles S. Singleton (Garden City, New York: Doubleday, 1959), 248.

38. "The New Atlantis" in *Francis Bacon: A Selection of His Work*, ed. Sidney Warhaft (New York: Macmillan, 1985), 444.

39. Bray, *Homosexuality*, 71–73; and "Friendship," 53–56.

40. Robert Shepherd, "Sexual Rumors in English Politics: The Cases of Elizabeth I and James I," in *Desire and Discipline: Sex and Sexuality in the Premodern West* (University of Toronto, 1996), 108–118.

41. David M. Bergeron, ed., *King James and Letters of Homoerotic Desire* (Iowa City: University of Iowa, 1999), Letters J20 (14 June 1623) and B17 (20 August 1623). These letters and their context are also discussed in Jonathan Goldberg, *King James and the Politics of Literature* (1983; reprint, Stanford, 1989), 143–46. That James called himself "dad" to Buckingham does not mean that the relationship with Buckingham was "fatherly" but that "fatherhood" was one way James conceived of his erotic relationship with Buckingham: in another letter James calls Buckingham his "sweet child and wife" and himself Buckingham's "dad and husband" (J29 [December 1623?]). The same could be said of the "fatherly" voice to the young man in the sonnets, especially in the sonnets advising the young man to marry and have children (numbers 1–17).

42. Bergeron, 119–23.

43. Katherine Duncan-Jones, *Sir Philip Sidney: Courtier-Poet* (New Haven: Yale, 1991), 199–201, 230–31.

44. *Oxford English Dictionary*, "tender," sb2, 1b ("An offer of money or the like in discharge of a debt or liability").

45. Jonathan Goldberg, "Fatherly Authority: The Politics of Stuart Family Images," in *Rewriting the Renaissance: The Discourse of Sexual Difference in Early Modern Europe*, ed.

Margaret W. Ferguson, Maureen Quilligan and Nancy J. Vickers (University of Chicago, 1986), esp. 12.

46. See, for example, *Shakespeare's Sonnets*, ed. Louis B. Wright and Virginia A. LaMar (New York: Washington Square, 1967), xv. W.H. Auden, in his introduction to the sonnets, gives as one reason for his dismissal of homosexual desire in the poems a related reason: that Shakespeare was married (*Shakespeare: The Sonnets and Narrative Poems*, ed. William Burto [New York: Signet, 1989], xxix). This idea is repeated more recently in Dympna Callaghan, *Shakespeare's Sonnets* (Oxford: Blackwell, 2007), 20.

47. Sonnet 8's vision of the harmonious family — "sire, and child, and happy mother" — is the closest the sonnets get.

48. On women's roles in arranged marriages, however, see Sara Mendelson and Patricia Crawford, *Women in Early Modern England, 1550–1720* (Oxford: Clarendon, 1998), 112–13.

49. Thomas M. Greene, "'Pitiful Thrivers': Failed Husbandry in the Sonnets" in *Shakespeare and the Question of Theory*, ed. Patricia Parker and Geoffrey Hartman (New York: Routledge, 1985), 234.

50. See *Oxford English Dictionary*, "engraft," v., 2a and "graff," n. An important reflection on the natural or unnaturalness of the graft occurs in *A Winter's Tale*, in a passage that brings together the legitimacy of both art and cross-class sex and marriage. King Polixenes defends the "art" that lets "conceive a bark of baser kind / By bud of nobler race," since "the art itself is nature" (4.4.94–95). But he is furious when shortly after this remark he learns his son is in love with the woman to whom he has been speaking, whom he believes is a mere shepherd's daughter (4.4.405–408).

51. Edwin Haviland Miller, *The Professional Writer in Elizabethan England: A Study of Nondramatic Literature* (Cambridge: Harvard, 1959), 94–136. Richard Helgerson, *Self-Crowned Laureates: Spenser, Jonson, Milton and the Literary System* (Berkeley: University of California, 1983), 26–28, 55–67; on the uncertain social value of poetry during the period see my *Defending Literature in Early Modern England: Renaissance Literary Theory in Social Context* (Cambridge, 2000). Thomas Bodley quoted in *Elizabethan-Jacobean Drama: The Theatre In Its Time*, ed. G. Blakemore Evans (New York: New Amsterdam, 1988), 17.

52. See also Alan Sinfield, *Shakespeare, Authority, Sexuality: Unfinished Business in Cul-*

tural Materialism (London: Routledge, 2006) for a particular emphasis on social and sexual positions in the sonnets (162–80).

53. Anna Bryson "The Rhetoric of Status: Gesture, Demeanour and the Image of the Gentleman in Sixteenth- and Seventeenth-Century England" in *Renaissance Bodies: The Human Figure in English Culture, c. 1540–1660*, ed. Lucy Gent and Nigel Llewellyn (London: Reaktion, 1990), 136–53. See also Joan Kelly, "Did Women Have A Renaissance?" in *Women, History, Theory: The Essays of Joan Kelly* (University of Chicago, 1984), 44–45.

54. On Shakespeare's erotic emphasis on the young man's physical beauty, see Joseph Pequigney, *Such Is My Love: A Study of Shakespeare's Sonnets* (University of Chicago, 1985), esp. 65–68.

55. C.S. Lewis, *The Allegory Of Love: A Study in Medieval Tradition* (New York: Oxford, 1958), 2.

56. Gloss, *Norton Anthology of English Literature*, ed. Abrams et al., sixth ed., vol. 1 (New York: Norton, 1993), 440.

57. Gordon Braden, *Petrarchan Love and the Continental Renaissance* (New Haven: Yale, 1999), 99–105; Michael Rocke, *Forbidden Friendships: Homosexuality and Male Culture in Renaissance Florence* (Oxford, 1996), 6, 139; Christopher Ryan, *The Poetry of Michelangelo: An Introduction* (Madison, NJ: Fairleigh Dickinson, 1998), 6, 102–103.

58. Barnabe Barnes, *Parthenophil and Parthenophe: A Critical Edition*, ed. and intro. Victor A. Donyo (Carbondale: Southern Illinois, 1971), 132. Spenser promises an eternity in verse to Charles Howard and Henry Carey. Other dedicatory sonnets refer to the commemorative power of poetry.

59. Wendy Wall, *The Imprint of Gender: Author and Publication in the English Renaissance* (Ithaca: Cornell, 1993), 38–40; Kelly, 36–47; Arthur Marotti, "'Love Is Not Love': Elizabethan Sonnet Sequences and the Social Order," *ELH* 49 (1982): 396–428. Marotti in his *Manuscript, Print, and the English Renaissance Lyric* (Ithaca: Cornell, 1995), observes that women were more able to participate in manuscript than print circulation (48–49). It's worth noting, however, as Sasha Roberts does (*Reading Shakespeare's Poems in Early Modern England* [Houndsmills: Palgrave Macmillan, 2003]), that in the sonnets themselves, the young man is described as participating in the circulation of verse, but the black mistress is not (172). Roberts also notes that the evidence

of the circulation of Shakespeare's own sonnets in manuscript point to a primarily male audience (177). The first notice we have of the sonnets, after all, is Meres' reference to Shakespeare's "sugred Sonnets among his private friends." Hyder Rollins, ed., *A New Variorum Edition of Shakespeare: The Sonnets (Vols. 24–25)*, 2 parts (Philadelphia, J.B. Lippincott, 1944), 2:53.

60. Callaghan is incorrect to call the love triangle in them "singularly scandalous" (3). The story is anything but singular. Besides the dramatic and prose examples listed below, in poetry contemporary with the sonnets there's Richard Barnfield's "The Affectionate Shepheard" (1594).

61. I draw here on Eve Kosofsky Sedgwick's influential reading of this love triangle in her *Between Men: English Literature and Homosocial Desire* (New York: Columbia, 1985), 28–48.

62. Laurie Shannon, *Sovereign Amitie: Figures of Friendship in Shakespearean Contexts* (University of Chicago, 2002), 38–39.

63. Wither's emblem reproduced in Shannon, 39.

64. Lorna Hutson, *The Usurer's Daughter: Male Friendship and Fictions of Women in Sixteenth-Century England* (New York: Routledge, 1994), 63–64; Stewart, *Close Readers*, xxxiv, 124–25, 152–54, and Shannon, 128–29.

65. *The Book of Common Prayer, 1559: The Elizabethan Prayer Book*, ed. John E. Booty (Washington, DC: Folger Shakespeare Library, 1976), 291. The echo is noted in, among others, Katherine Duncan-Jones, ed., *Shakespeare's Sonnets* (London: Thompson Learning, 2001), 342.

66. Shannon, 39n54 and 91 notes the relevance of Renaissance ideas of friendship to sonnet 116. See also 2, 8–9.

67. *The Poems of Sir Walter Ralegh: A Historical Edition*, ed. Michael Rudick, Medieval and Renaissance Text Studies 209 (Tempe: Arizona State, 1999), poem 17, lines 1–4.

68. In the anonymous sonnet sequence *Zepheria* (1594), for example, the mistress both frowns and is likened to the sun (canzon 27).

69. For this reading of sonnet 116 see Gordon Braden, "Shakespeare's Petrarchanism," in *Shakespeare's Sonnets: Critical Essays*, ed., James Schiffer (New York: Garland, 2000), 174–75, 181n12. Arguably, the possibility that either person in the relationship could be the "remover" restores mutuality to the sonnet. But a story of each lover's determination to

hold tight in the face of the other's "remove" remains a troubled one.

70. *A Critical Edition of Sir Thomas Elyot's The Boke Named the Governour*, ed. Donald W. Rude (New York: Garland, 1992), 154–68; quote 154.

71. John Lyly, *Euphues: The Anatomy of Wit*, ed. Edward Arber (London: Alex Murray and Son, 1866), 50; Thomas Heywood, *A Woman Killed with Kindness*, ed. R.W. Van Fossen (Cambridge: Harvard, 1961), 6.76–79. Caught by Frankford having sex, Anne eventually dies of grief, while Wendoll leaves England in shame. Frankford and Anne are reunited just before Anne's death; and, in an eerie repetition of Frankford's disastrous relationship with Wendoll, Anne's brother stresses his compensatory friendship with Frankford: "all the near alliance / I lose by her shall be supplied in thee" (17.101–102.).

72. Sonnet 99 bears similarities to a sonnet by Henry Constable, published in 1592 (*Shakespeare's Sonnets*, ed. Barbara A. Mowat and Paul Werstine, The New Folger Shakespeare Library [New York: Washington Square, 2004], 329–30, 353). There is a much stronger suggestion of theft, and possibly sin, in Shakespeare's sonnet, however.

73. Hallet Smith, for example, in his introduction to the sonnets in the *Riverside Shakespeare* calls the sonnets an instance of "platonic love" (ed. G. Blakemore Evans, 2nd ed. [Boston: Houghton Mifflin, 1997], 1840); Joseph Pequigney, *Such Is My Love: A Study of Shakespeare's Sonnets* (University of Chicago, 1985), notes the degree to which, on the contrary, the sonnets emphasize the young man's physical beauty (64–80).

74. I've followed Pequigney, 42–46, in this reading.

75. Bray, "Friendship," 56.

76. Bray, "Friendship," 53–56. E.K., the commentator on Edmund Spenser's poem *The Shepheardes Calender*, has no trouble hearing a hint (if only to condemn) of "horrible sins of forbidden and unlawful fleshiness" (*Spenser: Poetical Works*, ed. J.C. Smith and E. De Selincourt [Oxford, 1912], 422–23) in the description of the one male youth's love for another — even while that love is associated with the perfectly proper language of classical friendship. Richard Barnfield had to protest that his homoerotic verse was just an imitation of Virgil's second eclogue (*Richard Barnfield: The Complete Poems*, ed. George Klawitter [Selinsgrove, PA: Susquehanna, 1990], 115–16). Thomas Nashe accused Gabriel Harvey

of writing poetry that courted Philip Sidney (a potential patron) as if "he were another Cyparissus or Ganymede," referring to the beloveds of Apollo and Jupiter (quoted in Katherine Duncan-Jones, *Sir Philip Sidney: Courtier Poet* [New Haven: Yale, 1991], 156). In addition to these examples, see also the summary comments of Hammond 60–61, the Oldisworth's poem cited by Hammond (note 80 below) and Pequigney, 65–66.

77. Pequigney links sonnet 20 to the boy actors who played the women in Renaissance theater (37).

78. Smith, too, notes that Shakespeare may simply be preferring some other part of the young man's body. He also perceptively observes that did the speaker's "purpose" with the young man not include sexual interest, nature's addition of a penis would be irrelevant, rather than frustrating (250). Valerie Traub in her excellent essay "Sex Without Issue" similarly observes the way sonnet 20 rediscovers gender difference and exclusive heterosexuality only at the sonnets' end and only (and improbably) based on the presence or absence of a penis (Schiffer, *Shakespeare's Sonnets*, 435).

79. The sense of "love" as sexual love is not anachronistic. The OED witnesses this meaning of the word from as early as the fourteenth century ("love," n1, 6) See also "love" in Gordon Williams, *A Glossary of Shakespeare's Sexual Language* (London: Athlone, 1997), 194. In addition to William's examples from *Antony and Cleopatra* and *Othello*, I would add Cassio's remark in *Othello* that he hopes Othello will arrive soon in order to "make love's quick pants in Desdemona's arms" (2.1.81).

80. Hammond quotes a manuscript poem by Nicholas Oldisworth (1611–1645) which describes just this situation. The subject of the poem (said to be so holy that he thinks even sleeping and drinking is "too carnall") takes offense at the writer's expression of "friendship" until he is assured that the friendship is "pure" (37–38; for Oldisworth and his poetry more generally see 32–38.) Also see Hammond more generally on the fluidity of desire in the sonnets.

Section III

1. Hallett Smith, "Sonnets," *The Riverside Shakespeare*, ed. G. Blakemore Evans, 2nd ed. (Boston: Houghton Mifflin, 1997), 1840.

2. Douglas Bush, introduction to *Shakespeare's Sonnets*, ed. Bush and Alfred Harbage,

The Pelican Shakespeare, rev. ed. (Baltimore: Penguin, 1970), 13.

3. Hallett Smith, 1840.

4. E.K.'s gloss in *Spenser: Poetical Works*, ed. J.C. Smith and E. De Selincourt (Oxford, 1912), 422–23.

5. Sara Mendelson and Patricia Crawford, *Women in Early Modern England, 1550–1720* (Oxford: Clarendon, 1998), 62.

6. Stephen Booth, *Shakespeare's Sonnets* (New Haven: Yale, 1977), 438.

7. Booth, 439; see also *Oxford English Dictionary*, "Jack," n1, I.2a.

8. Booth, 439.

9. As Joseph Pequigney argues in *Such Is My Love: A Study of Shakespeare's Sonnets* (University of Chicago, 1985), 62.

10. Juan Luis Vives, *The Education of a Christian Woman*, ed. and trans. Charles Fantazzi (University of Chicago, 2000), 85. For the textual history see Juan Luis Vives, *The Instruction of a Christian Woman*, ed. Virginia Walcott Beauchamp et al. (Urbana: University of Illinois, 2002), lxxvii; on learning and chastity see lii in Beauchampt et al., and 72 in Fantazzi's modern translation.

11. Mendelson and Crawford, 37.

12. "Homily of the State of Matrimony," rpt. in Joan Larsen Klein, *Daughters, Wives and Widows: Writings by Men about Women and Marriage in England, 1500–1640* (Urbana: University of Illinois, 1992), 6. See also Mendelson and Crawford, 60–61, for the coincidence of popular and elite opinion on female inferiority.

13. Klein, 16; Ian Maclean, *The Renaissance Notion of Woman: A Study in the Fortunes of Scholasticism and Medical Science in European Intellectual Life* (Cambridge, 1983), 50–51.

14. Joseph Swetnam, *The Arraignment of Lewd, Idle, Froward and Unconstant Women*, rpt. in *Female Replies to Swetnam the Woman-Hater*, ed. Charles Butler (Bristol: Thoemmes, 1995), 54. I quote Swetnam because of his notoriety and because he brings many antifemale stereotypes into one place. Because Swetnam recycles much from other writers and proverbial wisdom (Butler, xiv–xv; xx), the work's composition after the sonnets does not matter. Earlier writers such as Lyly and Nashe could be adduced (Butler, xx), not to mention a whole intellectual tradition surveyed by Maclean.

15. Laura Gowing, *Domestic Dangers: Women, Words, and Sex in Early Modern London* (Oxford, 1996), 59–67. On the increase in slander suits and its causes see Gowing, 32–

38, and Martin Ingram, *Church Courts, Sex and Marriage in England, 1570–1640* (Cambridge, 1987), 165–67, 299–300. For the quote see Gowing, 129.

16. Gowing, 195–98; Mendelson and Crawford, 48.

17. Anne Laurence, *Women in England: 1500–1760: A Social History* (New York: St. Martin's, 1994), 65–67. Lawrence Stone, *The Family, Sex and Marriage in England 1500–1800*, abridged ed. (New York: Harper and Row, 1979), 311. *The Autobiography of Thomas Whythorne*, ed. James S. Osborne (Oxford: Clarendon, 1961), 24. Whythorne quoted in Stone, *Family*, 311.

18. Thomas Nashe, "Christ's Tears Over Jerusalem," *The Works of Thomas Nashe*, ed. Ronald B. McKerrow, 5 vols. (Oxford: Basil Blackwell, 1958), 2:138.

19. Caroll Camden, *The Elizabethan Woman* (Houston: Elsevier, 1952), 235; Gowing, 86, 90–91.

20. Swetnam, 25.

21. The idea goes back to the Christian medieval period. See Maclean, 16–17.

22. *Hamlet*, 5.1.179. Hamlet's remark is prompted by his recollection of kissing the jester Yorick ("I know not how oft") when he was alive. So this passage fits into a pattern that I explore in this section, of casting anxieties about male-male relations onto women — in this case anxieties about loss, and possibly eroticism.

23. Swetnam, headnote, p. 14.

24. Baldesar Castiglione, *The Book of the Courtier*, trans. Charles S. Singleton (Garden City, NY: Anchor, 1959), 217.

25. *Romeo and Juliet*, 3.1.108–109. Romeo does not even hold Juliet's love but her "beauty" responsible for his effeminacy. Romeo stresses — and blames — Juliet's sexual attractions. For this reading of *Romeo and Juliet* evocative of male fears of effeminacy see Elizabeth A. Foyster, *Manhood in Early Modern England: Honour, Sex and Marriage* (New York: Addison Wesley Longman, 1999), 56. On effeminacy see also Ian Frederick Moulton, *Before Pornography: Erotic Writing in Early Modern England* (Oxford, 2000), 28 and 70–109.

26. Mary Beth Rose, *The Expense of Spirit: Love and Sexuality in English Renaissance Drama* (Ithaca: Cornell, 1988), 20–21. Moulton, 28, 51.

27. Mendelson and Crawford, 60.

28. On the question of female authorship see Butler, introduction to *Female Replies to Swetnam the Woman-Hater*, xxiii–xxvi. At least one of the respondents to Swetnam, Rachel Speght, is identifiable. Other women's names (such as Ester Sowerman) appear to be pseudonyms, and so could disguise male authorship, or just the identity of the female writer.

29. These works have been collected and edited by Simon Shepherd as *The Women's Sharp Revenge : Five Women's Pamphlets From The Renaissance* (New York: St. Martin's, 1985). I've relied on his glosses and excellent introduction throughout my discussion of these writers.

30. [Anonymous], *Swetnam, The Woman-Hater, Arraigned by Woman* (1620) in *Female Replies to Swetnam the Woman-Hater*.

31. Sowerman in Shepherd, 103.

32. Anger in Shepherd, 38.

33. Sowerman in Shepherd, 113.

34. Sowerman in Shepherd, 103.

35. Sowerman in Shepherd, 89.

36. Stone, *Family*, 100–102.

37. Speght in Shepherd, 71.

38. "Homily of the State of Matrimony," esp. 22.

39. On the ways in which Protestant marriage both hardened and softened the husband's authority see Anthony Fletcher, "The Protestant Idea of Marriage," in *Religion, Culture and Society in Early Modern Britain: Essays in Honour of Patrick Collinson*, ed. Fletcher and Peter Roberts (Cambridge, 1994), 161–181. See also Mendelson and Crawford's concise statement of this issue at 135.

40. Anger in Shepherd, 33.

41. Anger in Shepherd, 38.

42. Sowerman in Shepherd, 103.

43. *The Norton Shakespeare*'s gloss.

44. This pun may be intentional and meant as an insult. That is, Shakespeare is saying that the black mistress is the kind of woman everyone knows, both as a familiar type of person, and carnally (Booth 475). In the very insult, however, Shakespeare admits that he is associating the black mistress with a type of woman, which we may be inclined to see as a stereotype.

45. "Bed-vow" is usually taken to mean "marriage vow," but it is not always interpreted as a vow to a husband rather than a lover, perhaps Shakespeare (Hyder Rollins, ed., *A New Variorum Edition of Shakespeare: The Sonnets* [Vols. 24–25], 2 parts [Philadelphia, J.B. Lippincott, 1944], 1:390–91); see also *The Norton Shakespeare* gloss. The *Oxford English Dictionary*'s two witnesses for "bed-vow" as marriage vow — one the "bed-vow" from this son-

net, another from Joyce's *Ulysses*— are not conclusive (see "bed," n. 19). For the "virginal" as the name of the instrument in this sonnet, see Booth, 438.

46. Booth, 467.

47. Eve Sedgwick observes the anonymity of the men in sonnets 135 and 136 (*Between Men: English Literature and Homosocial Desire* [New York: Columbia, 1985], 37).

48. Katherine Usher Henderson and Barbara F. McManus, *Half-Humankind: Contexts and Texts of the Controversy about Women in England, 1540–1640* (Urbana: University of Illinois, 1985) also point to this echo (101–102).

49. On the shift of this sonnet from love in the general sense to the mistress as beloved, see also Booth, 520–21, especially his gloss on line 13.

50. Booth, 148. For "fault" as slang for vagina see Gordon Williams, *A Glossary of Shakespeare's Sexual Language* (London: Athlone, 1997), 121.

51. On Aristotle's theory of sex difference see Maclean, 8–9.

52. Booth, 521. I read "men's eyes" in line 8 to refer to males and not to all people, men and women. If "love's eye" does refer to the vagina, then it makes sense that Shakespeare would compare this female eye to specifically gendered male eyes. Moreover, much other language in this sonnet implies an opposition of male and female. "Judgement" and "sun" are often understood to be masculine in the Renaissance, while what clouds both is punningly described in this sonnet as feminine. It would seem odd then for Shakespeare to be thinking of "men" in only gender inclusive terms in line 8.

53. On sex and venereal disease see Booth, 500 and 533.

54. Quoted in Moulton, 51. On the source of this poem and its misogyny see Moulton, 17.

55. *The Norton Shakespeare* gloss.

56. *Othello*, 4.2.89, 134–37.

57. I rely on Booth, 530, for his careful consideration of the possibilities.

58. Maclean, 29, 45. Nonetheless Galenists believed that women, though not incomplete men, are however inferior to them (35).

59. Foyster, 77–88, discusses evidence for the double standard and its limits.

60. On Protestant criticism of the double standard see Keith Thomas, "The Double Standard," *Journal of the History of Ideas* 20 (1959): 203–204, and Fletcher, 181.

61. *OED*, "dildo," 1. McKerrow's 1905 edition was the first regular printing of the poem. There was a privately printed edition in 1899. Also see McKerrow's notes for the alternate title "Nashe his dildo."

62. Daniel Javitch, *Poetry and Courtliness in Renaissance England* (Princeton, 1978), 124–32; Lauro Martines, *Society and History in English Renaissance Verse* (Oxford: Basil Blackwell, 1985), 86–91, 99–104. Also see chapters 3 through 6 in this book.

63. "Oh let me not serve so," *John Donne: The Complete English Poems*, ed. A.J. Smith (Harmondsworth, England: Penguin, 1973), lines 1–3.

64. "A Hymn to Christ, at the Author's Last Going into Germany," *John Donne: The Complete English Poems*, line 28.

65. *The Poems of Sir Walter Ralegh: A Historical Edition*, Medieval and Renaissance Texts and Studies 209, ed. Michael Ruddick (Tempe: Arizona State, 1999), p. 17, lines 29–32. For more information on Ralegh's betrayal and downfall, see Raleigh Trevelyan's discussion of the "Main" and "Bye" plots and ensuing trial in *Sir Walter Raleigh* (New York: Henry Holt, 2002), 356–97.

66. See for example Dympna Callaghan, *Shakespeare's Sonnets* (Oxford: Blackwell, 2007), 53–56.

67. Phyllis Rackin demonstrates that, contrary to many editors' explanation of the word "reeks" as the more neutral "gives off," "reeks" could already mean "smells" in a negative sense (*Shakespeare and Women*, Oxford Topics [Oxford, 2005], 102–103). I disagree with Rackin, however, that this sonnet is ultimately positive because it celebrates the fleshly woman over the inhumanly idealized one (105–106). For one thing, in the Renaissance being "fleshly" could not be a compliment. For another, female fleshliness and ideal beauty are two sides of the same stereotyping coin. One can also hardly assert that sonnet 130 "deserves much closer attention than it has usually received" because it challenges the Petrarchan ideal (106). Sonnet 130 gets lots of attention because it is mildly positive, in ways that appeal to contemporary readers. It's the other sonnets to the black mistress, most of which are far less positive, that rarely get attention (Rackin notes that 130 is an "anomaly" [110]).

68. David R. Carlson, "Reputation and Duplicity: The Texts and Contexts of Thomas More's Epigram on Bernard Andre," *ELH* 58 (1991): 268.

69. Martines, 104. See also 93–94.

70. Maclean, 2–3. Also see Sedgwick, *Between Men*, 30–31.

71. *Poems of Walter Ralegh*, p. 17, lines 37–42.

72. A copy of this poem from the second quarter of the seventeenth century makes the animus against women in these lines even more explicit. The copyist has changed "under which many childish desires / And conceits are excused" to "under which their ungrateful sex, and hard hearts are excused" (*Poems of Walter Ralegh*, 145, 228).

73. Swetnam, 33.

74. Booth, 447.

75. Booth, 497–98.

76. Sedgwick, *Between Men*, 31.

77. *Macbeth*, 1.1.10.

78. For examples of the young man's negative qualities, see sonnets 1, 33–55, 40, 84, 87, and 92–96. See also Arthur Marotti, "'Love Is Not Love': Elizabethan Sonnet Sequences and the Social Order," *ELH* 49 (1982): 412.

79. See Margreta de Grazia, "The Scandal of Shakespeare's Sonnets," *Shakespeare's Sonnets: Critical Essays*, ed. James Schiffer (New York: Garland, 2000), 101–103, and also my discussion of social mobility in the sonnets in chapter 6.

80. This change of course is already anticipated by the slightly negative cast of even the praises of 127.

81. Kim Hall, *Things of Darkness: Economies of Race and Gender in Early Modern England* (Ithaca: Cornell, 1995), 90.

82. See this book's introduction.

83. See Hall, *Things of Darkness*, 73–85 for the colonial background to other Elizabethan sonneteers.

84. Ania Loomba, *Shakespeare, Race and Colonialism*, Oxford Shakespeare Topics (Oxford, 2002), 22–24, 32–35; see also Jonathan Goldberg, *Tempest in the Caribbean* (Minneapolis: University of Minnesota, 2004), 120–21.

85. Kim Hall, "'These Bastard Signs of Fair': Literary Whiteness in Shakespeare's Sonnets," in *Post-Colonial Shakespeares*, ed. Ania Loomba and Martin Orkin (New York: Routledge, 1998), 72–73; see also Goldberg, *Tempest*, 121–24.

86. Callaghan suggests that the "black beauty" of the sonnets is the "aesthetic detritus of the unimpeachable beauty of the young man" (44). I agree, but would add that the aesthetic cannot be separated from the social or sexual in the sonnets.

87. Colin Burrow, ed., *The Complete Sonnets and Poems*, The Oxford Shakespeare (Oxford, 2002), 134.

88. Burrow, 134–35.

89. Most studies of the dates of composition of the sonnets suggest some overlap in the periods during which Shakespeare wrote the sonnets to the black mistress and some sonnets to the young man (see my introduction).

90. My sense of this dynamic has been shaped by Thomas Greene's excellent "'Pitiful Thrivers': Failed Husbandry in the Sonnets," *Shakespeare and the Question of Theory*, ed. Patricia Parker and Geoffrey Hartman (New York: Routledge, 1985), esp. 243; and Sedgwick, *Between Men*, 41–46.

91. John Rainolds, *The Overthrow of Stageplays* (1599; reprint, New York: Johnson Reprint, 1972), 10 See also Bray, *Homosexuality in Renaissance England* (N.p.: Gay Men's Press, 1982), 14.

92. See de Grazia, "Scandal." While de Grazia argues that the "scandal" of Shakespeare's sonnets is cross-race desire, she gives too little attention to the (related) scandal of cross-class desire.

93. See Nashe's "Choice of Valentines" (discussed in chapter 22), John Donne's "Farewell to Love" or George Gascoigne's "Gascoigne's Lullaby."

94. Bray, *Homosexuality*, 130–31 n77. A connection between effeminacy and homosexuality was made in the Renaissance (for stress on this point see Michael B. Young, *King James and the History of Homosexuality* [New York: NYU, 2000], 69–73) but then even more than now this connection was not inevitable. Moreover, as Bray suggests, that connection may have had to do with a link between women and luxury, rather than with one man playing the woman's role.

95. Moulton, 73; for an example of this point see Baldesar Castiglione, *The Book of the Courtier*, trans. Charles S. Singleton (Garden City, NY: Anchor, 1959), 36.

96. Alan Sinfield, *Shakespeare, Authority, Sexuality: Unfinished Business in Cultural Materialism* (London: Routledge, 2006), interestingly suggests that the poet calls the young man a woman because the young man has tried to make the poet one, as the recipient in anal sex. There is a struggle over who will be in the position of the "mistress." Sinfield notes the social implications of this struggle as well: is it the older but socially lower poet or the young but aristocratic man who's "on top"? (170). I don't think, however, one has to posit

an actual struggle over sexual positions, as Sinfield does, to get at Shakespeare's motives for manipulating anxieties about being the mistress.

97. Not only is the woman associated with darkness in the sonnets and Renaissance culture more generally, but also the praise of the young man in sonnet 20 for being "with nature's own hand painted" recalls the ideain the Renaissance that the whiteness of women was a cosmetic deceit that covered their darkness (see Hall, *Things of Darkness*, 86–90).

98. Sowerman in Shepherd, 106.

Section IV

1. In addition to *Shakespeare in Love*, the sonnets have recently been featured in heterosexual relationships in movies from the highbrow *Venus* (2007), the literary *Sense and Sensibility* (1995), the teen flick *10 Things I Hate About You* (1999; an adaptation of *The Taming of the Shrew*), to the lowbrow comedy *Sorority Boys* (2002). Despite its overarching heterosexual love plot, *Sorority Boys* like a Shakespearean comedy of cross-dressing, foregrounds the homoerotics of the sonnets; its sonnet of choice is 20. Katherine Duncan-Jones notes the anachronistic use in *Sense and Sensibility* of the sonnets as a token of love (Introduction, *Shakespeare's Sonnets*, ed. Duncan-Jones, [London: Thompson Learning, 1997], 78).

2. See for example the editions *Shakespeare and Love Sonnets*, ed. O.B. Duane (1996; reprinted New York: Gramercy, 1999); *Thy Sweet Love Remembered: The Most Beautiful Love Poems and Sonnets of William Shakespeare*, ed. Dorothy Price, illus. Bill Greer (Kansas City, MO: Hallmark, 1968); *Shakespeare on Love*, ed. Benjamin Darling (Paramus, NJ: Prentice Hall, 2000).

3. *Shakespeare and Love Sonnets*, 20–21. Since sonnet 3 refers to the recipient's "husbandry" of an "uneared womb," that recipient is clearly a man.

4. *Shakespeare in Love: The Love Poetry of William Shakespeare* (New York: Miramax/Hyperion, 1998), 70–71.

5. *Sonnets: William Shakespeare* (New York: State Street, 2000), dust jacket.

6. *Shakespeare in Love: The Love Poetry of William Shakespeare*, 73.

7. Stephen Greenblatt, "About That Romantic Sonnet...," *The New York Times*, Feb. 6, 1999: A15.

8. W.H. Auden, Introduction, *Shakespeare: The Sonnets and Narrative Poems*, Signet Classic Shakespeare (New York: Penguin, 1964, 1989), xxix.

9. David Bevington, Introduction, *William Shakespeare: The Poems*, Bantam Shakespeare, ed. Bevington et al. (New York: Bantam, 1988), 189. For a criticism of the distinction between sexual love for the black mistress and spiritual love for the young man, see chapters 16, 17 and 24. The Bantam *Poems*, for example, glosses "treasure" as having a sexual sense in sonnets 20 and 136, where the "treasure" is female, but not 52, where it is presumably male. Joseph Pequigney (*Such is My Love: A Study of Shakespeare's Sonnets* [University of Chicago, 1985]) points to ways in which editors bias their glosses (49–51). He is correct to a degree, but I also think that Shakespeare's sonnets to the young man are generally less sexual in their language — which as I argue in chapter 17 does not really tell us anything about how Shakespeare experienced sexual desire for the young man, as opposed to the black mistress.

10. Louis B. Wright and Virginia A. LaMar, *Shakespeare's Sonnets*, Folger Library General Readers Shakespeare (New York: Washington Square, 1967), xv.

11. *Shakespeare's Sonnets*, ed. Barbara A. Mowat and Paul Werstine, New Folger Shakespeare Library (New York: Washington Square, 2004), xiv–xv, 366–67.

12. Quoted in Sasha Roberts, *Reading Shakespeare's Poems in Early Modern England* (Houndmills: Palgrave Macmillan, 2003), 154.

13. *Short-Title Catalogue of Books Printed in England, Scotland, Ireland, Wales, and British America and of English Books Printed in Other Countries,1641–1700*, ed. Alfred W. Pollard and Donald Goddard Wing (http://eureka.rlg.org). Roberts (143) and Rollins (in *A New Variorum Edition of Shakespeare: The Sonnets (Vols. 24 and 25)*, 2 parts [Philadelphia: J. B. Lippincott, 1944], 2:326) make similar comparisons.

14. Duncan-Jones surveys the low number of verbal borrowings from the sonnets in the introduction to her *Shakespeare's Sonnets* (69–74). Statistics on allusions to the sonnets are from Rollins, 2:327–329.

15. Roberts, 172; Arthur Marotti, "Shakespeare's Sonnets as Literary Property," *Soliciting Interpretation: Literary Theory and Seventeenth-Century English Poetry*, ed. Elizabeth D. Harvey and Katharine Eisaman Maus (University of Chicago, 1990), 151. Dympna

Callaghan is incorrect that "many" of Shakespeare's sonnets are to be found in seventeenth-century commonplace book collections, and that this "demonstrates their early popularity" (*Shakespeare's Sonnets* [Oxford: Blackwell, 2007], 8).

16. Rollins, 2:326–327.

17. Paul Hammond, *Figuring Sex Between Men from Shakespeare to Rochester* (Oxford, 2002), 84–87. Duncan-Jones, *Shakespeare's Sonnets*, 43, 69, 74. While Margreta de Grazia is not wrong, in contrast to Hammond and Duncan-Jones, to emphasize the cultural acceptance of the language of male friendship in Shakespeare's sonnets, she overemphasizes the extent to which this acceptability was secure, especially when friendship involved social unequals ("The Scandal of Shakespeare's Sonnets," *Shakespeare's Sonnets: Critical Essays*, ed. James Schiffer [New York: Garland, 2000], 101–104). On this issue see chapters 9–10 of this book. For the black mistress sonnets as the source of readers' rejection of the sonnets, see Roberts, 153, 176.

18. Arthur Marotti, *Manuscript, Print and the English Renaissance Lyric* (Ithaca: Cornell, 1995), 246–47.

19. Lisle Cecil John, *The Elizabethan Sonnet Sequences* (New York: Russell and Russell, 1964), 21–22; *The Concise Cambridge History of English Literature*, ed. George Sampson (Cambridge, 1959), 150–52.

20. Katherine Duncan-Jones, *Shakespeare's Sonnets*, 29–31.

21. See Marotti, "Shakespeare's Sonnets," 157–58; and *Manuscript*, 227–28, 286–88.

22. Marotti, "Shakespeare's Sonnets," 159.

23. "To the Reader," *Poems: Written by Will. Shakespeare*, ed. John Benson (London, 1640), sig. *2r. Josephine Waters Bennett, "Benson's Alleged Piracy of *Shake-Speares Sonnets* and Some of Jonson's Works," *Studies in Bibliography* 21 (1968): 242–43. Marotti, "Shakespeare's Sonnets," 159–160; Margreta de Grazia, *Shakespeare Verbatim: The Reproduction of Authenticity and the 1790 Apparatus* (Oxford, 1990), 166–67; Marotti, *Manuscript*, 288.

24. Rollins, 2:29. Malone caused a major change in the reception of the sonnets when he went back to the 1609 quarto for his edition. See chapter 27 below.

25. Rollins, 2:20–21. The other sonnets besides 18 omitted by Benson were 19, 43, 56, 75, 76, 96, 126.

26. Rollins, 2:20–21.

27. Roberts, 163, 165. Roberts concurs with de Grazia that Benson was not trying to conceal the sonnets' address to a man ("Scandal," 89–91), and that the real "scandal" of the sonnets is their account of the black mistress. Critics who see Benson's edition as marking an end to the Renaissance acceptance of male-male love include Bruce Smith (*Homosexual Desire in Shakespeare's England* [University of Chicago, 1994], 268–70) and Hammond, 102–104. The view that Benson intended to erase the male beloved from the sonnets has been the longer held one. See Rollins, 2:133 and Duncan-Jones, *Shakespeare's Sonnets*, 42–43.

28. Dennis Kay, *The English Funeral Elegy from Spenser to Milton* (Oxford: Clarendon, 1990), 126, 138–41, 155–57.

29. Rollins, 2:22.

30. *Poems*, sig. D6v.

31. This is the suggestion of Raymond MacDonald Alden, "The 1640 Text of Shakespeare's Sonnets," *Modern Philology* 14 (1916): 25.

32. As de Grazia, "Scandal," herself suggests (90). The alterations to gender identifiers occur in sonnets 101, 104 and 108.

33. What counts as a substantive change versus what Benson might have seen as just a change in spelling is debatable. The following is a list of what appear to be Benson's most substantive changes (by sonnet number: quarto version, Benson version). Of these eleven changes, five relate to gender, including two of the three greatest departures from the original (104 and 108; the third is 83): 9: Is It, It is; 83: for, of; 101: him, her; 101: him, her; 101: he, she; 104: friend, love; 108: sweet boy, sweet-love; 111: harmful, harmlesse; 128: thy fingers, their fingers; 139: mine, my; 142: thy, my.

34. For example, sonnet 69, included in "The Glory of Beauty," is an insulting sonnet about the difference between the young man's beauty and his behavior. Sonnet 29 is grouped with sonnets 27 and 28 under the title "A Disconsolation," even though, as opposed to the previous two sonnets, it is consolatory. Inaccurate titles include "Youthful Glory" for sonnets 13–15. Rollins, 2:22, notes that many of Benson's changes were "inept." G. Blakemore Evans in his edition of the sonnets hypothesizes Benson recognizing midway the homoerotic implication of the sonnets and beginning at that point to change pronouns (*The Sonnets: The New Cambridge Shakespeare* [Cambridge, 1996], 284).

35. De Grazia, "Scandal," cites the phrase "god in love" in sonnet 110 as one example of

Benson's indifference to the male beloved of the sonnets (90). More generally, de Grazia argues that Benson changed male to female or gender neutral words in order to correct grammar or style errors, rather than to avoid the suggestion of same-sex desire. Unless we assume that these grammar and style errors were somehow especially compelling to Benson, this argument does not fit with the carelessness of his changes elsewhere in his edition, especially because the "solecisms" (90) de Grazia suggests he corrected are more subtle than errors he let stand.

36. These instances from Roberts, 170–77. Roberts notes that the copyist who changed the male pronouns in 68 nonetheless retained "the amorous language applied to the male beloved" when copying 107. The "he/him" in that sonnet is Death, however, not the beloved, and the language about him is not amorous! An early eighteenth-century edition by Charles Gildon similarly asserted that "most" of the sonnets were to Shakespeare's mistress (quoted in Rollins, 2:38). And, as I outline below, when Malone at the end of the eighteenth century pointed out that the first 126 sonnets formed a group for the young man, he was making a point that seemed new and controversial.

37. Rollins, 2:29–40; Marotti, "Shakespeare's Sonnets," 162–63; de Grazia, *Shakespeare Verbatim*,165.

38. Marotti, "Shakespeare's Sonnets," 158; de Grazia, *Shakespeare Verbatim*,165.

39. Marotti, "Shakespeare's Sonnets," 157–59, 162–63.

40. De Grazia, *Shakespeare Verbatim*,164; Marotti, "Shakespeare's Sonnets," 161.

41. David Baker, "Cavelier Shakespeare: The 1640 *Poems* of John Benson," *Studies in Philology* 95 (1998): 163; de Grazia, *Shakespeare Verbatim*, 163.

42. Marotti, *Manuscript*, 135–208, 212–18.

43. Marotti, *Manuscript*, 217–18 and "Shakespeare's Sonnets," 154, 158; de Grazia, *Shakespeare Verbatim*, 172.

44. Editors also alter words that are not as clearly compositorial errors but that don't seem to make sense (see e.g. Duncan-Jones's discussion of 12.4 on p. 134 of her edition).For ways modern editorial practices continue to shape, often invisibly, readers' understanding of Renaissance texts see Leah S. Marcus, *Unediting the Renaissance: Shakespeare, Marlowe, Milton* (London: Routledge, 1996).

45. *Poems*, sig. *2v.

46. Rollins, 2:331–336. See also Samuel Schoenbaum, *Shakespeare's Lives*, new edition (Oxford, 1991), 118–21 and de Grazia, *Shakespeare Verbatim*, 166–68.

47. Rollins, 2:335, 336, 337, 353.

48. Francis Gentleman, *Poems Written by Mr. Will Shakespeare* (London, 1774), sig. C6v. Also cited in Rollins, 336.

49. Gentleman, sig. C6v.

50. See Rollins, 2:37–39, 2:333 and de Grazia, *Shakespeare Verbatim*, 162–63.

51. In Edmond Malone, vol. 1 of *Supplement to the Edition of Shakespeare's Plays Published in 1778* (London), 582, 606.

52. Malone, *Supplement*, 582, 684, 685. Rollins notes Malone's "tepid" responses to Steevens (2:337).

53. Terry Eagleton, *The Function of Criticism from "The Spectator" to Post-Structuralism* (London: Verso, 1984), 21–24. Eagleton notes the effective limits on participants in this reader-criticism, and argues that by the end of the eighteenth century (the time of Malone's edition) the strain of a larger public of readers produced more explicitly politicized debate and the first development of the literary professional (29–39). De Grazia's account of the editorial activism of the eighteenth century provides a nice example of the relatively empowered reader-critic who does not treat the authors' text as hallowed ground (*Shakespeare Verbatim*, 63–71).

54. Colin Franklin, *Shakespeare Domesticated: The Eighteenth-Century Editions* (Aldershot, Hant, England: Scholar, 1991), 3–5, 24, 26.

55. Franklin, 71–134; *The Dunciad* quoted on 84.

56. James Boswell, *The Plays and Poems of William Shakspere*, 20 vols. (London: C. Baldwin, 1821), 1:lvii–lix; quotes on lix. Boswell's neutrality in the account of what transpired cannot be assumed.

57. George Steevens, Advertisement, vol. 1 of *The Plays of William Shakespeare*, ed. Steevens and Samuel Johnson (London, 1793), vii. Also quoted in Rollins, 2:337–338. De Grazia, *Verbatim*, observes Malone's pointed inclusion of "poems" in the title to his works edition (154).

58. Nathan Drake, *Literary Hours, or Sketches Critical and Narrative*, vol. 1 (1800; reprint, New York: Garland, 1970), 108. Also quoted in Rollins, 2:348.

59. "The Life of Shakespeare," in vol. 5 of *The Works of the English Poets, from Chaucer to Cowper*, ed. Alexander Chalmers and Samuel Johnson (London: J. Johnson, 1810), 15. Also

quoted in Rollins, 2:349. Readers interested in lots more disparagement or faint praise of the sonnets that now seems wrongheaded should see Rollins, 2:335–356.

60. Boswell, 20:2 Also quoted in Rollins, 2:353.

61. A. Bosker, *Literary Criticism in the Age of Johnson*, second ed., rev. (1954; reprint, Folcroft, PA: Folcroft, 1969), 25–27, 38–42; Rollins, 2: 33–339; Eagleton, *Function*, 25–26.

62. [John Nott?], *New London Magazine* 5 (April 1789), 212; anonymous reviewer, *The Annual Review* 2 (1803), 564. Both cited in Rollins, 2:340.

63. Malone, *Supplemenet*, 624–25, 682.

64. De Grazia, *Shakespeare Verbatim*,155.

65. Warton's remarks appeared in a manuscript continuation of his history of English poetry (*A History of English Poetry: An Unpublished Continuation*, Augustan Reprint Society 39 [Los Angeles: William Andrews Clark Memorial Library, 1953], 8); Malone, *Supplement*, 596.

66. Edmond Malone, vol. 10 of *Plays and Poetry of William Shakespeare* (London, 1790), 207. See also de Grazia, "Scandal," 93 and Peter Stallybrass, "Editing as Cultural Formation: The Sexing of Shakespeare's Sonnets," *Modern Language Quarterly* 54 (1993): 93–94.

67. On the increasing centrality of the bourgeois nuclear family and its limits on earlier homosociality see Bray, *The Friend*, 209–18; John Tosh, "The Old Adam and the New Man: Emerging Themes in the History of English Masculinities, 1750–1850," *English Masculinities, 1660–1800* (London: Longman, 1999), 219–23, and for his qualification of the shift from homosociality to marriage, 228–30. Tim Hitchcock, "Redefining Sex in Eighteenth-Century England," interestingly suggests that an increasing emphasis on sexual intercourse over more generalized sexual "play" favored procreative, heterosexual sex over "male kissing" and "physical signs of affection" (*History Workshop Journal* 41 [1996]: 84). De Grazia attributes Malone's dismay at the male addressee to an eighteenth-century shift in the medical understanding of gender from a relationship of symmetry and hierarchy (men and women are like one another, but men are better) to one of absolute difference and complementarity (men and women are "opposite sexes" and therefore need one another) (de Grazia, "Scandal," 98–99). I am skeptical that medical theory alone had such impact on the understanding of sex and gender, or that the transition was as neat as de Grazia implies.

68. See chapters 10 and 15 for a critique of this argument. See also Stallybrass, 93–94.

69. On Malone's commitment to historicism, see de Grazia, *Shakespeare Verbatim*, 94–131, especially 124 with reference to the sonnets.

70. Malone, *Plays*, 207, 296; the latter quote also *Supplement*, 685.

71. Stallybrass, 94. Boswell does not, as Stallybrass also asserts, argue the familiar line that the poems are really about patronage rather than love. Rather, he argues that no poet would ever write to a patron in "terms of such familiarity" and "in one instance [probably sonnet 20], of such grossness" (20:219). For Boswell, this tone is an argument against the idea that the sonnets are written to a noble or that they are autobiographical.

72. Boswell, 20:219, 20.

73. Rollins, 2:134; see also Schoenbaum, 181–82.

74. "Scorn Not the Sonnet," *Complete Poetical Works of William Wordsworth*, intro. John Morley (London: Macmillan, 1928), 655.

75. Rollins, 2:133; de Grazia, 155–163; Malone, 191, 265–68. Malone is more qualified in his own biographical speculations than de Grazia's account suggests, but certainly the general change she charts from Benson to Malone is correct.

76. Augustus William Schlegel, *Course of Lectures on Dramatic Art and Literature*, trans. John Black, rev. A.J.W. Morrison (1864; reprint, New York: AMS Press, 1965), 352. Also cited in Schoenbaum, 182.

77. "Essay, Supplementary to the Preface" (1815), *William Wordsworth*, The Oxford Authors, ed. Stephen Gill (Oxford, 1984), 647. Also cited in Schoenbaum, 182.

78. Anna Jameson, *Memoirs of the Loves of the Poets* (1831; reprint, Boston: Houghton Mifflin, 1900), 182. Rollins, 2:186–7, 195.

79. Eric Eisner, "Literary Celebrity and Lyric Intimacy in Nineteenth-Century British Poetry," unpublished book ms. London newspaper publisher Daniel Stuart quoted in Judith Pascoe, "Mary Robinson and the Literary Marketplace," *Romantic Women Writers: Voices and Countervoices*, ed. Paula R. Feldman and Theresa M. Kelley (Hanover, NH: University Press of New England, 1995), 253, 258.

80. Nathan Drake, *Shakespeare and His Times*, 2 vols. (London: T. Cadell and W. Davies, 1817), 2:74–82, 62–71; Jameson, 184. James Boaden, *On the Sonnets of Shakespeare*

(London: Thomas Rudd, 1837), 31–59. See also Schoenbaum, 182–83.

81. Paula R. Feldman and Daniel Robinson, Introduction, *A Century of Sonnets: The Romantic-Era Revival, 1750–1850* (Oxford, 1999), 3–4, 12–13. See also Stuart Curran, *Poetic Form and British Romanticism* (Oxford, 1986), 39. Byron quoted in Rollins, 2:341.

82. Wordsworth, "Essay," 647; *Coleridge's Miscellaneous Criticism*, ed. Thomas Raynor (Cambridge: Harvard, 1936), 455. For the sonnet as an instance of the Romantic part for the whole, see Curran, 36–37.

83. Drake, *Shakespeare*, 2:70. Also note Schoenbaum's note of this, 197.

84. *Coleridge's Miscellaneous Criticism*, 159. My discussion of Coleridge draws on Stallybrass, 97–100.

85. *Table Talk*, ed. Carl Woodring, vol. 14 of *The Collected Works of Samuel Taylor Coleridge* (Princeton, 1990), 376, 377–78.

86. De Grazia, "Scandal," 92–93; Stallybrass, 93.

87. Henry Hallam, *Introduction to the History of the Literature of Europe in the 15th, 16th and 17th Centuries*, Vol. 3 (1873; reprint, New York: Frederick Ungar, 1970), 40, 39. Originally published 1839.

88. "House" (1876), *Robert Browning's Poetry*, ed. James F. Loucks (New York: Norton, 1979), 416.

89. Gary Taylor, *Reinventing Shakespeare: A Cultural History from the Restoration to the Present* (Oxford, 1991), 175–79, 182–83. On Shakespeare and Victorian hero-worship see Aron Y. Stavisky, *Shakespeare and the Victorians* (Norman, OK: University of Oklahoma, 1969), 61–63, 69; Richard Altick, *Lives and Letters: A History of Literary Biography in England and America* (New York: Alfred A. Knopf, 1969), 82–84. Not all Victorians, however, were sympathetic to a biographical approach. For example, the poets Browning and Tennyson objected to it (Adrian Poole, *Shakespeare and the Victorians* [London: Thompson Learning, 2004], 161–62).

90. Thomas Carlyle, "The Hero as Poet," *On Heroes, Hero-Worship, and the Heroic in History*, ed. Michael K. Goldberg (Berkeley: University of California, 1993), 92.

91. *King Lear* (conflated text), 4.1.6.

92. Taylor, 173–82; Schoenbaum, 357–58. *Shakspere* was a simplified and more student-friendly version of Dowden's 1875 *Shakspere: A Critical Study of His Mind and Art* (Schoenbaum, 355–57).

93. Edward Dowden, ed., *The Sonnets of*

William Shakespeare (London: C. Kegan Paul, 1881), xv.

94. Dowden, xlix–lix, lxi, xxv.

95. Francis Palgrave, ed., *Songs and Sonnets, by William Shakespeare* (London: Macmillan, 1865), 243.

96. William Sharp, ed., *The Songs, Poems and Sonnets of William Shakespeare*, The Canterbury Poets (London: Walter Scott, 1885), 16, 15, 36.

97. F.J. Furnivall, Introduction, *The Leopold Shakespeare* (London: Cassell, Petter and Galpin, 1877), lxviin.3, lxiv.

98. Taylor, 162–82; Schoenbaum, 290–92, 296, 349–51; Stavisky, 23–24, 47, 53; David Amigoni, *Victorian Biography: Intellectuals and the Ordering of Discourse* (New York: St. Martin's, 1993), 124–30.

99. Dowden, xvi; Gerald Massey, *Shakespeare's Sonnets, Never Before Interpreted: His Private Friends Identified* (London: Longmans, Green, 1866), 19.

100. John A. Heraud, *Shakspere: His Inner Life, as Intimated in His Works* (London: John Maxwell, 1865), 4.

101. Thomas Tyler, introduction to *Shakespeare's Sonnets* (London: David Nutt, 1890), 10–11.

102. Schoenbaum, 329, tells this story.

103. Schoenbaum, 329.

104. Rollins 2:201–202. Tyler defended against the grime theory in his *The Herbert-Fitton Theory of Shakespeare's Sonnets: A Reply* (London: David Nutt, 1898), 16.

105. Thomas Carlyle, "On History," *The Works of Thomas Carlyle in Thirty Volumes*, ed. H. D. Traill (New York: Charles Scribner's Sons, 1907), 27:85–91, 95. On Carlyle's resistance to positivist biography see also Amigoni, 47–61.

106. Rebecca Laroche, "The Sonnets on Trial: Reconsidering *The Portrait of Mr. W.H.*," Schiffer, *Shakespeare's Sonnets*, 395.

107. Massey, 152–59.

108. Massey, 205–24, 330–66. For sonnet 130 see 343.

109. Schoenbaum, 328; Rollins, 2:260.

110. Massey, 348.

111. Duncan-Jones, *Shakespeare's Sonnets*, 53.

112. Massey, 317–19, 335.

113. See Robin Gilmour, *The Victorian Period: The Intellectual and Cultural Context of English Literature, 1830–1890* (New York: Longman, 1993), 58–59. This idea of progress is suggested in Heraud's comments above.

114. D. Barnstorff, *A Key to Shakespeare's*

Sonnets, trans. T.J. Graham (London: Trüb-ner, 1862), 14, 16, 20, 47.

115. Ethan Allen Hitchcock, *Remarks on the Sonnets of Shakespeare: with the Sonnets. Showing that they belong to the hermetic class of writings, and explaining their general meaning and purpose* (New York: James Miller, 1865), 24.

116. Heraud, 24, 26, 23.

117. Barnstorff, 10; Massey, 104.

118. Massey, 118. Charles Knox Pooler in his early twentieth-century edition suggests that Massey labels as "dramatic" the morally disturbing sonnets (*Sonnets*, The Arden Shakespeare [London: Methuen, 1918], xxix).

119. Michael S. Foldy, *The Trials of Oscar Wilde: Deviance, Morality and Late-Victorian Society* (New Haven: Yale, 1997), 31.

120. Foldy, 1–47.

121. H. Montgomery Hyde, *The Trials of Oscar Wilde*, 2nd edition (1962; reprint, New York: Dover, 1973), 101, 115.

122. Linda Dowling, *Hellenism and Homosexuality in Victorian Oxford* (Ithaca: Cornell, 1994), 1. My account of Wilde's trial and especially of the place of male love in Victorian culture owes much to Dowling's remarkably intelligent, expansive and graceful book. See also Dowling, 81; and Alan Sinfield, *The Wilde Century: Effeminacy, Oscar Wilde and the Queer Moment* (New York: Columbia, 1994), 60–62; Travers Humphrey's Foreword to *The Trials of Oscar Wilde*, 2nd edition, ed. H. Montgomery Hyde (1962; reprint, New York: Dover, 1973), 13–14 and Hyde, *The Trials*, 15, 201; Richard Ellman, *Oscar Wilde* (New York: Vintage, 1987), 463.

123. Wordsworth quoted in Rollins, 347. Drake, *Shakespeare and His Times*, 2:72. Boswell, 20:220. H. C. Beeching, Introduction, *The Sonnets of Shakespeare* (Boston, London: Ginn, 1904), lxvi. Drake almost a hundred years earlier likewise wished that these sonnets "had never been published" (2:72).

124. Dowden, xxiv.

125. Furnivall, lxiv. Furnivall quotes from the King James Bible, 2 Sam 1:26.

126. *In Memoriam, A.H.H., Alfred Tennyson: A Critical Edition of the Major Works*, ed. Adam Roberts (Oxford, 2000), lxi. Furnivall, lxvi.

127. Sinfield, *The Wilde Century*, 59.

128. Peter N. Stearns, *Be a Man!: Males in Modern Society*, second edition (New York: Holmes and Meier, 1990), 47–51; Herbert Sussman, *Victorian Masculinities: Manhood and Masculine Poetics in Early Victorian Literature and Art* (Cambridge, 1995), 4–5, 55–56;

Dowling, 30–31, 35, 67–86. On Victorian anxieties about progress see Gilmour, 2–3, 19–22 and Richard D. Altick, *Victorian People and Ideas* (New York: Norton, 1973), 40–47, 106–13, 229–42, 245–46.

129. *Rugby Magazine*, 2 vols. (London: Pickering, 1835), 1:148–49. Thanks to William Weaver for this reference.

130. Sinfield, *The Wilde Century*, 111–13; Sussman, 4–6; Jeffrey Weeks, *Coming Out*, Rev. ed. (London: Quartet, 1990), 34; John Chandos, *Boys Together: English Public Schools 1800–1864* (New Haven: Yale, 1984), 202–302.

131. Oscar Wilde, "The Portrait of W.H.," *Complete Works of Oscar Wilde*, 5th ed., contrib. Owen Dudley Edwards et al. (Glasgow: Harper Collins, 2003), 302. Further references to this story are cited parenthetically in the text.

132. Ellman, 296; Hyde, 11; Dowling, 124–26. Sinfield, *The Wilde Century*, argues that the evasiveness of the "Portrait" about homosexuality represents not self-censorship on Wilde's part, but his reluctance to define "the homosexual" as a recognizable kind (18–21). Nonetheless, Wilde and his trial produced just this sort of definition (122–26).

133. The "Portrait" thus extends a critique of overly positivistic biography that Amigoni locates in the playful biographical fictions of Thomas Carlyle (47–57).

134. Schoenbaum, 323–24; for contemporary examples see Pequigney 233n.17 and Rictor Norton, who praises Wilde's "persuasive evidence" and "erudite and critical argument" for Willie Hewes as the boy actor to whom Shakespeare wrote the sonnets (at http://www.infopt.demon.co.uk/shakespe.htm).

135. Weeks, 15; Wilde, "The Decay of Lying," *Complete Works*, 1071–92; 1090; Murray G. Pittock, *Spectrum of Decadence: The Literature of the 1890s* (New York: Routledge, 1993), 21; Chris Baldick, *The Social Mission of English Criticism, 1848–1932* (Oxford, 1983), 40–41.

136. Charles Knox Pooler, *Sonnets*, The Arden Shakespeare (London: Methuen, 1918) xxxii.

137. George Wyndham, ed. *The Poems of Shakespeare* (London: Methuen, 1898), vii, ix, xviii.

138. Lee Patterson, "Literary History," *Critical Terms for Literary Study*, ed. Frank Lentriccia and Thomas McLaughlin, 2nd ed. (University of Chicago, 1995), 254. Wyndham, cviii–cxxxii.

139. Israel Gollancz, ed. *Shakespeare's Sonnets* (London: J.M. Dent, 1896), vii, ix. Gollancz is strikingly transitional: he assumes the

sonnets tell a coherent story in the manner of Victorian editions of the sonnets, but the agent of those stories has become a personified figure — "love" — rather than a specific person (xvii–xxix).

140. John Dover Wilson, ed. *The Sonnets*, The Works of Shakespeare (Cambridge, 1966), xvii.

141. Wilson, xiii.

142. Shakespeare Association of America, Bulletin, June 2002, 4.

143. Baldick, 18–19, 31, 207; Terry Eagleton, *Literary Theory: An Introduction* (Minneapolis: University of Minnesota, 1983), 22–24.

144. Baldick, 66–67, 95–100, 228–29; Terence Hawkes, *That Shakespeherian Rag: Essays on a Critical Process* (London: Methuen, 1986), 111–16; Eagleton, *Literary Theory*, 24–25.

145. *The Teaching of English in England*, Sir Henry Newbolt et al. (London: HMSO, 1921), 252–53. Quoted in Baldick, 96. See also Baldick's discussion of Wilson, 98–100 and Hawkes, 111–16.

146. On the latter point see for example Chinua Achebe, "Colonialist Criticism," in *The Post-Colonial Studies Reader*, ed. Bill Ashcroft, Gareth Griffins, Helen Tiffin (New York: Routledge, 1995), 57–61.

147. John Fekete, *The Critical Twilight: Explorations in the Ideology of Anglo-American Literary Theory* (London: Routledge and Kegan Paul, 1977), 68–73, 85–87; Gerald Graff, *Professing Literature: An Institutional History* (University of Chicago, 1987), 148–52; Eagleton, *Literary Theory*, 48–50.

148. Graff, 173; Eagleton, *Literary Theory*, 50.

149. Beeching, xiii; W.H. Hadow, Introduction, *Shakespeare's Sonnets and a Lover's Complaint*, ed. Hadow (Oxford: Clarendon, 1907), vii. An exception is J.W. Lever, who praises Shakespeare for seeing that sonnets to a male patron could provide the occasion for a greater range of experience than sonnets to a female courtly beloved (*The Elizabethan Love Sonnets*, second ed. [London: Methuen, 1966], 167). However, this suggestion sounds similar to Douglas Bush's comment that the love between men in the Renaissance was better than love between men and women (see my chapter 16).

150. Duncan-Jones, *Shakespeare's Sonnets*, 32; Wright and LaMar, *Shakespeare's Sonnets*, xv.

151. T.H.W. Crosland, *The English Sonnet* (1917; reprint, Norwood, PA: Norwood Editions, 1975), 213.

152. See for example Drake, who refers to the "remaining 28 sonnets" as "the residue" and wishes "these sonnets had never been published" (*Shakespeare and His Times*, 2:72), Boaden, who agrees with Drake that the sonnets reveal the (hetero)sexual excesses of Herbert and Shakespeare (39, 42) and the editions of Furnivall (1877), Dowden (1881), Wyndham (1898) and Beeching (1904). It is Beeching who gives the black mistress sonnets one dismissive paragraph and calls them an "appendix" (lxii).

153. Based on my survey of over 2000 instances of anthologizations of the sonnets from 1803 to the present. The comparison pie charts of young man versus black mistress sonnets show the ratio of average anthologizations for each group.

154. Feldman and Robinson, 12, 16. While major growth in the popularity of these sonnets occurs in the Victorian period, such growth is characteristic of the sonnets as a whole. I suspect that sonnets 33 and 98 have a "leg up" at a time that all the sonnets are being reprinted more frequently because of their earlier, romantic popularity.

155. Conversation between Rowse and Katherine Duncan-Jones quoted in Duncan-Jones's *Shakespeare's Sonnets*, 51.

156. Eagleton, *Literary Theory*, 46–47; Graff, 149.

157. Wilson, vii.

Coda

1. The paradoxically exclusionary force of universalism is well put in Michael Bérubé's remarkable *Life as We Know It: A Father, A Family and an Expectional Child* (New York: Vintage, 1998), 65.

2. Stephen H. Balch and Gary Crosby Brasor, "Losing the Big Picture: The Fragmentation of the English Major Since 1964" (National Association of Scholars, 2000; available at http://www.nas.org/reports2.html), 21.

Bibliography

Achebe, Chinua. "Colonialist Criticism." *The Post-Colonial Studies Reader*. Ed. Bill Ashcroft, Gareth Griffins and Helen Tiffin. New York: Routledge, 1995.

Agnew, Jean-Christophe. *Worlds Apart: The Market and the Theater in Anglo-American Thought, 1550–1750*. Cambridge University Press, 1986.

Akrigg, G.P.V. *Shakespeare and the Earl of Southampton*. Cambridge, MA: Harvard, 1968.

Alden, Raymond MacDonald. "The 1640 Text of Shakespeare's Sonnets." *Modern Philology* 14 (1916): 17–30.

Altick, Richard. *Lives and Letters: A History of Literary Biography in England and America*. New York: Knopf, 1969.

————. *Victorian People and Ideas*. New York: Norton, 1973.

Amigoni, David. *Victorian Biography: Intellectuals and the Ordering of Discourse*. New York: St. Martin's, 1993.

The Annual Review 2 (1803), 564 [anonymous reviewer].

Archer, Ian. "Material Londoners?" *Material London, ca. 1600*. Ed. Lena Cowen Orlin. Philadelphia: University of Pennsylvania Press, 2000.

Auden, W.H. Introduction. *Shakespeare: The Sonnets and Narrative Poems*. In Burto.

Bacon, Francis. *Francis Bacon: A Selection of His Work*. Ed. Sidney Warhaft. New York: Macmillan, 1985.

Baker, David. "Cavelier Shakespeare: The 1640 *Poems* of John Benson." *Studies in Philology* 95 (1998): 152–73.

Balch, Stephen H., and Gary Crosby Brasor. "Losing the Big Picture: The Fragmentation of the English Major Since 1964." National Association of Scholars, 2000. Available at http://www.nas.org/reports2.html.

Baldick, Chris. *The Social Mission of English Criticism, 1848–1932*. Oxford University Press, 1983.

Baldwin, T. W. *Shakspere's Small Latine and Lesse Greeke*. 2 vols. Urbana: University of Illinois Press, 1944.

Barnes, Barnabe. *Parthenophil and Parthenophe: A Critical Edition*. Ed. and intro. Victor A. Donyo. Carbondale: Southern Illinois University Press, 1971.

Barnfield, Richard. *Richard Barnfield: The Complete Poems*. Ed. George Klawitter. Selinsgrove, PA: Susquehanna, 1990.

Barnstorff, D. *A Key to Shakespeare's Sonnets*. Trans. T.J. Graham. London: Trübner and Co., 1862.

Bates, Catherine. "Literature and the Court." *The Cambridge History of Early Modern English Literature*. Ed. David Loewenstein and Janel Muller. Cambridge University Press, 2002.

Battle of Maldon. Norton Anthology of English Literature, Volume 1. 6th ed. Ed. Abrams et al. New York: Norton, 1993.

Beeching, H. C. Introduction. *The Sonnets of Shakespeare*. Boston: Ginn, 1904.

Bennett, Josephine Waters. "Benson's Alleged Piracy of *Shake-Speares Sonnets* and Some of Jonson's Works." *Studies in Bibliography* 21 (1968): 235–48.

Benson, John. *Poems: Written by Will. Shakespeare*. London, 1640.

Beowulf: A New Prose Translation. Trans. E. Talbot Donaldson. New York: Norton, 1966.

Bergeron, David M. ed. *King James and Letters of Homoerotic Desire*. Iowa City: University of Iowa Press, 1999.

Bérubé, Michael. *Life as We Know It: A Father, a Family and an Exceptional Child*. New York: Vintage, 1998.

Bevington, David. Introduction. *William Shakespeare: The Poems*. Bantam Shakespeare. Ed. Bevington et al. New York: Bantam, 1988.

Boaden, James. *On the Sonnets of Shakespeare*. London: Thomas Rudd, 1837.

Bolger, R.R. *The Classical Heritage and Its Beneficiaries*. Cambridge University Press, 1954.

Bond, Ronald B., ed. *Certain Sermons or Homilies (1547) and A Homily Against Disobedience and Willful Rebellion (1570): A Critical Edition*. University of Toronto Press, 1987.

Booth, Stephen. *Shakespeare's Sonnets*. New Haven: Yale University Press, 1977.

Booty, John, ed. *The Book of Common Prayer, 1559: The Elizabethan Prayer Book*. Washington, DC: Folger Shakespeare Library, 1976.

Bosker, A. *Literary Criticism in the Age of Johnson*. Second ed., rev. 1954; reprint, Folcroft, PA: Folcroft, 1969.

Boswell, James. *The Plays and Poems of William Shakespeare*. 20 vols. London: C. Baldwin, 1821.

Braden, Gordon. *Petrarchan Love and the Continental Renaissance*. New Haven: Yale University Press, 1999.

_____. "Shakespeare's Petrarchism." In James Schiffer, ed., *Shakespeare's Sonnets: Critical Essays*.

Braun-Ronsdorf, M. *The History of the Handkerchief*. Leigh-on-Sea, England: F. Lewis, 1967.

Bray, Alan. *The Friend*. University of Chicago Press, 2003.

_____. "Homosexuality and the Signs of Male Friendship in Elizabethan England." *Queering the Renaissance*. Ed. Jonathan Goldberg. Durham: Duke University Press, 1994.

_____. *Homosexuality in Renaissance England*. N.p: Gay Men's Press, 1982.

Brewer, Leighton. *Shakespeare and the Dark Lady*. Boston: Christopher, 1966.

Bryson, Anna. "The Rhetoric of Status: Gesture, Demeanour and the Image of the Gentleman in Sixteenth- and Seventeenth-Century England." *Renaissance Bodies: The Human Figure in English Culture, c. 1540–1660*. Ed. Lucy Gent and Nigel Llewellyn. London: Reaktion Books, 1990.

Burke, Peter. *The Fortunes of the Courtier*. University Park: Pennsylvania University Press, 1996.

Burrow, Colin. Introduction. *The Complete Sonnets and Poems*. The Oxford Shakespeare. Ed. Burrow. Oxford University Press, 2002.

Burto, William. ed. *Shakespeare: The Sonnets and Narrative Poems*. New York: Signet, 1989.

Bush, Douglas. Introduction. *Shakespeare's Sonnets*. The Pelican Shakespeare, rev. ed. Ed. Bush and Alfred Harbage. Baltimore: Penguin, 1970.

Callaghan, Dympna. *Shakespeare's Sonnets*. Oxford: Blackwell, 2007.

Camden, Caroll. *The Elizabethan Woman*. Houston: Elsevier, 1952.

Cantarella, Eve. *Bisexuality in the Ancient World*. Trans. Cormac Ó Cuilleanáin. New Haven: Yale University Press, 1992.

Cantor, Norman F. *The English: A History of Politics and Society to 1760*. New York: Simon and Schuster, 1967.

Carlson, David R. "Reputation and Duplicity: The Texts and Contexts of Thomas More's Epigram on Bernard Andre." *ELH* 58 (1991): 261–80.

Carlyle, Thomas. "The Hero as Poet." *On Heroes, Hero-Worship, and the Heroic in History*. Ed. Michael K. Goldberg. Berkeley: University of California Press, 1993.

_____. *The Works of Thomas Carlyle in Thirty Volumes*. Ed. H.D. Traill. New York: Charles Scribner's Sons, 1907.

Castiglione, Baldesar. *The Book of the Courtier.* Trans. Charles S. Singleton. Garden City, NY: Anchor, 1959.

Chalmers, Alexander. "The Life of Shakespeare." Vol. 5 of *The Works of the English Poets, from Chaucer to Cowper.* Ed. Chalmers and Samuel Johnson. London: J. Johnson, 1810.

Chandos, John. *Boys Together: English Public Schools 1800–1864.* New Haven: Yale University Press, 1984.

Charlton, Kenneth. *Education in Renaissance England.* London: Routledge and Kegan Paul, 1965.

Coke, Edward. *The Third Part of the Institutes of the Laws of England.* 1797; reprint, Buffalo, New York: William S. Hein, 1986.

Coleridge, Samuel Tayor. *Coleridge's Miscellaneous Criticism.* Ed. Thomas Raynor. Cambridge, MA: Harvard University Press, 1936.

_____. *Table Talk.* Ed. Carl Woodring. Vol. 14 of *The Collected Works of Samuel Taylor Coleridge.* Princeton University Press, 1990.

Colie, Rosalie. *The Resources of Kind: Genre-Theory in the Renaissance.* Ed. Barbara K. Lewalski. Berkeley: University of California Press, 1973.

Correll, Barbara. "Malleable Material, Models of Power: Woman in Erasmus's 'Marriage Group' and *Civility in Boys.*" *ELH* 57 (1990): 241–62.

Crewe, Jonathan. *Trials of Authorship: Anterior Forms and Poetic Reconstruction from Wyatt to Shakespeare.* Berkeley: University of California Press, 1990.

Crosland, T.H.W. *The English Sonnet.* 1917; reprint, Norwood, PA: Norwood, 1975.

Curran, Stuart. *Poetic Form and British Romanticism.* Oxford University Press, 1986.

Darling, Benjamin, ed. *Shakespeare on Love.* Paramus, NJ: Prentice Hall, 2000.

de Grazia, Margreta. "The Scandal of Shakespeare's Sonnets." In James Schiffer, ed., *Shakespeare's Sonnets: Critical Essays.*

_____. *Shakespeare Verbatim: The Reproduction of Authenticity and the 1790 Apparatus.* Oxford University Press, 1990.

Devereux, Walter Bourchier. *Lives and Letters of the Devereux, Earls of Essex.* 2 vols. London: John Murray, 1853.

Donne, John. *John Donne: The Complete English Poems.* Ed. A.J. Smith. Harmondsworth, England: Penguin, 1973.

Donno, Elizabeth Story. *Elizabethan Minor Epics.* New York: Columbia University Press, 1963.

Dowden, Edward, ed. *The Sonnets of William Shakespeare.* London: C. Kegan Paul, 1881.

Dowling, Linda. *Hellenism and Homosexuality in Victorian Oxford.* Ithaca: Cornell University Press, 1994.

Drake, Nathan. *Literary Hours, or Sketches Critical and Narrative.* Vol. 1. 1800; reprint, New York: Garland, 1970.

_____. *Shakespeare and His Times.* 2 vols. London: T. Cadell and W. Davies, 1817.

Duane O.B., ed. *Shakespeare and Love Sonnets.* 1996; reprint, New York: Gramercy, 1999.

Dubrow, Heather. "'Incertainties now crown themselves assur'd': The Politics of Plotting Shakespeare's Sonnets." *Shakespeare Quarterly* 47 (1996): 291–305.

du Maurier, Daphne. *Golden Lads: Sir Francis Bacon, Anthony Bacon and Their Friends.* Garden City, NY: Doubleday, 1975.

Duncan-Jones, Katherine. Introduction. *Shakespeare's Sonnets,* ed. Duncan-Jones. London: Thompson Learning, 1997.

_____. *Sir Philip Sidney: Courtier-Poet.* New Haven: Yale University Press, 1991.

_____. *Ungentle Shakespeare: Scenes from His Life.* London: Arden Shakespeare, 2001.

_____. "Were the 1609 Shake-Speares Sonnets Really Unauthorized?" *The Review of English Studies,* n.s., 34 (1983): 151–71.

Eagleton, Terry. *The Function of Criticism from "The Spectator" to Post-Structuralism.* London: Verso, 1984.

_____. *Literary Theory: An Introduction.* Minneapolis: University of Minnesota Press, 1983.

Edmondson, Paul, and Stanley Wells. *Shakespeare's Sonnets.* Oxford Shakespeare Topics. Oxford University Press, 2004.

Eisner, Eric. "Literary Celebrity and Lyric Intimacy in Nineteenth-Century British Poetry." Unpublished book ms.

Elias, Norbert. *The Civilizing Process.* Rev. ed. Trans. Edmund Jephcott. Ed. Eric Dunning et al. Oxford: Blackwell, 2000.

Ellman, Richard. *Oscar Wilde*. New York: Vintage, 1987.

Elyot, Thomas. *A Critical Edition of Sir Thomas Elyot's The Boke Named the Governour*. Ed. Donald W. Rude. New York: Garland, 1992.

Erasmus, Desiderius. *De duplici copia verborum ac rerum*. Vol. 24 of *Collected Works of Erasmus*. Trans. Betty I. Knott. Toronto: University of Toronto Press, 1978.

_____. *De ratione studii*. Vol. 24 of *Collected Works of Erasmus*. Trans. Brian McGregor. University of Toronto Press, 1978.

Evans, G. Blakemore, ed. *Elizabethan-Jacobean Drama: The Theatre In Its Time*. New York: New Amsterdam, 1988

_____, ed. *The Sonnets: The New Cambridge Shakespeare*. Cambridge University Press, 1996.

Evans, Maurice, ed. *Elizabethan Sonnets*. Rev. Roy J. Booth. Vermont: Everyman, 1994.

Fekete, John. *The Critical Twilight: Explorations in the Ideology of Anglo-American Literary Theory*. London: Routledge and Kegan Paul, 1977.

Feldman, Paula R., and Daniel Robinson. Introduction. *A Century of Sonnets: The Romantic-Era Revival, 1750–1850*. Oxford University Press, 1999.

Fineman, Joel. *Shakespeare's Perjured Eye: The Invention of Poetic Subjectivity in the Sonnets*. Berkeley: University of California Press, 1986.

Fleissner, Robert. "Hebert's Aethiopesa and the Dark Lady." *College Language Association Journal* 19 (1976): 458–67.

Fletcher, Anthony. "The Protestant Idea of Marriage." *Religion, Culture and Society in Early Modern Britain: Essays in Honour of Patrick Collinson*. Ed. Fletcher and Peter Roberts. Cambridge University Press, 1994.

Fletcher, Giles. *Licia, or, Poems of Love in honour of the admirable and singular virtues of his Lady. To the imitation of the best Latin poets, and others* (1593). *Elizabethan Sonnets*. Ed. Sidney Lee. 2 vols. *An English Garner*. 1877–1890; reprint, New York: Cooper Square, 1964.

Foldy, Michael S. *The Trials of Oscar Wilde: Deviance, Morality and Late-Victorian Society*. New Haven: Yale University Press, 1997.

Foster, Donald. "Mr. W.H. R.I.P." *PMLA* 102 (1987): 42–54.

_____. "Reconstructing Shakespeare Part 2: The Sonnets." *The Shakespeare Newsletter*. Fall 1991: 26–27.

Foucault, Michel. *The History of Sexuality, Vol. I: An Introduction*. Trans. Robert Hurley. New York: Vintage, 1980.

Foyster, Elizabeth. *Manhood in Early Modern England: Honour, Sex and Marriage*. New York: Addison Wesley Longman, 1999.

Franklin, Colin. *Shakespeare Domesticated: The Eighteenth-Century Editions*. Aldershot, Hant, England: Scholar, 1991.

Frantzen, Allen. *Before The Closet: Same-Sex Desire from "Beowulf" to Angels in America*. University of Chicago Press, 1998.

Fuller, John. *The Sonnet*. London: Methuen, 1972.

Fulwood, William. *The Enimie of Idlenesse: Teaching a Perfect Platform How to Endite Epistles and Letters*. London, 1586.

Furnivall, F.J. Introduction. *The Leopold Shakespeare*. London: Cassell, Petter and Galpin, 1877.

Gentleman, Francis. *Poems Written by Mr. Will Shakespeare*. London, 1774.

Gilmour, Robin. *The Victorian Period: The Intellectual and Cultural Context of English Literature, 1830–1890*. New York: Longman, 1993.

Goldberg Jonathan. "Fatherly Authority: The Politics of Stuart Family Images." *Rewriting the Renaissance: The Discourse of Sexual Difference in Early Modern Europe*. Ed. Margaret W. Ferguson, Maureen Quilligan and Nancy J. Vickers. University of Chicago Press, 1986.

_____. *King James and the Politics of Literature*. 1983; reprint, Stanford University Press, 1989.

_____. *Sodometries: Renaissance Texts, Modern Sexualities*. Stanford University Press, 1992.

_____. *Tempest in the Caribbean*. Minneapolis: University of Minnesota Press, 2004.

Gollancz, Israel, ed. *Shakespeare's Sonnets*. London: J.M. Dent, 1896.

Gowing, Laura. *Domestic Dangers: Women,*

Words, and Sex in Early Modern London. Oxford University Press, 1996.

Graff, Gerald. *Professing Literature: An Institutional History.* University of Chicago Press, 1987.

Green, Janet M. "Queen Elizabeth I's Latin Reply to the Polish Ambassador." *Sixteenth Century Journal* 31 (2000): 987–1008.

Greenblatt, Stephen. "About That Romantic Sonnet...." *The New York Times.* February 6, 1999: A15.

———. Ed. *The Norton Shakespeare.* New York: Norton, 1997.

———. *Renaissance Self-Fashioning: From More to Shakespeare.* University of Chicago Press, 1980.

———. *Will in the World.* New York: Norton, 2004.

Greene, Thomas. "'Pitiful Thrivers': Failed Husbandry in the Sonnets." *Shakespeare and the Question of Theory.* Ed. Patricia Parker and Geoffrey Hartman. New York: Routledge, 1985.

Greg, W. W. *Some Aspects and Problems of London Publishing Between 1550 and 1650.* Oxford: Clarendon, 1956.

Hadow, W.H., ed. *Shakespeare's Sonnets and A Lover's Complaint.* Oxford: Clarendon, 1907.

Hall, Kim. *Things of Darkness: Economies of Race and Gender in Early Modern England.* Ithaca: Cornell University Press, 1995.

———. "'These Bastard Signs of Fair': Literary Whiteness in Shakespeare's Sonnets." *Post-Colonial Shakespeares.* Ed. Ania Loomba and Martin Orkin. New York: Routledge, 1998.

Hallam, Henry. Vol. 3 of *Introduction to the History of the Literature of Europe in the 15th, 16th and 17th Centuries.* 1873; reprint, New York: Frederick Ungar, 1970.

Hammer, Paul E. J. "The Earl of Essex, Fulke Greville, and the Employment of Scholars." *Studies in Philology* 91 (1994): 167–80.

———. *The Polarisation of Elizabethan Politics: The Political Career of Robert Devereux, 2nd Earl of Essex.* Cambridge University Press, 1999.

Hammond, Paul. *Figuring Sex Between Men: From Shakespeare to Rochester.* Oxford University Press, 2002.

Harrison, G.B. *Shakespeare at Work.* 1933; reprint with a new preface, Ann Arbor: University of Michigan Press, 1958.

Hawkes, Terence. *That Shakespeherian Rag: Essays on a Critical Process.* London: Methuen, 1986.

Heal, Felicity. *Hospitality in Early Modern England.* Oxford: Clarendon, 1990.

———, and Clive Holmes. *The Gentry in England and Wales, 1500–1700.* Stanford University Press, 1994.

Helgerson, Richard. *Self-Crowned Laureates: Spenser, Jonson, Milton and the Literary System.* Berkeley: University of California Press, 1983.

Henderson, Katherine Usher, and Barbara F. McManus. *Half-Humankind: Contexts and Texts of the Controversy about Women in England, 1540–1640.* Urbana: University of Illinois Press, 1985.

Heraud, John. *Shakespeare: His Inner Life, as Intimated in His Works.* London: John Maxwell and Co., 1865.

Heywood, Thomas. *A Woman Killed with Kindness.* Ed. R.W. Van Fossen. Cambridge, MA: Harvard University Press, 1961.

Hieatt, A. Kent, Charles W. Hieatt, and Anne Lake Prescott. "When Did Shakespeare Write Sonnets 1609?" *Studies in Philology* 88 (1991): 69–109.

Hitchcock, Ethan Allen. *Remarks on the Sonnets of Shakespeare.* New York: James Miller, 1865.

Hitchcock, Tim. "Redefining Sex in Eighteenth-Century England." *History Workshop Journal* 41 (1996): 72–90.

Honan, Park. *Shakespeare: A Life.* Oxford University Press, 1998.

Hotson, Leslie. *Mr. W.H.* New York: Knopf, 1964.

Howard, Skiles. *The Politics of Courtly Dancing in Early Modern England.* Amherst: University of Massachusetts Press, 1998.

Humphrey, Travers. Foreword. In H. Montgomery Hyde, ed., *The Trials of Oscar Wilde.*

Hunt, Marvin. "Be Dark But Not Too Dark." In James Schiffer, ed., *Shakespeare's Sonnets: Critical Essays.*

Hutson, Lorna. *The Usurer's Daughter: Male Friendship and Fictions of Women in Sixteenth-Century England.* New York: Routledge, 1994.

Hyde, H. Montgomery, ed. *The Trials of Oscar Wilde*. Second ed. 1962; reprint, New York: Dover, 1973.

Ingram, Martin. *Church Courts, Sex and Marriage in England, 1570–1640*. Cambridge University Press, 1987.

Jackson, MacDonald P. "Vocabulary and Chronology: The Case of Shakespeare's Sonnets." *The Review of English Studies*, n.s., 52 (2001): 59–75.

Jameson, Anna. *Memoirs of the Loves of the Poets*. 1831; reprint, Boston: Houghton Mifflin, 1900.

Jardine, Lisa, and Alan Stewart. *Hostage to Fortune: The Troubled Life of Francis Bacon*. New York: Hill and Wang, 1998.

Javitch, Daniel. *Poetry and Courtliness in Renaissance England*. Princeton University Press, 1978.

Jewell, Helen M. *Education in Early Modern England*. New York: St. Martin's, 1998.

Judson, Alexander. *The Life of Edmund Spenser*. Vol. 11 of *The Works of Edmund Spenser: A Variorum Edition*. Ed. Edwin Greenlaw, et al. Baltimore: Johns Hopkins University Press, 1954.

Katz, Jonathan Ned. *The Invention of Heterosexuality*. New York: Penguin, 1995.

Kay, Dennis. *The English Funeral Elegy from Spenser to Milton*. Oxford: Clarendon, 1990.

Keevak, Michael. *Sexual Shakespeare: Forgery, Authorship, Portraiture*. Detroit: Wayne State University Press, 2001.

Kelly, Joan. "Did Women Have a Renaissance?" *Women, History, Theory: The Essays of Joan Kelly*. University of Chicago Press, 1984.

Klein, Joan Larsen. *Daughters, Wives and Widows: Writings by Men about Women and Marriage in England, 1500–1640*. Urbana: University of Illinois Press, 1992.

Koller, Katherine. "Spenser and Ralegh." *ELH* 1 (1934): 37–60.

Laroche, Rebecca. "The Sonnets on Trial: Reconsidering *The Portrait of Mr. W.H.*" In James Schiffer, ed., *Shakespeare's Sonnets: Critical Essays*.

Laurence, Anne. *Women in England: 1500–1760: A Social History*. New York: St. Martin's, 1994.

Lawrence v. Texas, 539 U.S. (2003).

Lee, Sidney. *A Life of William Shakespeare*. New ed. New York: Macmillan, 1916.

Lever, J.W. *Elizabethan Love Sonnets*. Second ed. London: Methuen, 1966.

Lewis, C.S. *The Allegory of Love: A Study in Medieval Tradition*. New York: Oxford University Press, 1958.

Loomba, Ania. *Shakespeare, Race, and Colonialism*. Oxford Shakespeare Topics. Oxford University Press, 2002.

Loucks, James, ed. *Robert Browning's Poetry*. New York: Norton, 1979.

Lyly, John. *Euphues: The Anatomy of Wit*. Ed. Edward Arber. London: Alex Murray and Son, 1866.

Maclean, Ian. *The Renaissance Notion of Woman: A Study in the Fortunes of Scholasticism and Medical Science in European Intellectual Life*. Cambridge University Press, 1983.

Malone, Edmond. Vol. 10 of *Plays and Poems of William Shakespeare*. London, 1790.

_____. Vol. 1 of *Supplement to the Edition of Shakespeare's Plays Published in 1778*. London, 1780.

Malory, Sir Thomas. *Le Morte D'Arthur*. Intro. John Lawlor. Ed. Janet Cowen. 2 vols. New York: Penguin, 1969.

Marcus, Leah. *Unediting the Renaissance: Shakespeare, Marlowe, Milton*. London: Routledge, 1996.

Marlowe, Christopher. *Christopher Marlowe: Doctor Faustus and Other Plays*. Ed. David Bevington and Eric Rasmussen. Oxford University Press, 1995.

Marotti, Arthur. "'Love Is Not Love': Elizabethan Sonnet Sequences and the Social Order." *ELH* 49 (1982): 396–428.

_____. *Manuscript, Print, and the English Renaissance Lyric*. Ithaca: Cornell University Press, 1995.

_____. "Shakespeare's Sonnets as Literary Property." *Soliciting Interpretation: Literary Theory and Seventeenth-Century English Poetry*. Ed. Elizabeth D. Harvey and Katherine Eisaman Maus. University of Chicago Press, 1990.

Martines, Lauro. *Society and History in English Renaissance Verse*. Oxford: Basil Blackwell, 1985.

Massey, Gerald. *Shakespeare's Sonnets, Never Before Interpreted: His Private Friends Identified*. London: Longmans, Green and Co., 1866.

Matz, Robert. *Defending Literature in Early Modern England: Renaissance Literary Theory in Social Context.* Cambridge University Press, 2000.

McClatchy, J.D., ed. *Love Speaks Its Name: Gay and Lesbian Love Poems.* New York: Knopf, 2001.

Mendelson, Sara, and Patricia Crawford. *Women in Early Modern England, 1550–1720.* Oxford: Clarendon, 1998.

Miller, Edwin Haviland. *The Professional Writer in Elizabethan England.* Cambridge: Harvard University Press, 1959.

Montrose, Louis. "Of Gentlemen and Shepherds: The Politics of Elizabethan Pastoral Form." *ELH* 50 (1983): 415–59.

Moulton, Ian Frederick. *Before Pornography: Erotic Writing in Early Modern England.* Oxford University Press, 2000.

Mowat, Barbara, and Paul Werstine, eds. *Shakespeare's Sonnets.* The New Folger Shakespeare Library. New York: Washington Square, 2004.

Nashe, Thomas. *The Works of Thomas Nashe.* Ed. Ronald B. McKerrow. 5 vols. Oxford: Basil Blackwell, 1958.

Naunton, Sir Robert. *Fragmentia Regalia, or Observations on Queen Elizabeth, Her Times and Favorites.* Ed. John S. Cervoski. Cranbury, NJ: Associated University Press, 1985.

Newbolt, Sir Henry, et al. *The Teaching of English in England.* London: HMSO, 1921.

Norton, Rictor. "Enter Willie Hughes as Juliet Or, Shakespeare's Sonnets Revisited." Available at http://www.infopt.demon.co.uk/shakespe.htm.

[Nott, John?]. *New London Magazine.* 5 April 1789.

Orme, Nicholas. *From Childhood to Chivalry: The Education of the English Kings and Aristocracy, 1066–1530.* London: Methuen, 1984.

Osborne James, ed. *The Autobiography of Thomas Whythorne.* Oxford: Clarendon, 1961.

Palgrave, Francis, ed. *Songs and Sonnets, by William Shakespeare.* London: Macmillan, 1865.

Pascoe, Judith. "Mary Robinson and the Literary Marketplace." *Romantic Women Writers: Voices and Countervoices.* Ed. Paula R. Feldman and Theresa M. Kelley. Hanover, NH: University Press of New England, 1995.

Patterson, Lee. "Literary History." *Critical Terms for Literary Study.* 2nd ed. Ed. Frank Lentriccia and Thomas McLaughlin. University of Chicago Press, 1995.

Pequigney, Joseph. *Such Is My Love: A Study of Shakespeare's Sonnets.* University of Chicago Press, 1985.

Perry, Graham. "Literary Patronage." in *The Cambridge History of Early Modern English Literature.* Ed. David Loewenstein and Janel Muller. Cambridge University Press, 2002.

Petrarch, Francesco. *The Canzoniere.* Trans. Mark Musa. Bloomington: Indiana University Press, 1996.

Pittock, Murray. *Spectrum of Decadence: The Literature of the 1890s.* New York: Routledge, 1993.

Pollitt, Katha. "Adam and Steve — Together At Last." *The Nation.* 15 December 2003, p. 9.

Poole, Adrian. *Shakespeare and the Victorians.* London: Thompson Learning, 2004.

Pooler, Charles Knox. *Sonnets.* Arden Shakespeare. London: Methuen, 1918.

Price, Dorothy, ed. *Thy Sweet Love Remembered: The Most Beautiful Love Poems and Sonnets of William Shakespeare.* Illus. Bill Greer. Kansas City, MO: Hallmark, 1968.

Puttenham, George. *The Arte of English Poesie.* Ed. and intro. Gladys Doidge Willcock and Alice Walker. Cambridge University Press, 1936.

Rackin, Phyllis. *Shakespeare and Women.* Oxford Shakespeare Topics. Oxford University Press, 2005.

Rainolds, John. *The Overthrow of Stageplays.* 1599; reprint, New York: Johnson Reprint, 1972.

Ralegh, Walter. *The Poems of Sir Walter Ralegh: A Historical Edition.* Ed. Michael Ruddick. Tempe: Arizona State University Press, 1999.

Rappaport Steve. *Worlds Within Worlds: Structures of Life in Sixteenth-Century London.* Cambridge University Press, 1989.

Roberts, Sasha. *Reading Shakespeare's Poems in Early Modern England.* Houndsmills, England: Palgrave Macmillan, 2003.

Rocke, Michael. *Forbidden Friendships: Homosexuality and Male Culture in Renaissance Florence*. Oxford University Press, 1996.

Rollins, Hyder, ed. *A New Variorum Edition of Shakespeare: The Sonnets (Vols. 24–25)*. 2 parts. Philadelphia: J.B. Lippincott, 1944.

Rose, Mary Beth. *The Expense of Spirit: Love and Sexuality in English Renaissance Drama*. Ithaca: Cornell University Press, 1988.

Ryan, Christopher. *The Poetry of Michelangelo: An Introduction*. Madison, NJ: Fairleigh Dickinson University Press, 1998.

Salkeld, Duncan. "'Black Luce' and the 'Curtizans' of London." *Signatures* 2 (2000): 5–15. Electronic journal available at http://www.chiuni.ac.uk/info/Signatures.cfm.

Sampson, George, ed. *The Concise Cambridge History of English Literature*. Cambridge University Press, 1959.

Sanders, Stephanie A., and June Machover Reinisch. "Would You Say You 'Had Sex' If...?" *JAMA: Journal of the American Medical Association* 281 (1999): 275–77.

Schlegel, Augustus William. *Course of Lectures on Dramatic Art and Literature*. Trans. John Black, rev. A.J.W. Morrison. 1864; reprint, New York: AMS, 1965.

Schiffer, James, ed. *Shakespeare's Sonnets: Critical Essays*. New York: Garland, 2000.

Schoenbaum, Samuel. "Shakespeare's Dark Lady: A Question of Identity." *Shakespeare's Styles: Essays in Honour of Kenneth Muir*. Ed. Philip Edwards et al. Cambridge University Press, 1980.

_____. *Shakespeare's Lives*. New edition. Oxford University Press, 1991.

Sedgwick, Eve Kosofsky. *Between Men: English Literature and Homosocial Desire*. New York: Columbia University Press, 1985.

_____. *Epistemology of the Closet*. Berkeley: University of California Press, 1990.

Shakespeare, William. *The Norton Shakespeare*. Ed. Stephen Greenblatt, et al. New York: Norton, 1997.

Shakespeare Association of America. Bulletin. June 2000, 4.

Shakespeare in Love: The Love Poetry of William Shakespeare. New York: Miramax/Hyperion, 1998.

Shannon, Laurie. *Sovereign Amitie: Figures of Friendship in Shakespearean Contexts*. University of Chicago Press, 2002.

Sharp, William, ed. *The Songs, Poems and Sonnets of William Shakespeare*. The Canterbury Poets. London: Walter Scott, 1885.

Shepherd, Simon. *The Women's Sharp Revenge : Five Women's Pamphlets from the Renaissance*. New York: St. Martin's, 1985.

Shepherd, Robert. "Sexual Rumors in English Politics: The Cases of Elizabeth I and James I." *Desire and Discipline: Sex and Sexuality in the Premodern West*. University of Toronto Press, 1996.

Short-Title Catalogue of Books Printed in England, Scotland, Ireland, Wales, and British America and of English Books Printed in Other Countries, 1641–1700. Ed. Alfred W. Pollard and Donald Goddard Wing. Accessed at http://eureka.rlg.org.

"Silva Rhetoricae." Available at *http://rhetoric.byu.edu/*.

Sidney, Philip. *The Correspondence of Philip Sidney and Hubert Languet*. Ed. William Aspenwall Bradley. Boston: Merrymount, 1912.

_____. *Sir Philip Sidney: A Critical Edition of the Major Works*. Ed. Katherine Duncan-Jones. Oxford University Press, 1989.

Simons, Louise. "Rerouting the *Unfortunate Traveller*: Strategies for Coherence and Direction." *Studies in English Literature, 1500–1900* 28 (1988): 17–38.

Sinfield, Alan. *Shakespeare, Authority, Sexuality: Unfinished Business in Cultural Materialism*. London: Routledge, 2006.

_____. *The Wilde Century: Effeminacy, Oscar Wilde and the Queer Moment*. New York: Columbia University Press, 1994.

Smith, Bruce. *Homosexual Desire in Shakespeare's England*. University of Chicago Press, 1994.

Smith, Hallett. "Sonnets." *The Riverside Shakespeare*. Ed. G. Blakemore Evans. 2nd ed. Boston: Houghton Mifflin, 1997.

Sonnets: William Shakespeare. New York: State Street, 2000.

Spenser, Edmund. *Spenser: Poetical Works*. Ed. J.C. Smith and E. De Selincourt. Oxford University Press, 1912.

Stallybrass, Peter. "Editing as Cultural Formation: The Sexing of Shakespeare's Sonnets." *Modern Language Quarterly* 54 (1993): 91–103.

Stavisky, Aron. *Shakespeare and the Victorians.* Norman: University of Oklahoma Press, 1969.

Stearns, Peter N. *Be a Man! Males in Modern Society.* Second ed. New York: Holmes and Meier, 1990.

Steevens, George. "Advertisement." Vol. 1 of *The Plays of William Shakespeare.* Ed. Steevens and Samuel Johnson. London, 1793.

Stewart, Alan. *Close Readers: Humanism and Sodomy in Early Modern England.* Princeton University Press, 1997.

_____. *Philip Sidney: A Double Life.* New York: St. Martin's, 2000.

Stone, Lawrence. *The Crisis of the Aristocracy, 1558–1641.* London: Oxford University Press, 1965.

_____. *The Family, Sex and Marriage in England 1500–1800.* Abridged ed. New York: Harper and Row, 1979.

Sussman, Herbert. *Victorian Masculinities: Manhood and Masculine Poetics in Early Victorian Literature and Art.* Cambridge University Press, 1995.

Swetnam, Joseph. *The Arraignment of Lewd, Idle, Froward and Unconstant Women,* reprinted in *Female Replies to Swetnam the Woman-Hater.* Ed. Charles Butler. Bristol: Thoemmes, 1995.

Taylor, Gary. *Reinventing Shakespeare: A Cultural History from the Restoration to the Present.* Oxford University Press, 1991.

Tennyson, Alfred. *Alfred Tennyson: A Critical Edition of the Major Works.* Ed. Adam Roberts. Oxford University Press, 2000.

Thomas, Keith. "The Double Standard." *Journal of the History of Ideas* 20 (1959): 195–216.

Tosh, John. "The Old Adam and the New Man: Emerging Themes in the History of English Masculinities, 1750–1850." *English Masculinities, 1660–1800.* London: Longman, 1999.

Traub, Valerie. "Sex Without Issue." In James Schiffer, ed., *Shakespeare's Sonnets: Critical Essays.*

Trevelyan, Raleigh. *Sir Walter Raleigh.* New York: Henry Holt, 2002.

Tyler, Thomas. *The Herbert-Fitton Theory of Shakespeare's Sonnets: A Reply.* London: David Nutt, 1898.

_____. *Shakespeare's Sonnets.* London: David Nutt, 1890.

Vendler, Helen. *The Art of Shakespeare's Sonnets.* Cambridge, MA: Harvard University Press, 1997.

Vives, Juan Luis. *The Education of a Christian Woman.* Ed and trans. Charles Fantazzi. University of Chicago Press, 2000.

_____. *The Instruction of a Christian Woman.* Ed Virginia Walcott Beauchamp et al. Urbana: University of Illinois Press, 2002.

Wall, Wendy. *The Imprint of Gender: Author and Publication in the English Renaissance.* Ithaca: Cornell University Press, 1993.

Warton, Thomas. *A History of English Poetry; An Unpublished Continuation.* Augustan Reprint Society 39. Los Angeles: William Andrews Clark Memorial Library, 1953.

Weeks, Jeffrey. *Coming Out: Homosexual Politics in Britain from the Nineteenth Century to the Present.* Revised ed. London: Quartet, 1990.

Whigham, Frank. *Ambition and Privilege: The Social Tropes of Elizabethan Courtesy Theory.* Berkeley: University of California Press, 1984.

Wilde, Oscar. *Complete Works of Oscar Wilde.* Fifth ed. Contrib. Owen Dudley Edwards et al. Glasgow: HarperCollins, 2003.

Williams, Gordon. *A Glossary of Shakespeare's Sexual Language.* London: Athlone, 1997, 194.

Williams, Neville. *Elizabeth: Queen of England.* London: Weidenfeld and Nicholson, 1967.

Williams, Penry. *The Tudor Regime.* Oxford University Press, 1979.

Wilmot, John. *The Works of John Wilmot, Earl of Rochester.* Ed. Harold Love. Oxford University Press, 1999.

Wilson, John Dover, ed. *The Sonnets.* Cambridge University Press, 1966.

Wilson, Derek. *Sweet Robin: A Biography of Robert Dudley, Earl of Leicester.* London: Hamish Hamilton, 1981.

Winfield, Jess. *What Would Shakespeare Do?: Personal Advice from the Bard.* Berkeley: Seastone, 2000.

Wordsworth, William. *Complete Poetical Works of William Wordsworth.* Intro. John Morley. London: Macmillan, 1928.

_____. *William Wordsworth.* The Oxford Authors. Ed. Stephen Gill. Oxford University Press, 1984.

Wright, Louis B., and Virginia A. LaMar, eds. *Shakespeare's Sonnets.* Folger Library General Readers Shakespeare. New York: Washington Square, 1967.

Wyndham, George, ed. *The Poems of Shakespeare.* London: Methuen, 1898.

Young, Michael B. *King James and the History of Homosexuality.* NYU Press, 2000.

Index

237